# WONDROUS WORDS

# WONDROUS WORDS

## Writers and Writing in the Elementary Classroom

**Katie Wood Ray**

Western Carolina University

National Council of Teachers of English
1111 W. Kenyon Road, Urbana, Illinois 61801-1096

Prepress Services: Precision Graphics
Staff Editor: Zarina M. Hock
Interior Design: Precision Graphics and Mary C. Cronin
Cover Design: Jenny Jensen Greenleaf

NCTE Stock Number: 58161

**Library of Congress Cataloging-in-Publication Data**
Ray, Katie Wood, 1964–
    Wondrous words : writers and writing in the elementary classroom /
Katie Wood Ray.
      p.  cm.
    Includes bibliographical references (p.  ).
    ISBN 0-8141-5816-1 (pbk.)
    1. Creative writing (Elementary education)  2. English language-
-Study and teaching (Elementary)  I. Title.
LB1576.R38   1999
372.62'3—dc21                       99–31886
                                            CIP

*For my friends and colleagues through the years
at the Reading and Writing Project,
Teachers College, Columbia University*

# Contents

# Acknowledgments

There are many people to thank for helping to make this book possible. Thank you, my friends and colleagues through the years at the Teachers College Reading and Writing Project, to whom this book is dedicated. My history of conversations with you, of listening to you, and of watching you work has helped me to become the teacher I am today. Thank you for always welcoming me back into your thoughtful community.

Thank you to all the teachers who have welcomed me into their classrooms and let me work alongside them. And especially to those whose classrooms inform this book specifically: Lisa Cleaveland, Buffy Fowler, Chris Griffin, Connie McElrath, Donna Raskin, Mollie Robinson, and Sherry Seigel.

Thank you, Debbie Newton, for being a seamstress and for being wise enough to share that brilliant connection with me.

Thank you, teachers at P.S. 7 in the Bronx who, in 1993 and 1994, helped me craft the vision for writing instruction that I still follow today.

Thank you, Linda Kaufman, for helping me round up permissions from such a distance, and for supporting the good work at P.S. 95 in the Bronx.

Thank you, Isoke Nia, for the way you will argue with me for hours over a single word, a word that can make all the difference.

Thank you, Dixie Goswami, Beverly Busching, Heidi Mills, and Tim O'Keefe—my earliest mentors in the teaching of writing.

Thank you, Lester Laminack and Greg Owens, for being my readers during the summer. Your thoughtful comments were instrumental in helping me to shape the direction of this book.

Though I know they will probably never see this, I would like to thank all the authors who write, with such passion and dignity, such great books for children, especially Cynthia Rylant, who has made my teaching so much richer.

Thank you to the wonderful staff at NCTE for being so excited about this project right from the start. Karen Smith, Michael Greer, Zarina Hock, and Peter Feely are a tribute to our profession, and I am honored to have worked with each of them. Thanks especially to Pete, the lead editor of *Wondrous Words,* for all your help in making my dream for this book come true.

Thank you to my family, the Woods and the Rays, for believing in me and being proud of me and for telling everyone you see—whether or not they're interested—that "Katie's writing a new book." Thank you especially to Eric and Hannah, my nephew and niece (and two wonderful writers, I might add), for understanding when Aunt Katie couldn't come out to play because she had to work on her book. Thanks, Dad, for reading the early drafts and saying, "It makes sense to me."

And finally to my husband, Jim Ray, who just makes me so happy all the time. I write better when I'm happy. Thank you for always supporting whatever wild and crazy thing I want to do next. I'm finally finished. Let's celebrate.

# INTRODUCTION

*"Ms. Minifred liked wondrous words. She loved the beginnings of books, and the ends. She loved clauses and adverbial phrases and the descriptions of sunsets and death."*

—*from* Baby *by Patricia MacLachlan*

*Maybe it really is the boyfriend named "Rebel" who rides a Harley. Maybe so. My friends say that's the real reason I love Ms. Minifred so much. Ms. Minifred, the beloved school librarian in Patricia MacLachlan's book Baby. But I think it's because she has a soul like mine. We both love wondrous words. . . .*

So why don't you write a book?" The first time someone says this to you about your teaching, you are kind of flattered. You spend a few minutes—OK, maybe a few days—thinking, "Maybe I could write a book." And then one afternoon, when school is finally out for the summer, you sit down in front of your computer to start and you think, "I can't possibly write a book." And so instead of writing your book, you make a list of all the reasons you can't write it. Your list looks something like this:

1. I don't know enough about what I'm doing.

2. Even if I did know enough, I wouldn't know where to start.

3. I don't have the time or the energy.

4.  Everyone might think what I have to say is stupid.

5.  I might write it and then change my mind about what I'm saying after it's published.

6.  I'm sure someone else could write this better.

7.  I don't know enough about what I'm doing.

The list helps you with your resolve, and you decide that you will not, in fact, write this book after all, at least not right now. "Maybe later," you think.

Several years go by, and you're really excited about all you've been learning in your teaching. Other teachers you encounter are excited about it too, and someone else says, "Why don't you write a book?" So you go and dig out the list you made a few years ago, and you read it. Much to your surprise, every reason you had for not writing a book is still valid. But this time, *you* are different. This time you think maybe it's worth the risk to just get your ideas out there and speak up a little in the larger conversation about teaching and learning. So you do it. You just take a summer off and you do it. Pour your heart into it and see what happens.

This, of course, is exactly what happened to me, and I am hoping even now, as I prepare to send this off to my publisher, that *Wondrous Words* will be worth the risk it has been to write it. So much of who I am is wrapped up in what it's about, because so much of who I am is wrapped up in my identity as a teacher. Writing a book about your teaching feels a little like exposing yourself to strangers, letting them have a very intimate look at what's inside you, a good long look at what you don't usually have to parade around in front of other people. I hope that when you "glimpse my insides" you will see that I dearly love reading and writing and the wondrous exchange of words that is uniquely human. I can only hope that this book does justice to that love.

———————————

*Wondrous Words: Writers and Writing in the Elementary Classroom,* is a loud book. It is filled with the voices of writers, young and old, experienced and inexperienced. You will find several different kinds of ideas in this book. The first four chapters introduce the most important understandings that underlie how we teach students to learn to write from writers. Chapter 1, "Reading Like Writers," explores the central concept of how this kind of learning happens. Chapter 2, "The Craft of Writing," defines what is meant by "craft" by looking closely at examples of crafted text. Chapter 3, "Envisioning Text Possibilities," suggests that there may be a part of the writing process that we haven't nurtured enough in our teaching—the part where writers envision how they might write their texts. And in Chapter 4, "Reading Aloud," the role of reading aloud in the teaching of writing is explored.

Chapters 5 and 6 both describe kinds of inquiry that will help you and your students learn how to learn from writers. Chapter 5, "Studying Writers' Office Work," explores how good writing starts long before drafts are ever written, in the ways in which experienced writers select topics and develop them before drafts. And Chapter 6, "Organized Inquiry," explains a structure for looking at craft in actual texts which will teach your students how to learn to write from writers.

Chapters 7, 8 and 9 are resource chapters. Chapter 7, "An Invitation to My Library," is a glimpse at the books I own that help me show students many possibilities for how to structure their writing. Chapter 8, "Another Invitation to My Library," looks at my books again, this time in light of how they help me show students ways-with-words crafting techniques. And in Chapter 9, "Selecting Books for Craft Study," I take readers through the criteria I use to choose new books for my teaching of writing.

Chapter 10, "Growing Taller in Our Teaching," is a short chapter that examines the need to rethink teaching when we are under the influence of lots of new learning. In the four chapters that follow, I share some of the ways learning to write from writers has caused me to rethink my teaching. Chapter 11 looks at planning; Chapter 12, at focus lessons for the whole class; Chapter 13, at individual conferring; and Chapter 14, at assessment. In the final chapter I tell the story of a writer I encountered in a fifth-grade classroom, and I reflect on my own resolve to never again teach without the help of experienced writers.

There is a single bibliography at the end of the book for all the children's literature cited in *Wondrous Words*. References for adult writing and professional texts are found at the end of each chapter.

# READING
# LIKE WRITERS

I sat down beside Justin on a Friday morning. I was a guest writing teacher in his fifth-grade classroom, and I had brought with me that day a huge box full of books of poetry. Justin was looking at Georgia Heard's poetry collection *Creatures of the Earth, Sea, and Sky* (1992) and he had stopped on the poem "Frog Serenade," a poem for two voices. His fingers were moving back and forth across the widely separated lines of the poem. "I can't figure this out," he said to me as I moved in beside him. I knew what he was going through—I too remembered being unsure of the structure of one of these poems the first time I saw one. I explained to him how the left and right sides were for two voices, and then we began to read it together. When we finished, Justin called one of his friends over and we performed the poem again for him, and then again for a group of girls who had overheard and wanted their own reading. We were a hit because of our brilliant performance, of course, but also because we had introduced Justin's friends to this wonderfully exotic kind of poem. I moved on to other students and other poems and left Justin with Georgia.

As I was leaving his classroom later that morning, Justin caught me on my way out the door. Shyly, he slipped a piece of paper into my hands. "I wrote this," was all he said.

**Something Dead**

Boom
Boom
Boom
                    I hear a noise
Boom
                    a gun is firing
Boom
Boom
Boom
                    People are crazy
Boom
                    Something is dead
Boom
Boom
Boom
                    Cause buzzards are flying
Boom
                    That's not nice
Boom
Boom
Boom
                    People are cruel
Boom
                    Men come with deer.

As I read through "Something Dead" I knew that I was experiencing one of those moments we all live for as teachers. Right before my eyes I was watching a child do something he couldn't have even dreamed of doing only an hour before. I mean, he had never even *seen* a poem like this. In one short hour Georgia Heard had given Justin a new vision of what was possible in writing, and Justin had used that vision to see his way into saying a big important thing in his life: *People are cruel—Boom—Men come with deer.*

Something dead
~~the~~ Justin C.

Boom
Boom
Boom                    I hear a nasie

Boom                    a gun is firing

Boom
Boom
Boom                    People are crazy

Boom                    Something is dead

Boom
Boom
Boom                    cause buze tret ~~thing~~

Boom                    thats not nice

Boom
Boom
Boom                    People are crol

Boom                    Men come with deer

*Justin's poem*

# ADDING A NEW FOCUS

When I first began teaching writing, I found tremendous satisfaction in help-ing children like Justin find those big important things to say in their lives. I loved living in a classroom where, day after day through our writing, we laughed and cried and gasped in awe at our own storied lives. My students and I each used our writing to say, "This is who I am, this is what I wish for, and this is what I care about. . . ." There was a satisfaction in this that I had never known from school writing as a student myself, and so as a teacher of writing I found confidence in my ability to rise above what I had known as a student. That my students wrote about topics that really *mattered* to them was more important to me than anything else.

Time and experience haven't changed this focus. My number-one priority in teaching writing is still this: "Write what matters." But time and experience have shown me that helping students find what matters to write about just isn't enough. It's a good start, but it isn't nearly enough. To see what else there is, it helps to first go back in time. My "good start" teaching, without too much exaggeration, used to go something like this:

> So, you've decided to write about how much your mother means to you. Great idea—it'll be such a special piece! Have at it! Let me know when you're finished.

And then I was off to encourage the next child writing about the destruction of the rain forests or the death of a beloved pet. We all felt so good about our writing topics that it was easy to get a false sense that there couldn't possibly be anything more than this, anything more than writing about these dear, dear topics in our lives.

But that sense was false, and I saw it exposed more times than I'd like to mention on the faces of children who, when they finally shared their published writing with us, knew that writing just didn't convey the passion they felt for their topics. Kyle, a second grader, was one of those children. He was trying to write a piece for his mother for Mother's Day, to let her know how special he thought she was. He had all the good reasons a writer needs to write—an audience, an occasion, and a thing he wanted very much to say. He was editing his "final draft" when I came to confer with him.

> I hope you like the book. I love my mom and I will always love my mom and she will always love me too. Roses are red, violets are blue, I love you and that is true. Roses are red, violets are blue, you like flowers and that is true. I love you and you love me, you are my mom and that is true. You are my mom and I love you. Roses are red, violets are blue, you are my mom and I love you. I wish you a Mother's Day that you will always remember. I wish you a happy mother's day because that is what you deserve.

He read his piece to me, and I could see the look on his face. The poem wasn't doing what he'd hoped it would do. Kyle knew I couldn't see his mom in what he'd written. Despite its nice rhythm, he knew his poem didn't do the work of showing how special she was. Looking back, I know that Kyle was using all he knew of poetry at that time—the rhythm and rhyme of that one, classic, framing line—to write this piece about his mother.

"It sounded so good when I was thinking about it, it just didn't *turn out* that good," a writer finishing a memoir about the Dominican Republic once said to me. And I had to ask myself, "Where was I, his teacher of writing, while he was *turning out* this piece that mattered to him?" I had caught Kyle in the act of turning out his piece. What would I do to help him? What should I do?

Facing enough writers like Kyle finally made me realize something very difficult and important as a teacher: The ideas behind my students' topics were often way better than much of the actual writing they ever did about these topics. Quite simple—it's hard to admit—but there for me to face. How much power could my students' writing have to help them make waves or build bridges in the world if I only helped them to find good topics? Didn't I also have a responsibility to help them write about these topics *well*, to do these huge, important life topics *justice* with good writing?

The answer I found to this question was "of course." I had to start doing more to help my students write well. If they were brave enough to go for these life topics, then I had to match that with brave, bold teaching.

Coming to this realization and then coming to a place where I really felt like I was helping students to write well has been a long journey. What I have found on this journey is that helping so many students write *well* about so many important topics is an overwhelming job I can't do by myself. That's right. I can't help students to write well by myself. I need lots of help doing this teaching work, and I have found that help on the shelves of my library. Think about Justin, for instance. In his case, my really hard teaching work involved carrying all those heavy books from my truck to his classroom. Georgia Heard taught him to write that poem, not me. Georgia Heard showed him how to write well about this injustice he felt in his heart that morning. And day after day as I teach writing to many different students, I let writers like Georgia and Gary Paulsen and Cynthia Rylant and Jane Yolen help me do the important work of teaching students to write well.

Bravely, still new to bold teaching and still afraid to step on toes, I went and got the Eloise Greenfield book entitled *Honey, I Love, and Other Love Poems* (1986), the morning Kyle read his poem about his mother to me. I showed Kyle the title poem, and I showed him how Eloise Greenfield was also trying to show a love for something, how she was writing just like him, but the difference was that Eloise said very specific things about what she loved. Her "loves" applied only to her. After studying this poem a bit, making a list of specific things he might write about his love for his mother, Kyle began a completely new draft of his poem.

> Mom, I love a lot of things about you. Like you drive me to school when it rains and the way you let my friends spend the night. I love a lot of things about you. Like the way when I walk in the door you ask me did I have a good day at school and the way you kiss me good night before I go to bed. And the way you wash my clothes for me and the way you give me toys and the way you play with me when I don't have no one to play with. I love you mom for lots of things, but most of all you love me too.

There's Kyle! There's his voice, and there's his mother! Eloise Greenfield helped Kyle see a different way to describe something through poetry. Eloise Greenfield showed Kyle that poems can do more than rhyme; she showed him that poems can say things, big important things, about our lives. I believe we have a responsibility as teachers to get the Georgias and the Eloises into our students' hands to help them know how to write well about the things that matter most to them.

Many of us who teach writing have learned to let authors like these help us show our students how to write well. Reading-writing connections have gone beyond written responses into actual craft apprenticeships in the writing workshop. Rather than garnering ideas for *what* to write about from their reading, students are learning to take their own important topics and then look to texts to learn *how* to write well about those topics.

Writing well involves learning to attend to the *craft* of writing, learning to do the sophisticated work of separating *what it's about* from *how it is written*. Justin didn't get a new idea for writing something about frogs from Georgia's poem. He got an idea for a new way to structure a familiar genre. He was able to see the craft of Georgia's writing as separate from her meaning. Kyle didn't get an idea to write about love from Eloise Greenfield—he already had that topic in mind. Eloise just helped him see how to *show* love rather than *tell* about it.

When students are taught to see how writing is done, this way of seeing opens up to them huge warehouses of possibilities for how to make their writing *good* writing. The key is in learning how to learn to write from writers, and teaching students to do this is the instructional challenge faced by teachers who want to help students write well.

## LEARNING TO WRITE FROM WRITERS

As teachers it seems we have to spend a lot of time fighting against what our own educational histories have taught us to believe. We were not taught to learn to write from writers. Oh, in high school and college we analyzed the texts of brilliant (if not mostly dead) writers, but we always did it as an end in itself. No one ever said to us, "Hey, you could try and write *like* Robert Frost if you want." In this school world we were taught things like "everyone writes differently" and "everyone has her own unique style," and we were led to believe that good writing required nothing less than a writer inventing a new wheel to get attention. Who could write with that kind of pressure? Not many of us did, unfortunately.

So learning how to write from writers is a fairly new concept in many classrooms. Not surprisingly, however, it isn't at all new to professional writers. Countless interviews, articles, and memoirs by and about famous writers attest to the fact that writers learn to write from reading the work of other writers. In an article in *Workshop Two* (1990) about the teaching of writing, Cynthia Rylant says, "I learned how to write from writers. I didn't know any personally, but I read . . ." (19). Gary Paulsen would agree with her. Speaking at an NCTE conference he gave this advice to aspiring writers: "Just read for about four years before you even start. Read everything you can get your hands on." And in *Radical Reflections* (1993) Mem Fox talks about listening again and again as a child to the actor John Gielgud reading Shelley's "Ode to the West Wind" until she knew the poem by heart (113). Today, she says, she still has "Shelley in her bones" and his rhythms help her write. Like any other craftspeople, professional writers know that to learn their craft, they must stand on the shoulders of writers who have gone before them.

But how is this done? How does a writer learn to write from other writers? Is it a simple process of imitation? Or is it a more sophisticated gathering

of both explicit and inexplicit technical knowledge about writing craft that we find across many different kinds of texts?

I've spent the last six years in writing workshops, grades kindergarten through graduate school, where I've worked as both teacher and staff developer, trying to answer this question. Together, the teachers with whom I've worked and I have nudged students to learn from more experienced writers by studying the craft of their writing. We've developed habits of inquiry to engage students in learning to write from writers, and used our own growing knowledge of the craft of writing to help students, in focus lessons and conferences, to write well. These experiences have helped me to understand a lot about what it means to learn to write from writers in both explicit and inexplicit ways, both within classrooms and outside of them. *Wondrous Words* is a book that will help you teach yourself and your students how to learn to write from writers, outline for you many common crafting techniques that good writers use, and help you rethink your teaching of writing to incorporate the teaching of craft in conferences and focus lessons.

Before launching into explaining the classroom practices that teach students to learn to write from writers, it is important to establish what I think are three important concepts that form the foundation for this kind of teaching. These concepts are as follows:

1. What it means to read like a writer.
2. The difference between writing as unique and writing as individual.
3. The difference between a descriptive and a prescriptive approach to teaching writing.

## READING LIKE A WRITER

What does it mean to read *like a writer*? How does a writer read? To understand this it is helpful to think about how any craftsperson would study the techniques of others who practice the same craft—how a chef would visit a restaurant, for example, or a potter another pottery gallery, a painter an art exhibit. My husband is in the knife-making business, and recently one of his bladesmiths visited the shop of another bladesmith to study a particular technique of knife making. Reading is the writer's way of visiting another craftsperson's "gallery." If the writer knows what to look for, he or she can learn a lot from looking closely at another craftsperson's work, and the text, of course, is the writer's work "gallery."

To illustrate this point I often tell students about my friend who is a very accomplished seamstress. I explain learning a craft from a craftsperson this way:

> Because my friend is a seamstress, she goes to the mall or to the dress shops differently than the rest of us who aren't seamstresses. First, it takes her a lot longer than a normal person to make her way through the store. She turns the dresses and jumpers and shirts inside out, sometimes sitting right down on the floor to study how something is made. While the rest of us mere shoppers are looking only at sizes and prices, my friend is looking closely at inseams and stitching and "cuts on the bias." She wants to know how what she sees was made, how it was put together. And the frustrating thing for anyone shopping with her is that as long as it takes her, she hardly ever buys anything! You see, my friend's not shopping for clothes, she's shopping for *ideas for* clothes. After a day at the mall she goes home with a head full of new ideas for what she might make next on her trusty sewing machine.

This story about my seamstress friend helps students understand how a writer must read, gathering ideas from text to text to text about what the possibilities are for writing. Students can easily see how a writer in a library or a bookstore is like a seamstress in a dress shop.

The key part of the story is "the rest of us who aren't seamstresses" because it hints at the importance of identity in learning to read *like a writer*. My friend's identity as a seamstress means that she sees herself as someone who makes clothes. She knows that this act, making clothes, will be a part of her future, and so she lives with that expectation, watching clothes in the world to see what "clothes possibilities" exist. First-time expectant parents watch families differently for the same reason—they are looking for family possibilities. A man planning a garden looks at gardens on his way home from work for just the same reason—he's looking for garden possibilities. And when writers read, they can't help but see writing possibilities in the texts they encounter. If we know that a particular activity is something we will be doing (writing), if we see ourselves as someone who does this thing (writes), then we have a different way of looking at that thing (text) as we make our way through the world.

Now, conversely, if we do not see ourselves as the kind of person who would ever do a particular thing, then we do not live with this "craftsperson's vision" for this thing. Take for instance my interest in music. Music is something that I love purely as a spectator. I have no desire to be a musician. I do not see myself as a musician, and when I listen to music I don't hear what a musician hears when she listens to music because I do not *need* to hear it. Making music will not be a part of my future (I can hear those of you who have heard me sing saying "Thank God" here). And when my friend and I shop together I will always be only a shopper, a good shopper, but only that. Never a seamstress. I need only look at price and size to satisfy my needs as a shopper.

So what is essential here is to understand that for our students to learn to read like writers, they first have to see themselves as writers. They have to know that poems and letters and stories and editorials are a part of their futures. To learn from other writers, students have to live with the kind of expectations that come from being *people who write*. Once students see themselves this way, they are able to lay their work down alongside that of other writers and see habits and crafts mirrored there, and also extend their own understandings of what it means to write.

Lisa Cleaveland, a brilliant kindergarten teacher in western North Carolina, has done such a good job of helping her five- and six-year-olds see themselves as writers, that she routinely gets asked writerly questions from her young students at work. Recently, one of them asked her, "Ms. Cleaveland, when authors write, do they staple their books first and then write, or do they write first and then staple?" Sam was so sure that his stapling process was the work of a real writer that he wondered about the fine points of that process in other writers' work like Eric Carle and Ezra Jack Keats. Seeing his work as like the work of the writers he's read at home and in school causes Sam to think about what he reads as being like what he writes—the all-important connection necessary to read like a writer.

So in order to gather a repertoire of craft possibilities that will help a writer write well, that writer first has to learn how to read differently, how to read with a sense of possibility, a sense of "What do I see here that might work for me in my writing?" This is what reading like a writer means—to read with a sense of possibility.

# FRANK SMITH'S LEGACY

The whole idea of reading like a writer stands squarely on the shoulders of Frank Smith's work in learning theory development. Smith uses the expression "reading like a writer" in *Joining the Literacy Club* (1988) to describe how a writer must acquire the vast amount of knowledge necessary to write anything successfully. Smith points out that the knowledge needed to write successfully is so vast that it could never be covered or contained by a systematic instructional program. Quite simply, he says, students must learn what they will need to know about writing from reading. He is quick to point out, however, that this knowledge is only available to those who see themselves as part of "the club of writers." Smith calls on teachers to make it their main goal to help students see themselves as writers and then find the mentors students need. He says,

> Teachers must also ensure that children have access to reading materials that are relevant to the kind of writer they are interested in becoming at a particular moment. Teachers must recruit the authors who will become the children's unwitting collaborators. (26)

Smith focuses on the *vicarious* learning that takes place when a writer reads, and he points out that this learning happens at an overwhelmingly effortless and speedy pace as writers learn words, phrases, spellings, and authors' "stylistic idiosyncrasies" as they read. He goes on to say that "Teachers do not have to *teach* children to read like writers" (26). And I agree that writers cannot help but learn vicariously from their reading, and so in that sense they do not need to be taught to do this kind of vicarious learning.

I do believe, however, that there is a different kind of intentional and deliberate reading that writers can learn to do in order to grow in their knowledge of the craft of writing (Smith would call craft "stylistic devices"). While Eloise Greenfield and Georgia Heard were certainly "unwitting collaborators" as two young writers learned from them, Kyle and Justin were quite deliberate and intentional in their collaboration with these mentors. This kind of reading like a writer is undertaken by those who pursue writing as artists or craftspeople, writers who, like any other artists, jump at the chance to learn from a master craftsperson. But to learn from another craftsperson, it helps to know what kinds of things to be watching in that craftsperson's work. Imagine being in a gallery of oil paintings with an accomplished painter to show you around. The painter might show you things about the paintings that you would never see on your own. Smith talks about writers rereading something because "something in the passage was particularly well put, because we respond to the craftsman's touch" (24). I believe that writers can deepen their understandings of what it means when something is "particularly well put" or the result of "the craftsman's touch," know better what to watch out for, study more deliberately how a writer managed to "put it well," and in doing so be better able to imagine crafting writing this way in their own texts.

Smith goes on to say that when writers notice something and reread, it's also because "we have read something we would like to be able to write ourselves but also something we think is not beyond our reach" (24). My experience has shown me that many more things become "reachable" to writers who live in communities in which they read like writers and study together the craftsmanship of writers. The conversations that happen during an inquiry into craft make many techniques available to inexperienced writers that, without such inquiry, might have seemed out of reach. Slowing down to do more than simply reread something you've noticed an experienced writer doing in a text, slowing down to name it and figure out how it was done, helps you better imagine doing this kind of crafting in your own writing. If we travel back to my friend in the dress shop, we know that certainly she can gather ideas from simply walking through the shop, but true craft inquiry is the slowing down to sit on the floor and turn the dress inside out, not just seeing possibilities, but studying them as well.

So the inquiry structures we've been working with in writing workshops do simply this—they slow down and make more deliberate the reading like writers that happens vicariously when any writer reads. Slowing down lets writers apprentice themselves very deliberately to other writers, developing a line of thinking during inquiry that, with use over time, becomes a *habit of mind* that writers engage in without effort and without intentional inquiry. I have so developed my "reading like a writer" habit of mind that I can catch myself saying "Now look at how that's written" most every morning as I read the newspaper or look at billboards on the way to work.

As you will see explained in detail in Chapter 6, inquiry structures are used in classrooms to teach this reading-like-writers habit of mind to young writers.

And while lots of curriculum about good writing is generated from this kind of inquiry, the curriculum itself really isn't the point. The habit of mind, the habit that will outlive our moments in the classroom and continue to teach students throughout their reading and writing lives, is the point. So if we want to help our students write well, we first need to teach them to read like writers.

## WRITING IS INDIVIDUAL—IT IS NOT UNIQUE

For you and your students to learn to write from other writers, you will need to first think a little about "writing style." I'm defining style here as the manners of expression a writer uses, the ways in which a writer crafts words to make meaning on the page. Consider this: While any writer's style is individual, it is not unique.

The definitions for "unique" in my trusty old *Webster's* dictionary are

1. one and only; sole,

2. different from all others; having no like or equal,

3. singular; unusual; rare.

Once you begin to really look at texts and see how they are written, you soon realize how absurd it is to define writers' styles as "unique." As a matter of fact, the styles in which different writers write are more alike than they are different. Take for example the crafting technique of combining words with hyphens to make a new, just-right word. Lots of writers use this very handy technique. Jerry Spinelli uses it often in *Maniac Magee* (1990) to describe things like "That's why his front steps were the only *un-sat-on* front steps in town" (italics mine, all such). In *An Angel for Solomon Singer* (1992), Cynthia Rylant describes a waiter in a cafe as a "*smiling-eyed* waiter." And Libba Moore Gray uses this technique throughout *My Mama Had a Dancing Heart* (1995) in lines like "the sand stuck between the toes of our *up-and-down squish-squashing feet*." In the two chapters of this book which outline various structural techniques and ways of using words, you will see many different writers using words in exactly the same ways to make meaning in very different kinds of texts.

You see, when we write, we are not doing something that hasn't been done before. As a matter of fact, we are doing something that is very like what has been done for centuries. Our writing acts are all individual in that we are one person writing about one topic at one moment in time for some purpose, but the act of how we go about doing that is not unique. Language is defined by the very ways in which we *share* its use. So the decisions about which ways we will use language in a given piece of writing are individual, but the ways themselves are not unique.

When I'm explaining this concept to students I often go back to my story about the seamstress. I tell them that one of the reasons my friend likes to design and make her own clothes is that she never has to worry about showing up at church or at a restaurant wearing something that someone else is wearing. She hoards material of all sorts—linens and wools and gabardines—saving each piece for just the right plan for how to "make it up" into something snazzy and wonderful. Her material, and her exact plans for what to do with it, are what give her an individual style. But what she makes is not unique. Like anyone else who makes clothes, she makes vests and skirts and tops and little sarongs like she saw on her trip to the islands. How she makes clothes and the shapes and forms of what she makes are not unique, she shares the possibilities for these with all other seamstresses.

I tell my students that

[A]s writers, you're a lot like my friend. You have hoards of material, hoards of stuff you might write about. But how you go about writing about all that stuff will be in some way the same as writers who have gone before you. You'll write poems or stories or memoirs. You'll use lines that repeat and rhetorical questions and stunning verbs. Writing, like making clothes, is not a unique process each time someone engages in it. It is individual, but it's not unique.

We make a big mistake when we persist in this notion that every time someone writes it is an event that is unique in the history of the world—that everyone who writes has his or her very own style made up of totally unique ways of using words. Nonsense. Everything we do as writers we have known in some fashion as readers first.

A few years ago I worked with a group of middle school students in a summer writing camp. I asked the group during one of our first mornings together to talk about the writers whose styles matched their own. After they'd been talking a few minutes, Aaron, a brave soul in the group, spoke for the rest of them. "Katie," he said, "we were talking about it and we really don't think we write like anybody else. Everybody in my group—we all have our own unique style." They were really quite insulted that I had even suggested they might have something in common with others writers. That good writing was a unique act was something they had been taught in sometimes subtle, sometimes very direct ways in schools.

We spent a lot of time that summer rethinking the notion of a writer's style being something that is unique. I have learned from experience that making this false assumption and sticking to it shut down a writer's ability to learn from other writers in any intentional way, though the vicarious learning will still take place. Writers can't help the vicarious learning, and of course it is this vicarious learning that keeps writing style from being unique and makes language use (written or spoken) a shared commodity. We can't help the learning we do from other writers; what we can help is to help ourselves to even more of that learning! Once we embrace our individuality and let go of a misguided, impossible-to-fulfill need to have a unique writing style, we can get on to the business of really learning to write *well*.

## Descriptive versus Prescriptive Teaching

These two key understandings—reading like a writer and understanding the individual (not unique) nature of writing itself—are necessary for both students and teachers to learn to write from writers. The final key understanding is really only necessary for you (the teacher) to understand before pushing further—because it has to do with a shift in thinking about how we teach writing. If you are going to teach your students to learn to write from writers, you are going to have to switch from a *prescriptive* approach to teaching writing to a *descriptive* approach. What does this mean? I'll illustrate by sharing with you the classroom encounter I had years ago that taught me the difference in these two ways of teaching about writing.

When I first started using inquiry as a way to learn to write from writers, I didn't really know what I was doing, what we might find in this inquiry, or where we would go once we were under way. I just thought we needed to "learn to write from writers" the way Cynthia Rylant said she had learned to write. You might say I was teaching with a bit of blind faith. So since Rylant had gotten me into this, I decided we would use her texts to start our study. While looking at one of her texts, a fourth grader named Jennifer raised her hand, vigorously, in my face. I responded, and when I did she said, "Cynthia Rylant starts three sentences in this book with 'and' and my daddy told me you were not supposed to start sentences with 'and.' It's against the rules."

Uh-oh. The rules.

No fragments. No run-ons. No pronouns without antecedents. All paragraphs with topic sentences. No split infinitives. No ending sentences with prepositions. All stories with clear beginnings, middles, and ends. Don't repeat a word too often. And on and on and on.

We all know THE LIST, but incidents like this one early into my study of craft had me asking, "Didn't someone tell these award-winning authors about this list?" My students and I kept running into things involving language use that I had always been told not to do with my writing, and by that time in my teaching career I had "preached from the list" more than a few times myself. Now, I had seen enough student writing to know there were bad fragments that just left you hanging, run-ons that never ended, 'and's' used like marks of punctuation instead of conjunctions, and split infinitives so far apart you forgot what was happening in between. But that's not what we were seeing in these texts. We were seeing fragments that *were* complete thoughts, run-ons conveying a sense of desperation or excitement, texts that flowed beautifully but—belying clear beginnings, middles and ends—could have been organized in many different ways. And sentences starting with "and" that made perfect endings to perfect texts.

Through experiences looking at many different texts in inquiry with children, we came to realize that there was a difference between *describing* good writing and *prescribing* good writing. When we really engaged in *describing* good writing, we found ourselves talking about how it all works quite differently than we did when we only *prescribed* good writing, far away from the beautiful texts those prescriptions were meant to help create. And of course we had to face the fact that many of the things we had been taught about good writing simply were not true. As we looked and described what we saw, we were rewriting our own understandings about how good writing happens.

I would be lying if I didn't say that in these early describing days we (the other teachers and I) were at times fearful that what we saw writers doing signaled the end of the civilized world as we knew it. It wasn't until we looked at some of "the old masters" we'd read in school, and saw them doing the same things, that we realized using language in interesting ways has been going on as long as people have been writing. Crafting writing is nothing new. Describing the craft of writing was what was new to us. We were never taught to look at *how* Hemingway or Swift was writing. When it came time to learn how to write we were given prescriptions far removed from the texts we were asked to read.

Over time, as we *really looked* at writing, we found that there was nothing to fear. Good writers don't pursue their craft with a reckless abandon. Instead, they have come to realize that language is there to be used, in any manner possible, to make meaning. Human beings invented language. Its use is not a fixed, rule-bound principle of the universe that existed before us or outside of us. Its use is an exchange between human beings, and because of that, it is alive and changing and growing, and it is never static, never one thing or one way you can put your finger on. To learn to write from writers you will have to make peace with understanding language in use, rather than language in principle.

Once you do make peace with this and start describing what you see in beautiful texts, you may start celebrating as I have this new way of thinking about good writing. I am celebrating because finally I have found a fascination with language study. That's right—language study. Not mindless drudgery grammar and diagraming lessons, but language study that allows me to describe good writing and learn how craft happens.

Describing good writing requires you to get words into your classroom that let you talk easily about what you are seeing in texts. Usually young writers don't have the words I have to talk about writing, words like metaphor and simile, personification and alliteration, parts-of-speech names. But this inexperience with language terminology actually helps them more than it hurts them in the inquiry part of reading like writers. When we first started I found that I went to texts looking for things I knew the names of, rather than just looking at how the writing was done. So I might see what I was looking for, but I missed a lot of other things that the students were seeing. Early on, if I didn't have a name for it, I didn't see it. My expectations about what I thought I should see limited my ability to truly inquire as the children were. Many of the crafting techniques the students found did not have names in the literary devices I had known. I could describe them, often pulling up my parts-of-speech knowledge, but I didn't have a name for them in my adult repertoire.

For example, in Rylant's *The Relatives Came* (1985), a group of students was interested in "wrinkled Virginia clothes" and "hugging time." The students said things like "they sound neat" and "they sound weird together." And they did, but I didn't know a *name* to call what Rylant was doing. What I could do, however, was use my knowledge of parts of speech to first realize and then explain to the students that what made these phrases stand out was the fact that Rylant had used two words that aren't usually adjectives ("Virginia" is a proper noun and "hugging" is a verb, a present participle) as adjectives. Explaining it this way allowed us to think of other examples of our own such as "Tuesday was a sweating day" and "My dog gave me a jumping kiss." We could figure out how to do it; we just didn't know what to call it.

This language issue, this "what are the words we use to talk about writing" issue, was the source early on of another very significant insight into teaching writing from a descriptive rather than prescriptive stance. In these early inquiries I was finding many very natural opportunities to supply children with the language they needed to help them name what they were seeing. I was daily having to pull from my memory parts-of-speech names, pronoun categories, and names for literary devices to help children *and to help me* understand what we were seeing as we described texts. Embedded in all our talk about writing were many grammatical terms and usage concepts that the children picked up almost effortlessly, as they do most new words used in sensible ways within real contexts. Even kindergartners commenting that they loved a word like "luscious" were told, "Oh yeah, that's an adjective. It tells how something is. Isn't that one wonderful?"

I had always been taught concepts about how our language works in a way that was very removed from actual pieces of writing, from that language in use, and for this reason learning them was always hard. Some concepts never made much sense to me, and even with the ones that did make sense, I didn't see them as having an impact on my writing life beyond making my subjects and verbs agree. I was amazed that certain grammatical concepts, not named literary devices but grammatical concepts, could actually help me think about the craft of my writing. And this amazement grew from simple statements like, "It's got a lot of words that end in *-ing* in it" and questions like, "Do you think this really happened to Cynthia Rylant?"

Let me explain. Two stories.

Once, as a group of writers was looking at the Cynthia Rylant text *This Year's Garden* (1984), one of the things someone in the group noticed was, "It's got a lot of words that end in *-ing* in it." And he was right. Twenty-one to be exact. Words like *squatting, sitting, bending, digging, waiting,* etc. The group talked about this observation.

I said to them, "You call those 'participles.' They're verbs called 'present participles.'" That was about all I knew about participles. Someone in the group suggested that having all those *-ing* words in there made it feel sort of like you were planting the garden right along with them as you read it. Like you were "do-*ing*" all those things. A tiny whisper of a thought entered my mind. I shared it with the group. "I wonder if that's what 'participle' means? It sounds like 'participate' so maybe it means that when you use that kind of verb, it makes a piece of writing feel like you are participating in it?" This sounded promising, so we got a dictionary and looked it up and sure enough, "participate" and "participle" are closely related.

I felt slighted, cheated. I had only known participles as one of the conjugation columns on the board in my English classes. Why hadn't anyone ever shown me how functional they could be for me as a writer? Shown me that if I wanted to make a text feel participatory, I should use them, in abundance?

In another gathering of writers, an inquiry group raised this question to the whole class of third graders: "Do you think this [the story in *The Relatives Came* (1985)] really happened to Cynthia Rylant?" I thought this was an interesting question, so I asked the group how it became a question for them. One child explained, "Well, we noticed that in *When I Was Young in the Mountains* [1982], Cynthia says 'I' all the time so you know it is her own life memories. But in *The Relatives Came* she never says 'I,' but it still seems like it should be something that happened to her."

Guess what lesson I taught that day? You've got it—first-person pronouns, singular and plural. I knew that part, fed it to these third graders, and they got it in a snap. (Is that concept even *in* most third-grade curriculum guides?) But the understanding I didn't have, and what I figured out that day with that group of children, was what a difference the plural and singular forms of that pronoun make in a piece of writing. As a writer, if you want your piece to have an inclusive feeling, a feeling like it's anyone's story, any-one's essay, write in first-person plural as Rylant did in *The Relatives Came*, using "we" and "us" and "our." On the other hand, if you want it to sound very singularly "memoiry," you had better use the old standby "I." Did you learn pronoun cases this way? By what work they could do for you as a writer? This was radical to me.

So classroom encounters like these, happening over and over again, taught me that grammatical and usage concepts made a lot more sense when they came from the inside out, from looking at language and wondering, "How does this work?" And they also taught me what it means to know these concepts as a writer, something I had never been shown before. Language study had always been very separate from my actual work as a writer, and except for editing purposes, the concepts I learned in language study were never joined with my decision-making process as a writer.

A descriptive approach to teaching writing forces us to look at language as something that gets *used* by writers, and in this way it creates a marriage between the study of language and the teaching of writing that has been sadly absent from traditional, prescriptive approaches to language study. As you look at texts with students you discuss everything as a "writer's move." You form most every question about the text with the writer's name in it— "Why did Rylant choose not to use 'I' in this text?" Language is seen for what it really is, something that gets used in real ways by real people, not a land-mine field of "rules" set up for writers to cautiously make their way around. Language is beautiful, alive, wondrous, and studying the craft of it in use will remind you of this again and again.

## References

Fox, Mem. 1993. *Radical Reflections: Passionate Opinions on Teaching, Learning, and Living.* New York: Harcourt, Brace.

Rylant, Cynthia. 1990. "The Room in Which Van Gogh Lived." In *Workshop Two: By and for Teachers, Beyond the Basal,* edited by Nancie Atwell, 18–21. Portsmouth, NH: Heinemann.

Smith, Frank. 1988. *Joining the Literacy Club: Further Essays into Education.* Portsmouth, NH: Heinemann.

# THE CRAFT
## OF WRITING

We made a case in the last chapter for the idea that writing well involves learning to attend to the *craft* of writing, learning to do the sophisticated work of separating *what it's about* from *how it is written*. But what does this really mean? What is the "craft" of writing? In my work alongside other teachers during the past few years, I have learned that it helps to just go straight to this, to defining what we mean by craft, and then to work back out of that understanding and into thinking about how to help students read like writers so that they can see craft for themselves, both in the texts that writers publish and in the things that writers say about their processes. So that is what I'd like to do in this chapter: Define and give shape to what we mean by the craft of writing, both in process and in text, so we'll know what it is we're looking for as we learn to write from writers.

My dictionary defines a craft as a special skill or art, and that definition will work just fine to help us understand the craft of writing. A writer's craft is a particular way of doing something; it's a knowledge a writer has about *how* to do something. Competent writers need to know how to go about all aspects of the writing process, from ideas to finished texts, and we can learn from what they do, from the craft of how they do their work, in every step of the process.

Donald Graves is generally credited with bringing the writing process to contemporary classrooms. Graves and his colleagues studied closely what writers do, from ideas to finished texts, and then identified the mostly recursive steps that writers go through to write. The steps of this process are prewriting, drafting, revising, editing, and publishing, and without a doubt, all writers engage in each of these processes. For any one part of the writing process we have an opportunity to learn to write from writers by studying what writers do during each phase of the writing.

For the purpose of organizing classroom study, I have found it helpful to think about studying the craft of writing in two major categories. In one category I lump all the things there are to learn from writers about the craft of their "office work"—where they get ideas, how they do research, how they get response to drafts, how they set up their offices. In the other category I lump all the things there are to learn about how writers craft actual drafts, how they make the writing "come out" in powerful texts.

## THE CRAFT OF A WRITER'S OFFICE WORK

The particular ways writers engage with the writing process in their office work are varied and individual, but one thing is for sure—all writers have offices that extend way out into the world. "Office work" is simply a placeholder for the idea of "studio" or "workshop"—a place where a craftsperson practices his or her craft. Some writers keep notebooks for prewriting; others keep boxes of scraps of idea papers for prewriting. Some writers of fiction start with an idea for a character, others start with a setting, and still others start with a plot idea. Some writers draft fast and furiously, knowing they will return to the drafts later and do extensive revising. Other writers draft very slowly, sentence by sentence, revising as they go. Some writers have someone else look at their drafts throughout the process of writing; others won't let anyone see what they've written until they feel they are finished. The craft of this work is made up of all these different, individual possibilities for getting writing done that we see in the work of experienced writers.

For example, if we hear (as I did) Patricia MacLachlan speak and she says (as she did) that she will follow strangers an extra block or two down the street to finish eavesdropping on an interesting conversation they're having—because she might need it someday as a writer—we learn that she is thinking about her writing even when she's not writing (or in her office!), listening for interesting snippets of conversation she might use later as a writer. This kind of listening is part of the craft of her prewriting.

Or perhaps we learn that an author writes at the same exact time every day. The fact that he gets his writing done by having a regular writing time is part of his craft. Of course, other writers will tell you they only write when inspired, when moved to do so. This is part of their craft. It's how they get their writing done.

We might learn that an author belongs to a revising group of writing friends who trust each other enough to read each other's drafts and ask: "What would you do if this were your draft?" This would be part of that writer's revision craft.

Another writer might tell us that she cuts her drafts up into pieces, into meaningful chunks, and then tries arranging them in different ways, reading each arrangement aloud until she finds one she likes. This would be part of the craft of her drafting.

When we learn to write from the craft of writers' office work, we learn a variety of possibilities for how to go about getting our writing going and keeping it going. Studying office-work crafting helps us to imagine how to live our working lives as writers. A few years ago one of my student teachers at the university worked long and hard to set up a dentist's center in her kindergarten classroom. Much to her surprise (and dismay), many of the students really had no idea of what to do in this center. Unfortunately, many of them had yet to visit a dentist's office. They couldn't imagine the kind of work that would go on there. If we have writing workshops in our classrooms, we don't want our students to be at a similar loss to imagine what kinds of work should go on there. We need to study the ways in which writers engage in the craft of office work so we can see possibilities for our own writing office work. Chapter 5 will explore in detail ways to engage students in studying the office work of writers.

## THE CRAFT OF A WRITER'S TEXT

What does craft look like then in actual texts? The moves writers make in texts are not generally ones we can have explained to us, unless we have the opportunity to crawl inside a writer's head as he or she is drafting. We have to work backwards from what we see in a finished text to what we imagine the writer did to make it come out that way. Seeing and understanding craft in texts is a much more difficult process than imagining possibilities for your office work as a writer, so we will slow this part way down and really explore the meaning of craft in text.

When you see that a writer has crafted something in a text, you see a particular way of using words that seems deliberate or by design—like something that didn't "just come out that way" (an idea problematized in the next chapter). Crafted places in texts are those places where writers do particular things with words that go beyond just choosing the ones they need to get the meaning across. The "special skill or art" to writing is knowing more and more of these "particular things" to do with words. This is what helps writers write well when they have an audience in mind, it helps them garner attention for what they have to say, and it helps them find that place beyond meaning where words *sing* with beauty.

But how do we see that place beyond meaning? As you might imagine, it helps a great deal to look at some examples of crafting when you begin to define this for yourself. You can find craft anywhere, but for our purposes here, I'm going to point out some crafting found on just two pages (92 and 93) of a March 2, 1998 *Sports Illustrated* article by Gary Smith about the University of Tennessee women's basketball coach Pat Summitt. The title of the article is "Eyes of the Storm," and it is masterfully written in its entirety. It's a long article, but on these two short pages (shortened with inserts and pictures), Smith "shows off" in a glorious burst of lively, interesting language use. He's doing a lot more than just telling his story here—he's bringing that story to life, making it jump from the page with an attention to craft that is amazing. I'd suggest you go to your local library and find the article in its entirety. And by the way, *Sports Illustrated* always has very good writing in it.

## LOOKING CLOSELY AT GARY SMITH'S "EYES OF THE STORM"

## Making a Long Story Short

In the article, Smith writes about a young woman who's chosen another school but is wanting to transfer to the University of Tennessee. To describe the decision-making process that led her to choose another school, Smith writes this sentence:

> So Michelle agonizes, Michelle flip-flops, Michelle visits Tennessee a third time, hugs Pat, kisses the new baby . . . and signs with Notre Dame. (92)

The ellipses are actually in the sentence—I haven't used them to take the place of some of Smith's words. My students and I have come to call this kind of sentence "making a long story short." We've seen the technique in lots of places. A writer uses it to cover a lot of ground quickly and move a story along. Think about all the *life* that must have been happening to Michelle around those short noun-verb phrases that Smith just leaves out, cutting right to the chase as they say. Cynthia Rylant uses this same technique in her book, *The Relatives Came* (1985). She writes:

> So they drank up all their pop and ate up all their crackers and traveled up all those miles until finally they pulled into our yard. (n.p.)

She just gets through that whole long trip in one sentence and gets those relatives to their destination quickly. Knowing how to make a long story short is a writer's technique. This is craft.

## Using Print to Match Meaning

When Michelle realizes she has made a mistake by going to Notre Dame, Smith writes that she wants to transfer "rightthisveryminute." Smith runs those words together because he knows he can, and because of course he understands writers can manipulate print to match and make meaning.

Isn't running those four words together just perfect, squeezing time out of their meaning by squeezing the spaces out? This is a technique he probably learned when he was in kindergarten and saw a word like "hot" written in red letters or a word like "big" written in BIG letters. He's all grown up now, but he still knows how effective this can be. So do lots of other "grown-up" writers. In the newspaper I was reading just this morning, Chris Sheridan of the Associated Press had written an article about the NBA playoff game between the Indiana Pacers and the Chicago Bulls. He wrote, "nor were they the *UpsetableBulls* of Games 3 and 4" (C-1, col. 2). Sheridan also manipulated print and spelling and wordplay for effect. This is craft.

## Intentional Vagueness

In the next paragraph, Smith writes, ". . . almost everything between this lady and this girl is going to be complicated. . ." (92). Now why did he say "this lady and this girl" when it's already been well established that he's talking about Pat and Michelle? Why here did he choose not to use their names? My students and I call this "intentional vagueness"—being sort of general about something when you could be specific. Cynthia Rylant often uses this technique when she writes. "*The* relatives" in her book *The Relatives Came* (1985) is a classic example. And in *The Whales* (1996), she writes that the whales "are floating like feathers in *a* sky" (n.p.). "A" sky? Neat, huh? Not "the" sky. Angela Johnson does the same thing throughout her picture book *The Aunt in Our House* (1996) as she never names the aunt, just refers to her as "the aunt." This is a choice a writer makes about how to use words. This is craft.

## On-Your-Mark, Get-Set, Go Colon

In the next paragraph in Smith's article, the transfer is finally at UT and Smith uses a common writer's technique. He writes,

> It's the fall of 1993, and Michelle finally is living her dream, and here is how the dream begins: It begins with . . . (92)

What he's doing is using that colon to set us up for something. It's like an "on-your-mark, get-set, go" kind of colon. It's the same colon you see in Cynthia Rylant's book *Tulip Sees America* (1998) where she writes,

> And we left Ohio and went across America. This is what we saw: The farms in Iowa. (n.p.)

Both writers know what work a colon can do for them: It gets the reader ready for a listing of things that will follow. It's an organizational marker for a list. This is craft.

## Repeating Sentence Structures

What follows the on-your-mark, get-set, go colons in Gary Smith's and Cynthia Rylant's pieces is very similar. Both writers use a repetitive series of sentences to make the list. Smith repeats actual words, beginning six sentences in the next three paragraphs with the words, "It begins with . . ." as in

> . . . and here is how the dream begins: It begins with 4:30 a.m. wake-ups, with relentless wind sprints through the dark on the Tennessee track. (92)

*Six* more start just exactly the same way. Rather than repeating actual words, Rylant follows her colon with vignettes that each start with a repeated sentence structure—a noun phrase that names what Tulip and her owner saw on their trip and what will be described in each vignette. "The farms in Iowa." and "The skies in Nebraska." are two examples. What particular thing do both Rylant and Smith know about writing? They both know that repetitive patterns work to tie together a list of things that go together. This is craft.

## Close Echoes

In Smith's sentence quoted above—"It begins with 4:30 a.m. wake-ups, with relentless wind sprints through the dark on a Tennessee track"—he's using another fairly common writing technique when he uses the word "with" a second time. My students and I have come to call this technique a "close echo." A close echo is when writers repeat a word, usually a function-type word, that isn't necessary to repeat. Smith could have used "and" in this sentence, writing it this way: "It begins with 4:30 a.m. wake-ups and relentless wind sprints. . . ." He is joining two things together, and the first "with" can do the work for the second part of the sentence. He might have even included "and" and "with," writing it this way: "It begins with 4:30 a.m. wake-ups, and with relentless wind sprints. . . ." But leaving that "and" out, using the comma and another "with," lets you really hear that second "with" and gives the text a particular rhythm. Cynthia Rylant also frequently uses this technique in her writing. In her book *Night in the Country* (1986) she writes: "There is no night so dark, so black as night in the country" (n.p.). She uses a comma and repeats "so," echoing its sound, instead of connecting two like things with "and." This is craft.

## Effective Use of "And"

Believe it or not, we're only three paragraphs into our two pages, and there's still a lot more to see. Consider this line that Smith writes about Michelle's first visit to the UT locker room: ". . . stopping to stare at all the framed photographs on the National Championship Wall and the White House Visits Wall and the Final Four Wall and the All-Americas and Olympians wall." Look at all those "and's." Could it be that Gary Smith was absent the day his class learned to punctuate items in a series with commas and just one "and"? Of course not, he knows just what he's doing. He's doing the same thing Jane Yolen does in the afterword of *Welcome to the Green House* (1993) when she writes: "If we do not do something soon, there will be no more green house, not for the monkeys and fish and birds and bees and beetles and wild pigs and bats and kinkajous and all the hundreds of thousands of flowers and fruits and trees." When a writer wants to convey a sense not just of a list of things, but of the vastness of a list of things, he or she will frequently connect those things using "and" again and again, instead of commas, to get that vast sense across. This is craft.

## Runaway Sentence

Look a little further and try and read this *one* sentence that Smith writes. Try and read it without catching your breath:

> It begins with Michelle looking over her shoulder as she dribbles in a scrimmage
> and wondering what in blazes this woman is doing, three feet behind her, down

on one knee and squatting lower and lower as if the view at sneaker level might reveal some hidden flaw, slapping the floor with her palm at her latest find, hanging on Michelle's next decision as if life itself were riding on it, leaning right with her as she cuts and leans in for a lay-up, and then, *daggone it*, the anguish squinching Pat's cheeks and shaking fist if Michelle misses, the disappointment even sharper than Michelle's. (93)

Did you make it? That's a long sentence, and written on a classroom chalkboard it might be labeled "awkward," and you'd be trying to split it up into smaller, more manageable chunks. But in this article it has the wonderful feel of what my students and I call a "runaway" sentence. Its sheer length and its weaving its way in and out of the scene helps to convey its breathless, slightly out-of-control meaning. It's written long *on purpose*, to help us feel the desperation Michelle feels as she tries to figure out her coach's rather intense habits. Runaway sentences always convey some sense of either desperation, excitement, panic, or joy. Some sense of carried-awayness or out-of-control-ness (I made those words up; that's also craft). One of my favorite examples of another writer doing this is Sandra Cisneros, in her book *House on Mango Street* (1991) in the chapter entitled "Hairs." She writes this sentence to show the narrator's feeling of being carried away with the thought of her mother's hair:

But my mother's hair, my mother's hair, like little rosettes, like little candy circles all curly and pretty because she pinned it in pincurls all day, sweet to put your nose into when she is holding you, holding you and you feel safe, is the warm smell of bread before you bake it, is the smell when she makes room for you on her side of the bed still warm with her skin, and you sleep near her, the rain outside falling and Papa snoring. (6–7)

This, too, is craft.

## Commenting on the Text

After recounting a particularly poignant exchange between Coach Summitt and one of her players, Smith begins the next paragraph showing us his own shock at Summitt's tenacity. He starts with these words: "Whoo boy" (93). Whoo boy? It's as if, for just a moment, we are sitting next to Smith's computer as he writes. We get to hear his personal response to what he's writing. He starts the next paragraph in a similar way when he writes: "Imagine living with that" (93). Sometimes writers just sort of leave their texts for a moment, leave what they are saying alone for a moment, and have a word with their readers, person to person. Often, it's in the form of a command like "Imagine living with that." Cynthia Rylant does this in *Night in the Country* (1986) when she says directly to the reader: "Listen:" She stops right in the middle of her descriptions of the text and tells you (the reader) to listen. What these writers know is that it is OK to stop writing the "story" every now and then and use words just to talk to the reader. This is craft.

## Question Series

Right after "Whoo boy" Smith structures the entire next paragraph as a series of questions. All the questions start with "Who"—they are all about Pat, and four of the five of them start with "Who else . . .", as in

> Who else demands that her players sit in the first three rows of the classes and forbids them even a single unexcused absence? Who else finds out about every visit they make to the mall. . . . (93)

So that paragraph works out of a series of repeated words and a series of repeated sentence structures (questions). This is the second time in two pages Smith has written a series of sentences using a repeated phrase— remember the six "It begins with . . ." sentences we mentioned earlier? Repetition of a phrase or sentence structure is a very common textual structure, used frequently in longer texts to shape just a part of the text, as it does here, and used frequently in picture book texts to shape the entire text. If you know picture books well you can probably think of a dozen or so off the top of your head that use some sort of repeating pattern to structure the text. Reeve Lindbergh's book *What Is the Sun?* (1994) is a good example of an entire text being structured through questions. This is craft.

# Repetitions and Complete Sentence Fragments

OK, I'm almost finished. Just one more example and I think we'll have it. Look at how Smith writes about Pat Summitt's husband, R.B. Summitt:

> Imagine living with that. For the longest time even Pat couldn't imagine who could imagine it, until she found R.B. Summitt, whom she married in 1980, her sixth season at Tennessee. A man secure in his own profession as vice president of his family's bank, a man born to the first female pilot in Monroe County, Tennessee, a man unthreatened by a woman with a life all her own. (93)

Smith makes two interesting moves in this short passage. In one he decides to use the word "imagine" three times in a span of fifteen words, twice in a span of four words. Those of us who spent many a minute thumbing through thesauruses trying desperately not to repeat ourselves so close together may wish we had known what Smith knows. Using the same word several times *can* work just fine. It has an interesting sound to use it several times, and it adds to the importance of the word. He doesn't *mean* anything else but "imagine." And each time he uses it, that's what he means. So another word won't do. Jane Yolen knew this when she wrote *Welcome to the Green House* (1993). Again and again Yolen uses "green" to describe things in this text. It is OK to use a word repeatedly if that is the meaning you need, if that word dominates the meaning you want to convey. This is craft.

And how about the "a man" sentence? Those of you who are really sharp realized that this items-in-a-series sentence about R.B. Summitt has no verb. It's three noun phrases connected by commas with no "ands" and punctuated as a sentence. Jane Yolen does this in her text too. In *Welcome to the Green House* (1993) she writes a series of noun phrases (albeit much shorter than Smith's) and punctuates them each as an individual sentence. She writes,

> This is a loud house. A bright house. A day house. A night house. A wet house . . . (n.p.)

Smith and Yolen both understand that sometimes a description of something can stand quite on its own in a text—the understood connection to the other sentences around it holding it up and giving it enough meaning to be "complete." We all know about understood parts of sentences. We learned that the subject of a command was usually an understood "you." Experienced writers often work with understood connections within their texts. This is craft.

All this is craft.

All this is Gary Smith doing particular things with words that he knows how to do as a writer. It's his special "skill or art" coming through to help his writing come to life. I hope that our look at Smith's writing demonstrated what it means to look at how something is written and how that is different from thinking only of what it's about. Now let's take this close look at how this article was written and think through some significant aspects of what we did as we looked at Smith's writing.

# THE PROCESS OF SEEING CRAFT IN TEXT

## Reading Like a Writer

You may be wondering how much of that craft you would have seen if I hadn't slowed it down and pointed it out to you. Would you have seen it if you were just hanging out, sitting by the pool reading your latest issue of *Sports Illustrated*? I don't know. All I can do is tell you how I came to discover that amazing little span of writing in a long article. I *was* just hanging out at my parents' house, looking for something to read because both of them had fallen asleep on the couch and I didn't have anyone to talk to (this happens a lot!). So anyway, I was just reading along and the first thing I noticed that made me reread was "rightthisveryminute." I thought, "That's pretty clever." I love it when I see especially this technique in writing for adults because it's one that's so common in writing for children.

I kept on reading and the next thing I realized was happening was that Smith was repeating the "It begins with . . ." sentences. At that point I knew I was on to something, so I completely slowed down and started really looking at what he was doing as I read along. I saw several more things as I continued, but I copied the article the next day because I knew I wanted to study it even more. I took "Eyes of the Storm" to my class, and my students and I looked at it together. Through our discussions I was able to see even more of Smith's craft.

When you get some experience reading like a writer, this is usually how it happens. You see craft everywhere—even on billboards and restaurant menus. My husband frequently has to help me find the scissors in the morning because I need to cut something particularly well crafted out of the newspaper. Often, it's just one or maybe two things in an article or book that strike me and that I want to put in my collection. But every now and then I come upon a goldmine like Smith's article that I can tell is just full of interesting craft and I really want to study it. So I go back to these and really work at figuring out how the writer wrote that piece so well. This is a different engagement than the more routine, more vicarious "Well, would you look at that" kind of thing I notice in the natural course of my reading. This is the deliberate and intentional reading like a writer that I do because I want to study from master craftspeople. My students and I have learned so much from discovering these goldmine texts and then taking them and studying them closely.

## Connecting to Other Texts

Once you begin to study the craft of writing you will find that the more you know, the more you see. Lots of things that I notice in texts, lots of things that make me stop and reread them, are noticeable to me *because I've seen them before* in other texts. Being able to connect various crafting techniques that you see to other texts you know is one of the most significant understandings about learning to write from writers. Realizing, for example, that the "making a long story short" sentence in "Eyes of the Storm" is the same kind of sentence as the one we know well in *The Relatives Came* (1985) is a huge, huge insight. What work does being able to connect crafting techniques across texts do for us?

First, connections help us deepen our understanding of the "writing is individual but not unique" concept. Seeing different writers using words in exactly the same way in different texts shows us that the craft of writing is a part of the public domain, available to all who would write well. Related to this, these connections help us to see that while many crafting techniques are connected to a particular meaning—the runaway sentence, for example, is connected to some carried-away or desperate meaning—they are not connected to *topic*. Writers might use the runaway sentence technique in an information piece about basketball coaches or a memoir about the family's hair. Understanding that craft is not connected to topic helps us understand that we do not need to match our students' topics to texts that are *about* those same topics in order to help them write well. What we need to help them write well are texts that have writing in them that matches *the kinds of meanings* our students are trying to convey.

Now this is very sophisticated, so we'll slow it down a little. Think about all the connections I made to other texts as we looked at "Eye of the Storm." Not one of those texts I connected it to was about basketball coaches. One was about basketball, the "UpsetableBulls," but none of the others even came close to matching that topic. What did match in each connecting text were the kinds of meanings or the textual sounds (often related to meaning) or the organizational patterns the writers were using. Writers use similar crafting techniques to convey the same kinds of meanings, not to write about the same kinds of topics. This is such an important distinction.

Not long ago I was working in a fifth-grade classroom where a student had set up a story-within-a-story structure to write about his friends. The frame story was that he was home by himself one afternoon and he had gotten very bored, so he decided to clean out his closet. When he does, he finds an old yearbook and begins to look through it. As he sees each of his friends' pictures, he uses that as an opportunity to tell about that friend. When I saw what Carlos was working on, I thought of a book that he should look at— Gary Soto's *Snapshots from the Wedding* (1997). Now, Carlos was writing about schools and friends, and Soto's piece is about weddings. But *how* they were writing was the same. They were both writing as if they were looking at photographs, so I wanted Carlos to see how Soto did this, to see the ways in which Soto used words to make it sound like he was actually showing the reader the pictures. *Snapshots from the Wedding* really helped Carlos write his piece well. After reading it he added exclamations to his piece like the ones shown on the facing page, which make it really sound like someone looking at a yearbook.

What matched in Soto's and Carlos's work was not their topics but the kinds of meanings they were making. This understanding—that craft is connected to kinds of meanings, not topics—will help you so much as you begin to think about helping your students write well.

> I wish I could hang out with him today.
>
> Oh Look, there's Josh's picture.

> A picture of the lunchroom. God that lunchroom used to get gross!

> The yard was fun, though. Ah h/a picture of John.

> Boy Ian looks funny in his picture.

*Excerpts from Carlos's "My Yearbook"*

Connections like the ones we made above help us to realize that not only is craft not bound by topic, it is also not bound by genre or by intended audience. "Eyes of the Storm" is a very long, very detailed information piece written for a primarily adult audience. None of the connecting texts with similar crafts matched this kind of text. One connection was from a short wire-service newspaper article, and the others came from picture books primarily intended for children, written in genres of stories, poems, and memoirs. And, lucky for you I suppose, I only showed you a very small sampling of all the texts I know that could connect to each of Smith's crafting techniques—and hardly any of them match the *kind of text* he'd written. The crafts that writers use are just not bound by characteristics that otherwise set apart published texts—namely topic, genre, and intended audience or purpose.

So what does this mean for us as teachers? One thing it means is that we can feel comfortable in studying the craft of writing in any kind of text or choose any kind of text to help a given writer at a given time. Once students get past, say, third grade, many teachers worry about studying craft from picture books—unless they are in a specific picture-book genre study. But I find myself using picture books a lot, no matter what kind of writing my students are doing. I use them because I like them (they're pretty), because they're not so heavy to carry around, and because they're short and I can find the parts I want very quickly when I'm working with writers. And I understand that good writing is good writing whether it's in a picture book or a *Time* magazine article. I frequently use picture books in helping to teach adult students (who aren't writing picture books at all) how to write well. My A-Number-One choice for helping students to learn to show rather than tell is Cynthia Rylant's poetry in her and Walker Evans's *Something Permanent*

(1994). I use this poetry to help students see this whether or not they are writing poetry themselves. So, unless we are in a study of a very specific kind of writing, it just isn't important whether we match our learning to write from writers by genre, audience, topic, or intended audience.

Realizing that the craft of writing is ageless, genreless, and topicless can do another thing for us as well—it can help us to see the work of our youngest writers in a new light. Consider this piece by five-year-old Katie:

> I love my mom. My mom is sweet. My mom is pretty. My mom is good. My mom is kind. My mom is a pumpkin. My mom is my heart. Be my Valentine Mom. Afterword: My name is Katie. It feels good to be an author because I like it.

What Katie is doing here as a writer is no different from what Gary Smith does in "Eyes of the Storm," when he begins six sentences in a row with the words "It begins with. . . ." Both writers have a series of descriptions which go together to represent the essence of something—Katie's essence is her mom, while Smith's essence is Michelle's UT dream. Both writers know that repeating a phrase at the beginning of each line of description can glue those pieces together in the reader's mind and make them stick. Five-year-old Katie

*Pages from Katie's "My Mom"*

is doing exactly the same thing to craft her writing that Gary Smith does to craft his. Isn't that grand? The whole process of connecting craft across many different kinds of texts is very important to our understanding of how to learn to write from writers, even for our youngest writers.

## Know a Few Authors Well

You might have noticed that my connections drew heavily from my knowledge of the work of Cynthia Rylant. That's not an accident. I know Rylant's work like the back of my hand. She's my mentor. It's important for us to know the work of a few writers very well, to have what Lucy Calkins calls certain "touchstone" texts that we know almost by heart. What these writers and their well-crafted touchstone texts give us are benchmarks for the craft of writing. We need writers and texts that are so well crafted they can stand alongside many other texts we encounter and show us the way to the craft. Whenever I say "Show us the way to the craft," and I say it a lot in workshops, I always think of "Show me the money," that classic line from the movie *Jerry Maguire*. "Show me the craft." Cynthia Rylant shows me the craft every time she writes. So do Patricia MacLachlan, Jane Yolen, Gary Paulsen, Jerry Spinelli, Sandra Cisneros, and Eloise Greenfield. And these writers, because I've studied their work closely, have helped me to see craft in the work of many, many other writers. Although I'm sure there are many other fine writers who could "show me the craft," these are a few I've looked to repeatedly in the past.

Whose writing do you know like the back of your hand? Who is a writing mentor for you and your students? Be sure you know a few writers so well that their work has a chance of helping you to see craft as you read your way through the world.

## Creating Names for What We See

You may have noticed as we went through our close look at Gary Smith's writing that I frequently said, "My students and I call this . . .", and then you read about things like "close echoes" and "making a long story short" and "intentional vagueness." As you study the craft of writing, you will often see things that are most definitely techniques—you know they are because you can see the work they are doing in the text—but you won't know what to call them. Don't be afraid that because you don't know a name for them like "personification," that maybe they don't really exist and you're just delusional in thinking they are there. If you can describe the work you see a technique doing, if perhaps you've seen another writer doing this same thing with words, if you can imagine writing this way in a text of your own, then you are definitely seeing a technique of craft. Give it a name so you can refer to it easily in the future as you study craft and as you write your own texts.

As I mentioned in the last chapter, children have an advantage over adults in this aspect of reading like writers. Because they don't yet know the names of lots of things that do have names—things like alliteration and personification and metaphor and simile—they don't have the resistance to unnamed crafting techniques that adults often have. And, for the same reason, they can often see things in a text that adults don't see because they aren't looking for something that has a name. Think of the discovery of some technique you've never known before as being like the discovery of a new star or planet—you get the honor of naming it. You may find out later that someone else already knows about this and has given it another name, but that's OK. What's important is that, in seeing it and naming it for yourself, you have a new vision of what's possible when you try to write well.

You might also have noticed that the names for the various crafting techniques Gary Smith uses help us to understand the function of using words in that particular way: "making a long story short," for example, or an "on-your-mark, get-set, go colon." If we name and define the crafting techniques we see by the work they do in the text, then this will help us understand more clearly the situations where this technique might work for us or for our students when we are writing. For example, a student writing about something like a baseball game may know she needs to get through most of the innings of that game fairly quickly. She knows she needs to "make a long story short." The name matches the function of the technique, and the discussions she's had with her classmates about this technique, calling it by that name, will help her access it more easily when she finds herself in a writing situation that matches it.

## Seeing How It's Not Written

An important "skill" in learning to see and understand the craft of writing in texts is the ability to think about other ways the text might have been written, to think through the other options a writer had for how to write the text. We did this several times as we looked at Smith's text, most notably as we discussed his use of a close echo in the sentence, "It begins with 4:30 a.m. wake-ups, with relentless wind sprints on the dark Tennessee track." We imagined that Smith could have written this sentence with an "and," but he didn't.

Being able to think through other choices a writer had for how he or she might have written something does several things for you as you read like a writer. First, it often helps you to see why the writer chose to write something the way he or she did. When you think through other options, you say them aloud to yourself. Often, you can hear the difference in the text that choosing one way over another makes. This is clearly the difference with the choice to leave out the word "and" in Smith's sentence. It makes a clear rhythmic sound difference not to have the conjunction there.

Thinking of other options the writer had also helps you to understand writing more clearly as a process of decision making. Writers make choices about how to use words as they compose a text for an audience, and these choices go beyond simply what information to include—the choices extend into how that information will be presented. We often forget that writers make thousands of choices as small as whether or not to include an "and" in a sentence. Conversations about the decisions writers make as they craft their texts will help you and your students to better understand what decisions you have to make as you write your own texts. If you don't study the craft of writing, you may not even realize that you have many of the options you have for how to write something.

## Knowing Grammatical Names

You may have noticed that as we discussed Smith's article, there were many occasions to bring out our knowledge of grammatical names for things—particularly parts-of-speech names. Regardless of the grade you teach, you will need to brush up on your knowledge of the grammatical names for things. As mentioned in the first chapter, I throw in grammatical names for anything five-year-olds notice. And they notice parts of speech—they just don't know what they are called. If they notice, for example, in a text like Mem Fox's *Tough Boris* (1994), that each page "tells what the pirate was like," then I say, "Oh yes, you call those words adjectives. Those words that tell what something is like are adjectives." Throughout their school years, if students had conversations each year about writing and how it happens, and if they had a more knowledgeable language user discussing this with them, feeding them the words they need for the things they see, they would be quite savvy about how our language works.

You may be thinking, "But I'm not very savvy about how our language works." Most of us were taught about language from the outside in, off a chalkboard instead of from beautiful texts, and unless we've been teaching it for years, we don't remember much about grammatical terms because we just haven't used them enough. We weren't taught grammar or even usage alongside our writing, so we don't know things from a writer's perspective either. But the grammatical names for things are useful. They make it easier to talk about writing. "Adjective" is easier to say than "a word that describes a noun." And if you are going to reverse tradition and help your students learn about language as insiders, then they need to learn this insider's language from you, naming things for them whenever it makes sense in your reading like writers. So, brush up. Keep a grammar guide handy that can help you define something if you are unsure which part of speech it is or what to call a certain function of a word.

## What Do We Learn from the Study of Craft in Texts?

As I have studied texts with students and teachers throughout the years, I have found that we have learned two main kinds of things about the craft of these texts. One of these kinds of things is *structure*. A structural crafting technique is a way of using words that holds together either a whole text or a part of a text. Structural crafts are those that allow different parts of the text to work together. In Smith's article, the two structural crafts we see are the two series of sentences that begin the same way: "It begins with . . ." and "Who else . . ." These are structural because they allow several sentences to work together for effect. This same structural crafting technique is often used to hold entire picture book texts together; Rylant's *When I Was Young in the Mountains* (1982) is a classic example.

Structural crafts can be as big as the technique behind Karen Hesse's Newbery Award-winning book *Out of the Dust* (1997), in which the entire novel is a series of narrative poems that work together to tell the story of Billie Jo. The text works this way, it is assembled this way, as a series of poems, so this is the crafted structure of the text, the "how it's done" of its structure. Other authors have used this same text structure; Cynthia Rylant's *Waiting to Waltz, A Childhood* (1984) and Lee Bennett Hopkins's memoir *Been to Yesterdays* (1995) are notable examples.

But structural techniques can be smaller, fashioned only to make a certain part of the text work together, as we see in Smith's article. One common structural technique that is frequently used to hold entire picture book texts together is used just as frequently to balance parts of longer texts. The structural technique works a lot like a seesaw, consistently balancing pieces of information or pieces of story in a back-and-forth motion. Mem Fox's *Tough Boris* (1994) works this way: "He was tough. All pirates are tough. . . . He was massive. All pirates are massive" (n.p.). Consider this excerpt from the article "Where the Winston Cup Begins" by Stephan Wilkinson, found in the August 1997 issue of Delta Airlines's *Sky* magazine (yes, you can read like a writer when you travel too):

> Someday, he may be driving in a NASCAR (National Association for Stock Car Auto Racing) event at Daytona or Charlotte or Pocono. But tonight, he'll make $185 for winning the "feetch." Someday, his car may be covered with logos for the likes of McDonald's or DuPont or Quaker State. But tonight, it bears the sponsorship of Renze Hybrids, an Iowa seed-corn producer, and Cyberhair by Mr. Executive, a toupee franchiser. Someday, Jackson's car may be a pristine piece fresh-built for every race, waxed and decaled and rolled out of a multimillion-dollar shop into a $500,000 transporter by a platoon of bright-uniformed crewmen. But tonight, it is a battered 1984 Buick Regal bearing the number 2J and a roll cage that Jackson has welded up himself. (70)

The seesawing "someday–but tonight" structure holds only this opening part of Wilkinson's lengthy article together, but it is indeed the same structural craft Fox uses in *Tough Boris*. So structural crafts make parts of texts or entire texts work together in a particular way.

The other kind of thing we learn from the study of craft in texts are the particular *ways with words*. These are crafting techniques that stand by themselves and do not do any work in conjunction with other parts of the text. Gary Smith's article is full of these crafts: making a long story short, using print to match meaning, speaking directly to the reader, and intentional vagueness, to name just a few. Well-crafted texts are usually chock full of a variety of ways-with-words crafting techniques. Sometimes these techniques may be used more than once in a text, but they are not considered structural if they do not work in conjunction with another part of the text. For example, in *My Mama Had a Dancing Heart* (1995) by Libba Moore Gray, the writer uses a neat technique of creating adjectives and adverbs and verbs by hyphenating familiar words: "I'd slip-swish behind mama" and "eye-blinking blue air." She uses this technique throughout the text, but each instance of it stands alone, and this is why it is a ways-with-words technique and not a structural crafting technique.

Understanding these two kinds of things to learn from texts—structural possibilities and ways-with-words possibilities—has helped me organize learning both as a writer and as a teacher. I am careful to think about (as a writer) or teach about (as a teacher) structural crafting techniques when my students and I are planning how we will write something. We think about ways-with-words techniques more as we are drafting and attending carefully to each word, sentence, and paragraph.

Craft: a special skill or art. In this chapter, I hope that, with Gary Smith's help, I have given you some shape and definition to what I mean by "writer's craft." I believe that the only true definitions for writer's craft are found in the wondrous words of beautiful texts like Smith's, and searching these out has become the great passion in my teaching and writing life.

## References

Sheridan, Chris, "Bulls return to top form," *Asheville Citizen-Times,* 28 May 1998, C-1, col. 2.

Smith, Gary, "Eyes of the storm," *Sports Illustrated* 88, 2 March 1998, 88–93.

Wilkinson, Stephan, "Where the Winston Cup begins," Delta Airlines' *Sky,* August 1997, 70.

# ENVISIONING TEXT POSSIBILITIES

Now that we understand something of what it means to learn to write from writers, to read like writers and see the craft of how writing is done, it is time to think about exactly what this process will do for us and our students. What kind of learning, exactly, will we get from writers? How should we expect this learning to manifest itself in our own writing and in the writing of our students?

To understand the impact that all of this has on helping students to write well, it will be helpful to return to my beliefs about writing, which have been evolving over my entire lifetime. When I was a young girl in school, I believed that to be a good writer you had to have a good imagination. Now, to me at that time, having a good imagination meant having really good ideas for writing, being able to "think up" incredible plot lines or outrageous characters. Jeffrey, whose last name I won't mention to protect his guilt, was always the one with the great imagination in our class. We could hardly stand him when it came time to write because he was so far beyond the rest of us in his ability to imagine the truly unimaginable. His writing about aliens and outlaws left the rest of us panting in exhaustion (from hanging onto the edges of our seats) and dreading having to follow one of his stories with our own pitiful attempts at being "creative." We took our understandings of a good imagination from pop culture at that time, and from the topics we were given in school that steered us toward "imaginative" pieces of writing like "my most embarrassing moment" (surely that should be interesting) or "my life as a French fry."

In my early days as a teacher of writing, in those first days of writing workshops when we were so happy to be writing about what mattered in our lives, I became an "anti-imagination" advocate. I had learned that good writing didn't have to come from some far-out, insanely great idea. By reading the work of Graves and Calkins and Atwell, I had learned that writers can write about very ordinary things in their lives, small things that they treasure like mothers and morning glories and moon pies. The pressure was off—I no longer needed an imagination the size of Texas for outrageous ideas for making writing good. Whew, was I glad, and whew, did I rebel against the great imagination pieces.

But in my current teaching, surprisingly, I have returned to the notion that what a writer needs to write well *is* a good imagination. It's just that now, I am defining it quite differently. I believe that a good writer's imagination is made up not of incredible plot lines and outrageous characters, but of a sophisticated repertoire of ideas for how to go about writing and how, particularly, to fashion texts and parts of texts. Really good writers can imagine all kinds of things *to do with text*, and this imagination comes from their sense of craft, a sense garnered over time from reading like writers and from writing themselves—trying out the crafts they have come to understand.

## Including "Envisioning" in the Writing Process

I believe that in our attempts to match our teaching of writing to the actual processes that writers use, we may have been overlooking an important aspect of that process. In our schema for writing process, we understand that writers prewrite, draft, revise, edit, and publish, and that there are individual ways that writers go about each of these parts of the process, sometimes overlapping one part with another, as in revising and editing in the process of drafting. We've actually talked a great deal about revision, the ability to "re-see" what we are writing, because helping students revise well in any classroom is a challenge. But what I am thinking after studying writing in the ways outlined thus far in this book is that an important part of the writing process may have been missing from our conversations. We know about revision that comes after a draft has started, but what about *envisioning*, the ability to imagine what a draft could be before it is even started, or as it is in process, being able to envision how you might write the next words, and the next.

Experienced writers, those with a well-developed sense of craft, of how writing can be fashioned, have the ability to envision more possibilities for their writing than less experienced writers because, to put it simply, experienced writers know more things that they might do with writing. They have read like writers over time, and over time this reading has given them a storehouse of knowledge about how to write.

If I were to add the envisioning process to what we know about writing process, I would have to account for its recursive nature as well. I would want "envisioning" to somehow wrap around all the five other processes because I think that, at all the junctures along the way, from even before ideas to publication, the ability to envision what is possible to do with writing helps one to write well. In Chapter 5 as we look at studying the craft of writers' office work, we'll discuss helping students to better envision how they might go about gathering ideas for writing, having more images of what they might do as writers before drafts are even anticipated. Without a doubt, though, being able to envision possibilities for drafts during the prewriting and drafting part of the writer's process seems critical. At the writing workshops I've taught in during the past few years, we are seeing our greatest strides in helping students to write well come about when we slow down the prewriting process, nudge students to spend time envisioning possibilities for their writing before they begin drafts, and then help them make intentional decisions about how they will go about their writing.

I'd like to tell a teaching story now that will help to open up this idea of the importance of including attention to envisioning in our teaching of writing.

# HELPING WRITERS TO ENVISION

## A Study in Envisioning

Sherry Siegel and Donna Raskin had *large* classes of fourth and fifth graders at P.S. 95 in the Bronx last year, when I joined them for two weeks to teach writing. Having thirty-plus students in a writing workshop forces you to focus your teaching on one or two goals at a time that you will follow into the students' individual work. Our goal for those two weeks was to help these fourth and fifth graders be more intentional about envisioning the writing projects they were working on at the time.

When I arrived at P.S. 95, the students in Donna's and Sherry's rooms had already chosen seed ideas for their writing projects and had been collecting entries around those seeds and discussing them in small response groups for several workshop days. Needless to say, most of them were ready to start their drafts and get going on their projects. My first day there we spent some time having short assessment conferences with as many of the students as we could reach. Our goal was to assess what kinds of "visions" students had for how they might draft the material they had in their writers' notebooks (Calkins 1991). In these conferences we asked the same two questions again and again: "What is your seed idea?" (which is a form of "What are you going to be writing about?") and "How do you think you might go about writing that?"

As we reviewed the notes from those conferences and discussed them at the end of the day, we saw a pattern in the students' responses that is fairly common. Simply, the pattern we saw was that most students answered the two different questions in the same way; in other words, they gave the same answer for both questions. If a child's response to what he was writing about was "My dog," his answer to how he might write about that was "I'm going to tell about my dog." The students' answers to how they might write something were driven directly by what they were writing about. Their visions for what they might do with their topics matched the way the topics existed in their thinking.

If, in their thinking, their seed ideas were either a person, place, or thing, like "my dog" or "friends" or "my aunt's apartment" or "Lamborghinis," then their answers to how they might write about those were some form of "I'm going to tell about it." If, in their thinking, their seed idea was an event, like "The time I fell at the Bronx Zoo" or "When my father left," then their answers to how they might write about those events were, "I'm going to tell how it happened."

These two visions—telling about something and telling how something happened—were far and away the two most prominent visions the students had for how they might go about drafting their seed ideas. This is not uncommon in inexperienced writers. Often, these writers envision writing as matching thinking only—they know only to write about the subject as it exists in their thinking. And these two ways of writing, telling about it and telling how it happened, represent two of the most common text structures students learn in school—the essay and the story.

Corry, Anthony, and Mark were three of the writers in these two class-rooms. Corry was writing about his friends, and his response to how he would write about this was—you guessed it—he was going to tell about them. There were four of them, and Corry had something along the lines of a paragraph on each one in mind. He already had entries on each friend in his notebook, so drafting would be a fairly easy process of assembling that infor-mation into organized paragraphs. Anthony's seed idea was to tell about an event, the day his father left and moved away from the family. His answer to how he would write this was that he would tell about that whole day, explain what had happened the day his father moved out. Mark's seed idea revolved around his dreams for the world, and he had pages and pages of writing on this. Hinting that the task seemed overwhelming, Mark's response to how he would write about these dreams was "I'm going to explain them." Corry, Anthony, and Mark could all envision how they would draft, though in each case, these visions stayed fairly close to the nature of their topics.

For the next two weeks Sherry, Donna, and I held the students off from drafting, and we engaged them instead in looking at *how* many different texts were written. We looked at texts written as a series of diary entries and texts written as a series of poems. We looked at texts with repeating lines and texts that seesawed back and forth between bits of information. We looked at texts that shifted perspectives in the middle and texts that held one story inside another story. And all along the way as we looked, we engaged the students in envisioning their various topics written in all these varieties of ways. By the end of the two weeks we had nudged each student to envision (not write, only envision) his or her topic written in at least half a dozen different ways, and on their own many students had seen ways of writing that we hadn't discussed in class, and they had used those text possibilities for envisioning their own texts as well.

Our goal in this teaching was to help the students take the material they had gathered around their seed ideas and read like writers to find possibilities for how they might draft those ideas and write well. We wanted them to be able to envision doing many different kinds of texts with a single idea, to know that they didn't have to be limited to just "telling about" their idea in a draft. Our belief was that Sherry's and Donna's students weren't envisioning a range of possibilities for how they might write because they hadn't yet learned how writers find a range of possibilities for drafting their ideas. If we wanted the students to be able to write well, we had to help them see a range of possibilities for how they might do so. Envisioning was the part of the writing process that was really limiting the students, but the great writers of great texts we looked at during those two weeks helped the students break free of these limitations.

## Corry's Piece about Friends

When Corry saw Libba Moore Gray's *My Mama Had a Dancing Heart* (1995), he began to have a vision for how he might write about his friends. Gray's text is organized by a structure that moves the story through the four seasons, describing the "dancing relationship" between a mother and a daughter in each season. Corry liked the way this text worked, and he saw potential in it at first because he thought to himself, "I have four friends I want to write about and there are four seasons. I could write about one friend in each season." He started his draft this way and got frustrated fairly quickly. The structure worked out mathematically, but it caused "meaning" problems because the whole point of Corry's seed idea was to show how he and his four friends were virtually inseparable, hanging out together at every opportunity, in all seasons.

At this point Sherry and I helped Corry deepen his understanding of why someone would write something organized by seasons: "Because seasons change things in some way," we told him, and that was all the help Corry needed to go back to this vision and shape it so that it worked for his meaning. Here's his piece, "My Four Best Friends and Me," by Corry Merano:

### My Four Best Friends and Me

My friends Danny, Omar, Anthony and Adam, I think they are the best in the world. They enjoy spending time with me at any time of the year.

In the summer Danny, Omar, Anthony and Adam become my pool playing friends. We do splish splashing cannonballs and wrench wrecking dives. We have contests to see who can stay under water the longest and Daniel always wins. Adam always wins in the diving contests. But I always win in the cannonball contests because I make the biggest splash.

In the fall Danny, Omar, Anthony and Adam become my leaf playing friends. We take leafs and splatter them in each other's faces. When there are piles of red riding green sliding leaves we jump right through them. We become covered with leaves and we start to laugh.

In the winter Danny, Omar, Anthony and Adam become my snowball playing friends. We take big strong snowballs and do white-rolling air-rolling throws. We hit each other and fall on the floor laughing. We make tall-standing carrot-holding snowmen and name them after ourselves.

In the spring Danny, Omar, Anthony and Adam become my baseball playing friends. We slap the ball with our bats as hard as we can. It flies through the blue blinking flower-kicking air. We run as fast as we can and slide in the dirt into home base.

My friends Danny, Omar, Anthony and Adam are the best in the world.

In Corry's piece you will notice that looking closely at texts for two weeks had allowed him to envision all sorts of other possibilities for his text beyond its seasonal structure: matching beginning and ending lines, repeating phrases (his friends' names), repeating structures (giving the friends a seasonal name each time), and made-up language ("white-rolling"). Corry's teacher and I believe that his ability to envision this text, to know from his reading a range of possibilities for how his writing might be fashioned, helped him to write well about his friends in a lively burst of language.

# Anthony's Piece about His Father

Anthony first conceived his seed idea as being about the day his father left the family and moved away. Anthony was going to write the story of that day, but after slowing down to consider possibilities for how he might write it, he actually realized that the day itself was not really what was important. Our work at envisioning text possibilities not only helped Anthony write with a different vision, it gave him an opportunity to write something that more closely matched his meaning. You see, I believe that Anthony decided at first to write about the day his father left, not because the day itself was so important to him, but because he couldn't envision anything but *a story*. The day we looked at texts with two sides, however, Anthony began to hatch a new idea for how to go about his writing.

Texts with two sides are those that shift perspectives right in the middle—everything changes and goes in a different direction in the middle. The whole first half is about one thing and the second half is about another thing. The text fashioned like this that Anthony saw was *For the Love of the Game: Michael Jordan and Me* (1997) by Eloise Greenfield. In this text, the first half is about Michael Jordan playing the game of basketball, and the second half is about children playing the game of life. As we discussed this kind of "shifting perspective" text with Anthony and his classmates, insightfully, Anthony saw this kind of text as a possibility for his writing. Why? Because clearly his life had "gone in a different direction" right in the middle, right when his father had left. The idea of writing about how life used to be and then how life is now appealed to Anthony. Considering the structure of Eloise Greenfield's text had given him a vision for how he might write. Here is Anthony Perry's "My Father and Me":

### My Father and Me

Why did my father have to leave?

I looked at a picture of my father and started to cry quietly. Tears were dripping down my cheeks so I wiped them with my shirt.

When I was helping him pack his bags I asked him, "Are you really moving away?" My dad did not answer. I asked him again and he said, "yes." I asked him, "Is it because of me and Tyrone?" "No!" he said, "It's because me and your mother had a fight. I said, "Don't fight," as I was putting the bags in the car. That was when I was four years old.

I miss my father. He drives me to places like Pizza Hut. I love when we go to Pizza Hut. We eat bread sticks with sauce. I like when my father orders pizza with pepperoni and sausage.

When we play tag I like my father to get me. I try to run as fast as I can, but I always get tagged. Playing hockey with my father is fun. When I hit the puck in the goal my father laughs at me. Sometimes he hits the puck out of my stick and I try to get him back.

Things are not the same since my father left. He used to pack me donuts before I went to school. No one does that any more. Who is going to drive me places far away or who is going to buy me things that cost too much? No one. No one plays like my father. Who is going to play tag like my father? Who is going to play hockey like my father or play basketball like my father? I like when he plays basketball because he always blocks the ball when I shoot.

Why did my father have to move away from me?

**Author**
My name is Anthony Perry. I live in New York City. I got this idea from my father, the way I love him.

Being able to envision this kind of text helped Anthony do justice to this big, important topic in his life. When you look at the text closely, you will see that it is an intricate weaving of many sophisticated writerly moves. There is so much going on in the piece—the opening image of Anthony looking at the picture, the scene as the bags are being put into the car, the rhetorical questions that wrap their arms around the text, the thread-backs to tag and hockey near the end, and the subtle shifts in time which are such a challenge for any writer. The weeks spent looking at great texts helped Anthony match his vision for this piece to his passion for its topic.

# Mark's Piece about His Dreams

When Mark first told Donna and I that he was going to make an alphabet book about his dreams for the world, I have to confess that I was a little disappointed. He had such rich, rich material in his notebook about his dreams, and I was afraid that that richness would be lost if he wrote it this way. I tried hard not to show this to Mark, though. Our teaching goal had been to get the students to make deliberate decisions about how to write their pieces, and Mark certainly had done this. And as I so often discover, he was way smarter than I was about knowing what was best for his writing. Let's look at his piece first, and then we'll discuss it a little more in terms of Mark's envisioning of it:

### "Dreams from A–Z" by Mark Anthony Ramos

To my mom whom I love

Oh how I wish the world would be a better place and
Animals would not be killed.
Babies will not grow up in a bad world.
Caring would be a more popular thing to do.
Dogs and cats would be in peace.
Everyone will love each other.
Fighting will disappear.
Girls and boys will be created equal.
Honor will be brought to all.
Intelligence will be part of everybody.
Joy and happiness will bring peace.
Kindness will be in everyone's heart.
Love will be in the air.
Money will have no value.
Nothing will stand between caring and friendship.
Opposite attitudes won't cause fighting.
People will help each other.
Queens are little old ladies with wisdom.
Race won't matter.
Sun will beam into everybody's heart.
Teaching will help people be all that they can be.
Unity will join the world.
Voices will be heard.
Women will continue to succeed.
Xenophobia (fear of foreigners) will be no more.
Youth will provide for the future.
Zeal is what you will do for your nation.
Oh how our world would be if you just cared.

**About the author**

Mark Anthony Ramos is an 11 year old 5th grader. He likes to play basketball. He wrote this story because these are the things he wants in life.

I still go "wow" every time I read this. Mark knew that alphabet books are very sophisticated these days. The alphabetical structure allows writers to write about everything from Africa to deserts to butterflies to dreams for the world. A-B-C books aren't just about teaching the alphabet anymore, and once Mark saw this he was able to envision a new possibility for this huge topic in his life. My theory is that Mark saw the alphabet structure as perfectly suited to helping him overcome the problem of having *so much* to say. I remember how overwhelmed he sounded when we first started our study and his idea for how he would write about his topic was to "explain his dreams for the world." The task must have seemed overwhelming to him because of the sheer scope of what he wanted to say. But reading alphabet books like *A Is for Africa* (1993) by Ifeoma Onyefulu helped Mark to see a way of tackling this very big topic with dignity.

# Nurturing Envisioning in Writers' Processes

As we've said before, the ability to envision more of what you can do with writing comes from reading like a writer. It comes from going to the library the way my seamstress friend goes to a dress shop, searching for ideas and possibilities. Corry, Anthony, and Mark all wrote their pieces after some very intentional "shopping for ideas" trips to their classroom libraries. They and their classmates had topics, they had their material, but they needed ideas for how to "make up" that material in ways that were compelling and interesting, and so they looked to texts of all sorts to help them envision new possibilities. I'd like to think now about some of what is gained by helping students to become more intentional about envisioning what they will do as they write.

## Envisioning Gives Purpose and Energy

I haven't been able to get the image of Corry out of my mind. After he figured out how to make a seasonal structure work for his text, I saw him move to a corner of the floor with his workable plan in mind, his notebook and draft paper in hand, and the posture of someone who's about to start something big. I've searched my thinking to make meaning from what I saw in Corry that morning, and I've gone back to a very old memory to make sense of it. It's a memory you might share. Do you remember the feeling of a having a project to do when you were young? A poster on conservation for school, maybe, or muffins to make for a Girl Scout cook-off, or maybe a dam to build in the creek behind your house? Do you remember the energy of this? The way you went at collecting your supplies so you could get started— the glue and glitter and markers, the recipe and milk and sugar, the piles and piles of sticks and leaves? The way you dreamed and talked about what it would be like when you were finished? My next-door neighbor growing up, Sharon Kimble, and I used to literally fill our summers with one sort of project or another. There was energy in our work, and it was the same energy I saw in Corry that morning as he went to that draft.

I have come to believe that Corry's energy came from the same place that my childhood energy for projects came from. Corry's energy came from being able to envision how his writing project could work. Just as he might dream about what a tree house he was building would be like when he finished it, he could dream about all that his writing would become because he could see it through the structure that he had found for it. If young writers don't write with some vision for what their writing can be when it's all done, it makes it hard to find this type of project energy for their work as writers. Writers like Corry and Anthony and Mark have helped me to believe that the better a writer can envision how he might go about writing, the more intention and energy he is able to bring to drafting.

For example, a writer trying to capture the essence of her relationship with her sister can simply "write about" that relationship, but she also might handle the topic in myriad other ways. She might write a series of fictitious letters back and forth between sisters that capture essential elements of their relationship. She might fashion the text like a diary, writing entries that highlight moments in their relationship together. She might have an organizing thread running through the piece, like lyrics from songs they've loved together, which allows her to focus on various aspects of their relationship. The question this writer must ask is, "What can I imagine doing with this material I've got?" And her ability to imagine this comes from what she is able to envision.

Teachers who have been working with writers' notebooks (Calkins 1991) have found again and again that the move from writing in a notebook to drafting a piece for publication is a difficult one for many writers. It could be that this move is difficult because we haven't done enough work with writers on envisioning what they might do with their notebook material. In the example above, the "writing about" her relationship with her sister is what usually happens in a notebook, and with no vision, it is also what will end up in a draft. When a draft feels like a copy of notebook entries or a recording of exactly what's in a writer's head, the writer can quickly lose enthusiasm for the task at hand. Energy is drained because there is nothing new to look forward to. The draft won't be anything new when it "grows up" into a published piece.

My friend Isoke Nia talks about the need for writers to have plans in the writing workshop—not ideas, but *plans*. Planful work is more purposeful because it moves toward a vision of what will happen and of how things can be. Plans, in life and in writing, are a way of seeing into the future. Envisioning possibilities for writing is almost like looking at blueprint plans for how something could be made, and the ability to see in this way is what gives writers energy for their work.

## Staying with Topics over Time

Another benefit to being intentional about envisioning possibilities for writing is that it helps writers to see a single topic as having many different potentials. It is a mistake to think that every time a writer takes a piece to publication he or she needs a new topic to start writing again. Patricia MacLachlan says that, whether readers are aware of it or not, she writes about the same topic every time she writes—her love for the prairie. Could a writer *grow* and get better if he or she writes about the same topic again and again? Of course. It's not the topic that matters to the growth—it's the kinds of meanings made and the variety of ways a writer can go about writing that bring about the growth. If, for example, a writer like Mark wanted to stay with his topic of dreams, he could write about that in different genres. A collection of poetry about dreams, a persuasive essay about dreams, a work of fiction that has his dream world as its setting, or a memoir about moments in his life when he wished the world more closely matched his dreams. And then within any of these genres, he could try a number of different ways of writing. His fictional piece could be written as a series of diary entries or letters, or it could be fashioned as a story within a story. He might write one poetry collection in which each poem stands alone, and another poetry collection in which the poems work together in a more narrative way to tell a story about his dreams.

Mark can stay with a topic he loves as long as he can envision new ways of writing about that topic. As a matter of fact, if our teaching helps students envision many different possibilities for writing, they really only need one good topic during the year for us to help them grow as writers in our workshops. I'm not suggesting we make every student stick to one life topic; I'm just saying it is possible. I do, however, think it would be an important thing to have students write more than one piece during the year about the same topic. Doing so helps a writer understand how to shape and reshape an interesting topic in different ways, it shows a writer that any one topic doesn't dictate any one specific kind of writing, and the combination of these in a writer's understandings can give that writer great dexterity.

## Envisioning Helps a Writer Revise

What can a writer envision doing with text? As I mentioned at the beginning, envisioning is not just a part of prewriting, just something writers do before they write. Once writers have drafts in hand, then their ability to envision text possibilities can help them revise those texts. Envisioning has to do with being able to see what isn't there yet, and this is as much a part of revision as it is a part of planning for a draft.

I haven't met many teachers who didn't struggle with getting students to revise. Of course, part of the problem is that we often teach about revision as if it were like being sent back to clean your room again because you didn't do a good job the first time. We were taught revision this way, and unless we've written a lot we don't realize that writers don't really think of revision like this, as something they have to do because, surely, the writing wasn't good to start with.

Writers go back to drafts not because the drafts are bad and need fixing, but to see what else is possible. And to see what else is possible you have to be able to see what's not there yet. Writers revise both meanings and craft, and with the craft of their writing, this is where, again, their ability to envision helps them revise and write well. To help them revise for craft, inexperienced writers need to learn to ask, "What have I seen in my reading life that might be a possibility for the kind of draft I've written?" When Anthony finished the first draft of his piece about his father, he didn't have the closing question "Why did my father have to move away from me?" in the draft. He added this question later, and the addition of it came from a vision he had of texts that start and end the same way, and of rhetorical questions.

I think that our students often sit and stare at drafts during revision because they don't have any way of envisioning possibilities for what they might do to those drafts. "Make it better" or even "See what else is possible" is very difficult when you don't know much that you can articulate about how good writing is done. The conversations that come from students reading like writers and studying the craft of good writing help them know, in articulate ways, what possibilities exist for their drafts—and their classmates' drafts! In rooms where students regularly study craft, it is not uncommon to see them suggesting specific ways of rewriting to classmates during response-group meetings. The study of craft helps everyone in the room write and revise their writing with an exciting sense of possibility because the ways good writing happens have been demystified through the study of craft, putting more options within the reach of young writers.

Now, thinking about the relationship between envisioning and revision brings us to another important issue. The fact of the matter is, when students are led to spend time intentionally envisioning their texts before they write them, they usually need far less revision to make those texts work well. The reason is, of course, that students begin the drafts with some clear ideas about how they will write and shape those drafts. Revision then becomes simply a process of fine-tuning the plan that was in place before the writer began. Time spent envisioning helps the draft "just come out that way," better.

Now this leads us even further into thinking about envisioning. Legend has it that Cynthia Rylant, when asked at an NCTE convention to talk about her revision process in *When I Was Young in the Mountains* (1982), said to the accompaniment of an audible audience gasp, "I didn't revise that. It just came out that way." Many of those listening must have thought "poppycock" to that, that of course every piece of writing has to be revised many times over to be publishable. But could it be that Cynthia Rylant is so adept at envisioning text possibilities as she writes that her drafts do, in fact, just come out that way?

I believe this is very possible because I have seen it happen again and again in my own writing and in the writing of the students I teach. When we are first learning to study the craft of writing, we are very intentional in our reading like writers. We try to read like writers *on purpose*. And when we return to our own drafts, we often draft and craft *on purpose* in a particular way that we have come to know from our study. We do this because we are not yet as experienced as Cynthia Rylant, so we choose to do on purpose certain things with our writing that we trust will, over time and with experience, become far more automatic for us as we draft. We study now so that our writing will grow to be an intricate mix of some well-crafted text that just comes out that way because we write being able to envision it, and some text that we have deliberately reshaped during revision to be that way because we envisioned what wasn't there yet.

When I think of this I am reminded of my recent experience of taking a course to learn to ride a motorcycle. I had trouble with one of the essential parts of the course, how to go around a curve (an important skill when you live in the mountains). To do this, you are supposed to "slow, look, lean, and roll." This process was described to us in great detail, and we were told to think "slow, look, lean, and roll" as we went around the course. Once we were on the bikes, the instructors (having our best interests in mind, I'm sure) shouted at us as loudly as they could whenever we would round a curve, "SLOW, LOOK, LEAN, AND ROLL! SLOW, LOOK, LEAN AND ROLL!" When I was expressing to my husband my difficulty mastering this particular aspect of the course, he assured me that this would become very natural to me over time. He assured me that he never *thinks*, "slow, look, lean, and roll" when he rides, though this is in fact what he does every time he rounds a curve.

Much of a writer's ability to craft, much of what looks deliberate and by design, becomes over time as natural as "slow, look, lean, and roll" is for my husband who's ridden motorcycles for three decades. Experienced writers don't have to think as specifically about much of their crafting as inexperienced writers do. In our classrooms we do the intentional work of studying craft by reading like writers because we live with the expectation that once our students learn to envision writerly moves, they can do them on their own, purposefully at first, and almost effortlessly with experience.

This movement from intentional to natural and unintentional is a lot like the movement we see with more mechanical aspects of writing such as spelling and handwriting in our youngest writers. Our five- and six-year-olds find they have to spend a lot of their energy remembering how to make an "h" or what letters are in "the." Though we know they have to think about those things with intention when they are first beginning, we keep them at it because we know it is experience that will make those things more automatic for them. I believe the same is true of crafting techniques. When I first began to see and talk with students about crafting techniques like "close echoes," this was new to me, and I had to think about it in order to use this technique in my own writing. Now, I find that when I write, I write with close echoes slipping in when I'm not even thinking about them, not even trying to make them happen.

So we teach writing with the hope that the ability to write well will become a more and more natural course of action for our students. The craft of writing, as we defined it in the last chapter, is a particular way of using words that goes beyond just choosing the words we need to get the meaning across. Studying craft allows our students to envision more and more possibilities for how to use words in powerful ways, and it is this vision that will help them write well.

## Reference

Calkins, Lucy McCormick, with Shelly Harwayne. 1991. *Living Between the Lines.* Portsmouth, NH: Heinemann.

# READING ALOUD
## Filling the Room with the Sound of Wondrous Words

I used to read aloud to my students to get them to be good: "If you'll just be good this morning, I'll read to you after lunch." I thought of the read aloud as being like candy—the kids loved it, but it seemed not so good for them—like time away from what we *should* have been doing. I still think of the read aloud as something deliciously edible, only now I see it as a wonderful vegetable—something so good for us as a class that we need several helpings of it each day.

I begin every session I ever lead with teachers by reading something aloud. Even if my assigned topic is something like spelling or assessment, I still begin by reading aloud because I believe it is the single most important classroom structure there is, and so I demonstrate it wherever I go. The read aloud as a predictable, ritualized classroom structure does so much work in a classroom community, and it nurtures our individual and shared identities as readers and writers in so many complex and interesting ways.

To understand that reading aloud is important *teaching* time in the classroom, we must consider what it is offering our students as readers and writers. Becoming articulate about why this time matters to students' development will help us become more intentional about how we use that time. Here I'd like to consider briefly some of the central things that read aloud offers our students as a community of readers, and then move into considering what the read-aloud time offers our students as a community of writers learning from writers.

## LEARNING TO READ

First, and quite simply, reading aloud to students helps them learn to read for themselves. In *Joining the Literacy Club* (1988), Frank Smith reminds teachers that when students first begin reading like writers, they (the teachers) may have to do the actual reading for them, until the students can read with the teacher and then finally read for themselves (26). Of course, read-aloud time helps children of any age, in any classroom, who aren't yet reading for themselves to move more quickly toward independent reading. It is the purpose of some other book to explain *how* it happens that children learn to read from read aloud, but I'd like to consider for just a moment some of *why* it happens.

When I was a child first starting out in school, my older sister Shauna would read aloud to me from *Pippi Longstocking* at night before we went to bed, and the sound of her voice reading those words would transport me to another place, another life. Through Pippi, Astrid Lindgren gave me a life place I longed for, and I would travel across her words to get there as fast as my sister could read. The problem, though, was that she wasn't reading fast enough, doling out the story in pitifully small portions, enjoying, as all sisters must, having me completely at her mercy. Her merciless dribbles of this wondrous story made me realize it was time for me to learn to read for myself.

Reading aloud has made countless children throughout the ages long to read for themselves, to need to read for themselves so that they can get to the good parts faster—as I longed to as a child—faster to the little house on the prairie or more quickly to sit underneath the tree that grows in Brooklyn or hurry to cross the bridge to Teribithia. If we are sharing aloud great books that catch children in a carefully spun web of words, we can never read fast enough to satisfy them, and isn't that *grand*?

Because the teachers of our youngest students know that many of them are not yet reading for themselves, read aloud happens frequently in primary classrooms. But sadly, read-aloud time diminishes, or even completely disappears, in classrooms where most students are reading independently. And yet there are so many other reasons for readers to share great texts aloud.

## SHARED READING

Reading aloud has made countless children throughout time fall in love with a teacher (or a sister) who did it well and who did it often. And these teachers are never forgotten. Memories, some of them now decades old, of being read aloud to inhabit the dusty corners of so many of our minds, and though we may not remember any of the steps of mitosis, the positions of the planets, or the rest of our fourth-grade curriculum, we remember being read to. We recall the feeling of gazing up, gazing up at a teacher reading to us.

I remember the first time I realized students were gazing up at me while I was reading to them. I was overcome for a moment at how significant their gaze was, at how much trust I saw in their upturned faces. At how awesome my responsibility was to fill that space between them and me with words, wondrous words that would not disappoint them, words that would not let them down, words that they and I could stand on, walk across and meet one another in a place the ordinary words of our days forbid us to go. It was a journey of words we could make together through reading aloud.

As a classroom of readers and a classroom of people, journeys of words have so much to offer us. Beyond making us all long to read for ourselves, sharing the read aloud gives us new people in the room—Gilly and Sophie, Journey and May, Esperanza. In a room where reading aloud is a powerful force, it gets so hard to believe that these characters don't really live right there in the room with us. I never saw children love and care for characters as much as my seventh-grade students did for Cassie and her brothers in Mildred Taylor's moving *Roll of Thunder, Hear My Cry* (1978). What happened to those children in that book mattered to my students. It mattered so much to them, and crazy as it might sound, I really believe that it made them, my students, matter more to each other. We were so kind for so long after we read that book.

As readers and people, a shared journey of words gives us a new language to speak while we're together, an insiders' language. A man we see sitting alone each day while we're at recess becomes Solomon Singer to us. A Friday afternoon of free time becomes our "wild rumpus." We come to call that time when parents flock up to us after the writing celebration, reaching for hugs and kisses, "Hugging time!" And when someone tells a story about himself or herself that seems more fantasy than fact, more legend than truth, we say that person is "Maniac'd."

Our journey of words lets us inhabit parallel worlds together. You know how, when you are reading a book for yourself over several days, you are always sort of living in your everyday world and living in the world of that book at the same time? During the course of the day your mind will often slip into wondering about the world you left at home, between the pages of that book by your bed. When that feeling is shared in a classroom, it's like going on a field trip together every single day. And as Dr. Seuss would say, "Oh, the places you can go." My whole class and I, all thirty-five hearts and minds of us, can live parts of our days frightened and homesick together in a civil war camp, parts of our days working on a farm in the middle of a vast prairie, or lost and alone (together), struggling for survival in the great north woods, or parts of our days wandering through city streets, all of us without a home. Oh, the places we can go. . . .

As readers and as people, all of these aspects of reading aloud, shared characters, shared language, and shared journeys to new worlds bring us together in a way that nothing else we do during the day quite matches. What we are reading, our rituals of place and time and movement for reading aloud together, all of these become such an important part of how we are "us" in our classroom. So, in essence, what read aloud offers us as a classroom of readers is the opportunity to be a *community*. As teachers we know the whole rest of the instructional day is changed by the moments we spend gathered together around a powerful text. But what about sharing common texts as writers? What does the read aloud offer us when we live with the expectation that we will learn to write from other writers?

## READ ALOUD FOR WRITERS

When we read aloud, often and well, we fill our classrooms with the sound of words, well placed and well written, and that sound wraps its arms around the work of young writers who are hard at work learning their craft.

Of course, Mem Fox would disagree that reading aloud is just for very *young* writers:

> Even in my forties I have benefitted as a writer *directly* from hearing writing read aloud. The music, the word choice, the feelings, the flow of the structure, the new ideas, the fresh thoughts—all these and more are banked into my writing checking account whenever I am fortunate enough to be read to. (Fox 1993, 70)

Our students need to be just that fortunate, fortunate enough to be read to every single day by someone who values wondrous words and knows how to bring the sounds of those words to life in the listening writer's ears and mind and heart. Like Mem Fox, we want our students to have "full checking accounts" as writers, and our attention to read aloud in our classrooms will help to ensure that they have access to all the "funds" available in the texts around them. Our read-aloud time will form the roots for the study that will grow tall and branch out over the course of the year as we learn to write from writers.

## LISTENING LIKE A WRITER

As students gather on our carpets to listen to the read aloud, they bring with them their identities as both readers and writers. All of the benefits of reading aloud discussed above come about because the students' reading selves engage with the text as it's read aloud. But their writing selves are there too, listening in, and the stronger these identities are in our students, the more active their writing selves are in listening. Remember that, from our discussion in the first chapter, the writing self is the one who expects to be writing in the future, who lives with that expectation and, because of it, sees possibilities for that future writing everywhere.

You see, our engagements with the world are colored by the particular identity that most governs each engagement. Sometimes we are more a wife than a mother, more a cook than a gardener, more a teacher than an aerobics fanatic. Whoever we are most at a particular moment guides what we hear and see and feel, guides how we respond and what we say and do. But the other identities don't go away—they just hang out in the background.

As literate people, we each have both a reading self and a writing self. My favorite reading self is the one that sits on the porch in the evening and reads Lee Smith or Jane Hamilton or Barbara Kingsolver. That reading self forgets the real world and tries to inhabit the world the writer has made for me. But I am never cut off from my other selves, and this is why the writer in me often interrupts and says, "Hey, look at that. Look at how she wrote that!" If we and our students have strong identities as writers, if we have dreams of drafts we will someday write in our heads, then our writing selves are never far from consciousness even when we aren't ostensibly engaged as writers. As Cynthia Rylant says of writers as artists, we "go fishing as an artist and have relatives over for supper as an artist and walk the aisles of a Woolworth's as an artist" (1990, 19). What we hope is that our students' identities as writers will be so strong that they can't get away from those identities easily. We hope that they will allow their writing selves to listen to the read aloud with an attention equal to that of their reading selves. If they do, they will open up for themselves vast storehouses of knowledge about, particularly, what good writing *sounds* like.

## THE SOUND OF GOOD WRITING

*On the eve of your birth, word of your coming passed from animal to animal.*

—Debra Frasier, *On the Day You Were Born* (1991)

When I was reading this once to a group of children, and I had gotten halfway through that first page as the "marvelous news migrates worldwide" through all the various animals, a little boy started raising his hand like the school was on fire. I was really afraid he knew of some emergency the rest of us didn't, so I stopped the reading (something I almost never do) and asked, "Joel, what's the matter?"

"That. That sounds like the Bible," he said. And it does. Though I'd never really thought about it until he said it, the first page of Debra Frasier's book does sound very much like a biblical passage. It *sounds* like the Bible.

What of sound and writing? Have you ever written something, reread it to yourself, and then said, "That just doesn't sound right." How do you know? What sound are you listening for when you write? How do you know when writing sounds right?

Once when I was teaching a class in a summer institute for teachers in New York City, someone on the first day started introducing herself to the class, and before she'd hardly gotten a full sentence out, the others in the class said, almost as one, "You sound like Katie." The teacher introducing herself was from Texas, and I am from South Carolina, and so she learned the art and craft of speaking at the same school I did. She and I grew up surrounded by Southern voices that shared rhythms and intonations and pitches and ways with words, and we sound a lot alike, and a lot different from most voices you hear in New York City.

We so easily accept that in spoken-language learning, we learn to speak like the voices that surround us. But perhaps we haven't thought enough about this with written-language learning. Writing, like speaking, has voice in the sense that both are language going out from a person, as opposed to language coming in with listening and reading. Language going out, then, always has voice; that's how it gets "heard." Voice is made up of particular rhythms, intonations, pitches, and ways with words. In written voice, punctuation, sentence structure, and word selection do most of the work to give the writing its sound, its voice. And the sound of that voice that goes out, whether it's crafted through airwaves or with ink, is a *learned* thing. We sound like sounds we've heard before. If we immerse ourselves in new sounds, before long we can make those sounds on our own.

When I first moved back to the Carolinas after having lived in New York City for two years, people in the South thought the sound of my voice had changed significantly. While living in a place where I was surrounded by different sounding voices, I had tuned my voice to try and match it to the rhythms and sounds I heard around me in New York City.

The dialect I adopt as a speaker comes from the places I have lived as a listener. Could it not be equally true that the "dialect" I adopt as a writer comes from the places I have lived as a reader? When I heard Ashley Bryan speak at the 1996 NCTE Annual Convention in Chicago, he said, "I find my voice by reading aloud black poets who have gone before me." Think about that: I find *my voice* by reading aloud black poets who have gone before me.

In her memoir *Dear Mem Fox, I Have Read All Your Books, Even the Pathetic Ones* (1992), Mem Fox credits none other than the Bible for helping her to find the right sounds for her writing. She says that

> All of my childhood I was exposed to the music of the Bible. The sound of the often-repeated words in all the church services I attended affected me forever, as a speaker and a writer. The sonorousness, the position of words, the number of words per phrase, the rhythms of those phrases, and the placement of the pauses have been collected in a storehouse from which I draw constantly, particularly for opening and closing sentences. Listening to the Bible developed my need to read aloud every sentence I write in order to check its balance and meaning. When I write, I *hear*. The words I've read ring in my ears and reverberate against the ceilings of my storehouse, echoing their way into my own writing. (31)

We learn what writing sounds like from what we read. We tune our writing voices to the writing voices we have known, much as our speaking voices are tuned to the voices we've listened to in the past. And the beauty of this is, while we don't have much control over what our speaking voices sound like, because we don't have much control over where we live, we have lots of control over where we spend our reading lives. If I want my writing voice to sound like Patricia MacLachlan's or Gary Paulsen's or Eloise Greenfield's, all I have to do is sit still and read them aloud, read them aloud, read them aloud—getting the sound of their writing voices in my head so that I can tune my own writing to match that lovely sound.

A few months ago, as I read over an introduction I had written for my friend Isoke Nia's speech at the 1997 NCTE Spring Conference in Charlotte, I realized that Sandra Cisneros's writing voice had crept unawares into my own writing voice. In writing about Isoke, I penned these words:

When my students at Western read about her in Lucy's book and Shelly's book, "You know her?" they ask. "Yes," I say, and I am proud.

As I reread what I had written, I said to myself, "Bums! Bums in the attic!" You see, the ending of Cisneros's piece about bums in *House on Mango Street* (1991) goes like this:

> Some days after dinner, guests and I will sit in front of a fire. Floorboards will squeak upstairs. The attic grumble. Rats? They'll ask. Bums, I'll say, and I'll be happy.

"You know her?" they ask. "Yes," I say, and I am proud. When I read those lines I'd written about Isoke, I knew they sounded right, but I couldn't at that moment have told you how I knew that. I realized later that I knew the right sound because I had heard that right sound from Sandra Cisneros. I've read her work aloud so often that I now write with echoes of her voice in my head.

## ECHOES

In the last chapter we discussed at length the things writers can envision, the things they can see, but what about what writers can hear? Could it be that writers know when something is just right because the sound of it matches an echo of something they have heard before that was just right? I think this is more probable than possible, and I am talking to all the writers I now teach about the importance of writing with echoes of sounds of good writing in their heads.

You see, once we realize the importance of "sounding right" to good writing, how can we ever think of reading aloud again in the same way? Our students need to be so full of the sound of good writing that even if they tried, they couldn't write words without rhythm, without music in them. Our students will find strong writing voices for themselves when they hear good writing read aloud well and often. To find these voices they will need echoes of wondrous words thundering around in their consciousness as they write.

OK. I've said all this, but what if you are thinking, "I do read aloud to my students, but I just don't see it having an impact on their writing. I don't hear strong writing voices from my students. I'm not sure it's echoing loudly enough." Let's troubleshoot. There could be problems. There are better ways than others to share read-aloud time with writers. What might be the problem if you are reading aloud and you can't hear the sounds of the read aloud echoing in your students' writing?

## Time

First of all, you probably don't have enough read-aloud time in your room. I can safely say that because I don't think we could ever spend too much time at it. Remember that it's immersion in the sounds of good writing that makes a difference. Just like my Baptist buddies who believe you've got to be fully dunked under for the baptism to really take—just a sprinkling won't do—the same is true for read aloud. You've got to dunk yourself under those words for them to make a difference. In addition to a longer, regular time for read aloud, you might try shorter read alouds like a poem just before lunch, a short picture book before you come in from recess, or a particularly beautiful quote to end the day. Read more of your students' work aloud to them as you work alongside them in conferences during the writing workshop. Watch for opportunities to just break into reading something out loud so those around you can hear the sound of it. Read it more than once, in more than one way if you can.

Thinking about the need for more time to read aloud has led me to an important realization during the past year or so. It has occurred to me that one of the reasons my writing keeps getting better and better is because I'm the one who's doing the most reading aloud. I not only hear the words, I hear them in consort with seeing them laid out on the page. I really understand how words *happen* because I read aloud so much and have to think about the performance of words read aloud. So now I'm trying to get the students I teach to read aloud more. I assign reading aloud for homework. I encourage students to have a very short stack of books that they read aloud over and over during the year—so that they can almost read them by heart, like I do with *The Whales* (1996) and *Missing May* (1992) by Cynthia Rylant. Often, we schedule student read-aloud times in classrooms where they read these "by heart" texts to other students or make tapes of these beloved texts for listening centers. I invite very young children to read aloud with me when they know a text, and I tell them not just to match my words as I read, but to try and match the sound of my voice as it makes those words. Every writer in the room needs to be a part of read aloud, in one role or another, as often as absolutely possible. Later in this chapter I will describe a predictable structure for choral reading that gets students involved in filling the room with the sounds of the read aloud.

## EXPECTATIONS

If your read alouds aren't having an impact on your students' writing, it might be that they don't know how to listen to the read aloud like writers. I wish I had known how to do this when I was a child. I wish I had had dreams of drafts as I listened to Mrs. Wade read to us after recess every afternoon. We have already discussed the importance of identity in learning to read like a writer. If your students don't live with the expectations that come with being writers, then they've got no reason to search for their own writing voices in the voices of the writers that surround them. But an even larger question is, do YOU—their teacher—think of them as writers as they are gathered around you? What expectations do you have for them as writers? Do you expect the read aloud to make a difference?

Frank Smith explains that children learn to talk because they need to get a word in edge-wise in the conversations around them, and they learn to talk because the adults in those conversations fully expect that the children will begin to talk just like them any day now. Those of you who have infants live with this in a very immediate way. You absolutely believe that, before you know it, your children will start to talk back to you. You live with that expectation. You also expect that they will sound a lot like you. A family in the middle of Mississippi would be very surprised indeed if their infant daughter's first words sounded like someone from Queens speaking!

We expect children both to begin speaking and to begin speaking like the people they've been listening to as they were learning. But let me ask you this. Do you have this same expectation for your students as writers? Do you fully expect that if you read aloud to them often, the natural course of their development will be to begin to write like Jane Yolen or Margaret Wise Brown any day now? If you accept this connection between learning a speaking voice and a writing voice in similar ways, because of the voices that surround that learning, then you're going to have to read aloud with your students sitting in front of you knowing that you expect them at any minute to break out into some Paulsen-like prose. They need the confidence that comes from your expecting them to write well.

## READING ALOUD WELL

A third possibility for why your read alouds may be less than successful is that you're just not reading aloud well; maybe you're not honoring the sound of it as you should. Reading aloud needs to be recognizable as a sound that's different from all the other kinds of sounds in the room. The sound of good writing has to stand apart from other sounds if it's going to help your writers.

Are you making a space for that sound? I do. I read aloud at the beginning of every class I teach, and the rule is, if you're late to class, you do not interrupt the read aloud. You stand outside and wait until we're finished. We have a "Do Not Disturb" sign that helps us manage this. I tell my students, "When I'm reading aloud, I don't want to hear Velcro, bottle tops, zippers, potato chips. I don't even want you to sneeze while I'm reading aloud." We have to honor the sound space of the read aloud. We don't want the writing sound in our students' heads to be full of interruptions. They can't listen to it clearly when they write if it's been messed up in their memory banks with other sounds.

Connected to this, you're not reading aloud well if you switch too quickly from your teaching voice to your read-aloud voice. It just doesn't work to go directly from that to this:

> Marcus, if I tell you one more time to sit down and be quiet and leave him alone you are gonna have more trouble than you want buster. . . . *On the eve of your birth, word of your coming passed from animal to animal.*

The students are still reeling from Marcus's scolding—they haven't had time to tune their ears for the read aloud that comes next. I have to watch out for this. If I can, I take a timeout for myself before I start the read aloud, and I leave my teaching self at the edge of carpet. I like a few moments of silence—

some eye contact, but no words—just before we start. I tell the students that we're making a "space"s for the read aloud when we do this.

Read aloud well at all costs. Know the texts you read aloud inside out. Practice reading them aloud to yourself before you read them to students. But if necessary, cheat to make up for your miscues. Sound is so important to me that if I look back down at the text and realize I've misread, I'll rewrite it quickly if there's any way possible to make it come out right without messing up the sound. I cover my miscues as I go. Reading aloud isn't just about graphophonics. My students are often surprised to find that I do this, that I honor sound more than anything else. I once had to read a whole chapter of *Missing May* (Rylant 1992) saying "passed away" when the text said "passed on." I had mistakenly read it as "passed away" the first time it appeared in the chapter, and so to maintain that without correcting the miscue, I just continued to read "away" each time.

The importance of sound in text became really clear to my students and me one summer at the Teachers College Summer Writing Institute. Patricia MacLachlan was coming to speak, and so I chose her book *Baby* (1993) as a read aloud in my sections for the entire week before she came. During that time we had all come to know and love the character we called "Lalo"—L-A-L-O (with a long "a"). But when Patricia finally arrived and began to talk about the book, she referred to this same character as "Lalo" (with a low-back vowel as in "far"). We were shocked. We were dismayed. We still had three chapters to go. What would we do? We kept calling him Lalo (with our long "a" sound) as we had all week. Lalo had become a part of the sound of that text for us, and that sound, the sound of his name in that text, was way more important to us than getting our phonics to match hers.

Honor the sound. But also honor the absence of sound if you want to read aloud well—the absence of sound that's in the pauses, in between the words. And these aren't always marked by punctuation. There's an art to feeling the pauses as you read. You've got to take charge. Make a pause when it feels right to make one; don't wait for a comma or a period. Practice reading different lines in different ways, listening for natural pauses that feel right to you.

Read slowly. If you only have ten minutes to read, then only read for ten minutes worth—even if that's just a very few pages. It's not about just plodding through the words and getting them behind you. But oh, when they are behind you. There is nothing I love more than that tiny space of silence at the end of the reading of a beautiful text—that moment when the words are done but still echo in our ears. Hold that silence at the end. Wrap your arms around it. When I was in high school, I was a cheerleader. I loved cheerleading. I wanted to be a professional cheerleader, and as a teacher, I guess I sort of am. But one thing I learned as a cheerleader was to hold my endings. At the end of a cheer we would hold that last motion for three seconds and then, as one, release it. That's how I feel now when I read aloud and we hold our ending until, as one, we reluctantly let the words go.

## SELECTION

Fourth, if reading aloud isn't helping your students find their writing voices, maybe you're not reading the right kinds of things. Selection is terribly important if the read aloud is to make a difference. The books that will help your students the most as writers are the books that are written with an obvious attention to craft. In these books writers can write about anything, or hardly anything, and still make it sound good because they are consummate wordsmiths, showing off in a display of rich, interesting language that rings in the listener's ears after the text is finished. You remember these books not just because of what they're about, but because the sound of them stays with you. The beginning of Debra Frasier's *On the Day You Were Born* (1991), mentioned earlier, is an excellent example of this kind of text. If you want to nurture your writers' voices, you need to read aloud books that are good because the writing in them is so good.

So, while it may be enough for readers that the story is good, it's not enough for writers. Writers need well-crafted words. When I think about so many of my favorite read-aloud books for writers, especially picture books, I realize that many of them aren't *about* much, at least not in the traditional sense of story they're not. *The Whales* (1996) by Cynthia Rylant is a good example. After I had finished reading this aloud once, a student exclaimed, just as I closed the book, "Oh, good." Thinking I knew what she meant, I agreed that yes, this was a very good book. "No," she said. "I said 'good' because I thought something bad was going to happen to those whales. I'm glad nothing happened." And she's right. Nothing really *happens* in *The*

*Whales.* They swim around and court and inspire those who see them, but there's really no plot to the book; it's not what you would call a "story" in that traditional, plot-driven sense. *The Whales* is a very good book not because it's a great story, but because the writing in it just takes your breath away.

If you want your read alouds to get the sound of good writing into students' heads, then you've got to choose those books that will nurture them as writers on the basis of language use and language sound above all else. I might choose a book for my students as *readers* because the idea of the book or the plot of the story is something I know would really appeal to them. But their diet as writers has to include lots of books that are good because of the beautiful language. Look for language that is stunning, rereadable, read-aloudable.

## BELIEVING IN YOU, THE ONE WHO READS ALOUD

Finally, and probably most important, and most likely the hardest of all to think about, if your read alouds aren't having an impact on your students' writing, it could be because your students don't believe in you—they don't believe you really care that much about the words you're reading to them. Children have a remarkable sixth sense that tells them when we adults aren't what we seem to be. They're on to us so fast when we try to give them medicine disguised as candy. And they'll know if we are sharing words with them more out of duty than out of love, more to cover curriculum than to really sigh with them over words. And when that fundamental trust in us is broken, learning all but shuts down. The engagement is no longer about readers and writers sharing wondrous words—it's just about "doing more school."

What I'm saying probably seems very contradictory. This whole chapter has been about reading aloud in our teaching, reading aloud in the service of nurturing writers' voices, reading aloud on purpose, with ulterior motives. Am I now saying that you'll never get away with it?

Not really. Let me try and explain it this way. All of the things in this chapter that I've written about reading aloud are understandings I have about the act of reading aloud in classrooms. But not one of them is what *compels* me to read aloud. If I knew nothing of all the benefits of reading aloud, I would still do it. I read aloud because the writer in me truly, deeply loves the sound of words. I fill my life with reading aloud when I'm not teaching. I've read *On the Day You Were Born* (1991) at baby showers, I read Kim Stafford's *We Got Here Together* (1994) about a bubble and a raindrop in celebration of our newly remodeled bathroom, and on the first Valentine's Day with my husband, I gave him a book with this inscription:

> Dearest Jim,
>
> Since the day I met you you've been bringing me only good things. I wanted to give you something good in return, so in this book you'll find I've copied my favorite William Stafford poems. They come to you with a promise to read each of them aloud to you, and when we get to the end, I'll read them all again. Valentine's Day, 1996.

I'm not trying to teach my husband how to write. I read aloud because I cannot stay silent. I move through my world searching for words because I must have them, not for my students, but for me. And I know that when I teach, my students realize that as I read aloud to them the me that is a writer, a lover of words, stands up and my teaching self sits down. On that point we, my students and I, have absolute trust.

I'm not reading to them because it's good for them; I'm reading to them because it's good for me.

## INVITING STUDENTS TO FILL THE ROOM WITH WONDROUS WORDS

Up until this point we've mostly been discussing reading aloud in the most traditional and familiar classroom sense—the teacher reads and the students listen. But what about inviting students to help us fill the room with the sound of beautiful writing? The benefits of being a writer who reads aloud are as great or greater than being a writer who listens to read alouds. Remember Ashley Bryan saying that he finds his voice by reading aloud black poets who have gone before him? If we really are to help our students get echoes in their heads as they write, we need to think about meaningful ways to engage them in reading aloud too. I mentioned a few ways to do this earlier in this chapter, when we discussed making lots of time for read aloud. Now I would like to describe a predictable classroom structure for choral readings that I often use to engage students in reading aloud from beloved texts. This particular choral reading structure is also useful in beginning to turn students' attention past the meaning of the text to the actual writing of the text.

## Finding a Familiar Text

For choral reading I will need an already familiar text. It could be a text we have shared during read aloud, but it might be a text the students know from literature study or their independent reading—a text that has passed through the room in some way. It could be a text from the "required reading" basket. Because the number of books we'll need to learn from as writers are too numerous to all be shared during read-aloud time, I often have baskets of short texts of required reading that I have students read through early in the year. This lets students become familiar with these texts when I return to them to look at the writing in focus lessons and conferences. I could select a text from here. It doesn't matter where it comes from as long as it's familiar and as long as it's well crafted. With this choral reading we will reconstruct our favorite lines from the text and make them into a performance poem.

## Focusing on Wondrous Words

When every student has access to the text, I ask each of them to star the parts where they think the writing is best. Then I say to them:

> Find the part where the words are most *striking* to you. *Striking* might mean the words are so beautiful that they just melt in your mouth. *Striking* might mean you like the beat of the words, or the order of the words surprises you in some way. *Striking* could mean the words are so simple and yet so right. *Striking* means you want to read those words again and again. You like the way they sound.

I give them a few moments to find these striking parts, then I insist they do the really hard part:

> Now, find the part of all those parts that is *most* striking. Once you find this part, if it is more than fifteen words, get it down to fifteen words or less. Just select a part of it that is fifteen words or less.

They will moan and groan when you say this, trust me. You don't have to force kids to narrow down to fifteen words, but I've found the narrowing helps them to zero in on the words that are striking to them. More focused text selections from individual readers also make for a much better performance poem when we combine them through choral reading in the end. Many students will read several paragraphs of "the most striking part" if you don't force them to focus. I once had a student tell me, "I want to read the whole thing—it's all striking!"

When all students have identified the parts they think are most striking, it's time to practice reading them in our best read-aloud voices:

> Quietly, to yourself, but loud enough to hear it, I want you all to practice reading the part you've chosen in your best read-aloud voice. Try reading it several different ways until you find one you really like and one you think best conveys its sound and meaning.

Quickly, all around the room, voices are practicing "performances" of the beautiful pieces of text they have selected. I move about the room and very quietly check in with my struggling readers to see if they need any help with their parts.

## A Gathering of Voices

When we are all ready, we gather in a circle, a circle of voices, and we choose a starting place. I explain to the students that we will read our selected parts into the circle, one right after another so that it sounds as if we are reading one continuous text. "The beautiful portions of the text will echo all around us as we read," I say. The order in which we gather and where we start in the circle is completely arbitrary; as a matter of fact, usually no one really knows what part someone else is going to read. We are always amazed at the way so many of these completely arbitrary choral readings sound as if they were crafted quite deliberately.

Now, here is an important tip. After having several bad experiences with students screaming out in dismay, right in the middle of our performance, because someone who went before them read the same part they had chosen (you can imagine this happening, can't you?), I have learned to say some version of this:

> Oh, I hope the best thing happens. I hope several people have chosen the same part so we have a repeating refrain in our performance.

This usually sends the message that it is not a bad thing to be a person who is repeating a part that's already been read—it is an honor.

With this established, the person we have chosen to begin says the name of the text, say, *My Mama Had a Dancing Heart* (1995), and then follows this with, "a poem, by Libba Moore Gray." I call what we perform in the choral readings "poems" because that is the genre they most closely resemble. So, no matter what genre the text is written in, we transform it into a poem, a performance poem to be exact, with our choral readings.

When our poem has been announced and the author credited, we begin to read. Voice after voice joins in a celebration of the beauty of the text. As if carefully unveiling a piece of art, each new reader casts his or her line into the circle of voices. The excitement is contagious. We are always fascinated to see what will come next, and next, in the poem, and we marvel at how the lines we've thrown together mold and mesh their way into something new, something beautiful in a way that's different from the original text. When the last voice has shared the last line, we hold the silent sound still for just a moment, and then we almost always burst into applause. We can't help it.

## Why Choral Readings for Read Aloud?

So why choral readings of this sort? They are a lot of fun, but so is line dancing, and I wouldn't recommend that for the teaching of writing. "It's fun" is not a sufficient reason in itself to make something a part of your regular curriculum. We have to know, theoretically, why an activity makes sense in our teaching.

Beyond, again, filling the room with wondrous words, choral readings of this sort make a great first move toward getting students to think about the *writing* in a text. In a way, the choral reading is the first bit of research in later inquiry because it reveals to us the lines we should probably look to first in our study, the lines that are chosen as striking and repeated several times in the reading. The choral reading also forces students to really listen to text as they practice their own lines and hear the lines of others being read. This develops the sound of good writing in their heads which will help them so much as they write.

But if time allows, choral readings of this sort can give me even more mileage. Following this whole-group collaboration, we often break into small groups, arbitrarily formed, of anywhere from four to seven or eight students. The challenge now is for each group to craft a choral reading from the lines they identified and read in the large group. They can do anything they like with these lines—repeat them, break parts of them up, add movement to them, but they must use only the lines each group member brings. The students break apart to work on these, and we decide on a time limit, say, ten minutes, when we will all meet back to perform the choral readings they have planned.

What is decidedly different about this engagement and the whole-class choral reading is that now students have to draft and craft. The arbitrary nature of the first choral reading is gone. Students must look at what material they have to work with in their collected lines and make all sorts of decisions about how they will get them to work together as a performance poem.

If you walk about and listen to the groups as students are planning these, you will hear an amazing kind of talk. To make this happen, students have to engage in the decision-making kind of talk that is characteristic of very deliberate crafting of writing. You will hear things like "This would sound good at the end because it's sort of a quiet line," and "We could repeat this one between each of the others because what it says sort of brings them all together," and "I think these two lines go together, this one first, because . . ." and on and on. The students must work *with text* in a very deliberate fashion to accomplish this. They also craft and draft these poems with a clear vision for how this text will be when it's completed (published) because they know about these kinds of choral readings. In other words, they work with a clear sense of what they are making, a clear vision of where they are headed.

Later, when students are working with their own written texts, I will remind them of the talk they did when they planned these choral readings and nudge them to engage in this kind of talk around their own drafts. If I make time for students to work together, planning choral readings like this frequently, and if I make that connection to their own individual planning-drafting-crafting processes, they come to understand this decision-making aspect of writing in a highly theoretical way.

## A Choral Reading Experience

Now, I have to tell an interesting story. This story really happened, but it has become legendary in my teaching because I share it with all the writers I encounter. Once, when a group of students was planning and performing choral readings for the first time, it came time for everyone to perform. There were seven different groups. The first group performed and it was a lovely rendering of Cynthia Rylant's text, *Night in the Country* (1986). The group simply read it as we had in the large group, one voice contributing one line each, though it was very obvious they had put the lines in an order that made sense to them. When they finished, we applauded.

When the second group began their performance, however, we knew we were in for a treat. This group had one member in it who had a lot of experience with performance poetry. The second group's reading had lines they said in unison and lines they said in two's and three's. It had lines they said softly and lines they said loudly. Their poem had motion and sound effects and rhythmic accompaniment. The performance looked like something the Temptations (in the old days) might have choreographed. It was, to put it simply, stunning.

When they finished, we applauded. And then, almost in unison, the other groups who had not performed yet, cried, "Wait! We need more time! Please let us have more time to work on ours!"

Now, I ask you, what happened in that room as all those waiting in the wings to share their own versions of poems watched this group perform? What happened was those groups *got a new vision of what was possible* when they saw this performance. They were not reading like writers, but they were watching like performers of poems—and the principle is exactly the same. Because they saw themselves as the kinds of people who perform poems, because they had that collective identity, they couldn't help but watch this performance and see possibilities for their own poems in the crafting of it. Not one of these groups wanted to go back and do an exact rendering of what they saw, or even their own versions of it. They had their own material to work with, and they just wanted another go at crafting that material now that they had seen this. The performers could imagine more because they had seen what was possible.

This is precisely what learning to write from writers is all about. We want to teach students to read, just like that group of students who watched that stunning performance of a poem—with their eyes open for possibilities that will help them rethink their ongoing writing and imagine writing in the future. As teachers we don't want to forget a key part of this story. This group of observers was watching this performance with "drafts" of their own performance poems in hand. Studying the craft of writing in the active way that those students watched this performance only happens to someone whose life has drafts, or dreams of drafts, in it.

Choral readings, performance poems. Large groups, small groups. Playing around with a text to get the sound of it filling our classrooms. This is all so important. These kinds of engagements give students a working knowledge of texts which they can use as they do the closer study of reading like writers, and the drafting nature of the engagements makes a strong theoretical connection to the writing process itself, critical in workshop teaching.

Choral readings of performance poems can become an oft-repeated, predictable structure in your classroom. Your students can create their own (as described above) from any texts they encounter, including published student texts. Your students can also perform choral readings from the actual texts of books, portions of books, poetry, articles, etc., without changing the words at all—only adding the performance. In one classroom I know, Friday afternoons are reserved for choral readings of performance poems. On their own, students who want to participate plan poems to present to the class at this time, or they plan to bring a text to the class and get everyone involved in making it into a performance poem from favorite lines.

## The Bottom Line

The bottom line to all this read aloud stuff is this: Our students' work as writers needs to happen in an environment made noisy by the sounds of wondrous words. You read. They read. Everybody reads, reads (You knew that was coming, didn't you? The sound was already in your head).

# References

Fox, Mem. 1992. *Dear Mem Fox, I Have Read All Your Books, Even the Pathetic Ones: and Other Incidents in the Life of a Children's Book Author.* San Diego: Harcourt Brace Jovanovich.

————. 1993. *Radical Reflections: Passionate Opinions on Teaching, Learning, and Living.* New York: Harcourt, Brace.

Rylant, Cynthia. 1990. "The Room in Which Van Gogh Lived." In *Workshop Two: By and for Teachers, Beyond the Basal,* edited by Nancie Atwell. Portsmouth, NH: Heinemann.

Smith, Frank. 1988. *Joining the Literacy Club: Further Essays into Education.* Portsmouth, NH: Heinemann.

# STUDYING WRITERS' OFFICE WORK

## Powerful Writing Begins Long Before the Draft

In Chapter 2, I told the story of a new kindergarten teacher who set up a dentist's office center in her classroom and was dismayed when many of her students didn't know exactly how to role-play in the center. Many of them had never been to a dentist. Often, as I watch students at work in writing workshops, I feel like I am watching those kindergarten children. It looks like the students have very few ideas about how writers actually go about their office work, how they go about the process of writing. Now, part of this may be that a crowded classroom is so unlike the places writers actually work that it wouldn't matter if students *could* imagine the office work of writers, so unlike are the settings. But I think that's a bit of a cop-out. If I didn't believe I could get students involved in meaningful ways in a classroom writing workshop, then I'd have to leave this active kind of teaching behind, and I'm not ready to do that. No, I believe I can do a lot to help the students I teach better envision the office work of writers, and as I learn alongside them, I can do a lot to make my classroom more conducive to this kind of work.

What we and our students need is a better vision for how to go about our work as writers "behind the drafts." I've come to call the study of this work behind the drafts, "studying the craft of writers' office work." I use "office work" only as a placeholder. So much of the important writing work happens away from a writer's desk. Writers' offices extend out into their lives, into their worlds, but we need to understand what happens in these extended "offices" if we hope to write well.

In my experience, there are two main questions about the craft of writers' office work that seem to make the most difference in student writing. The first question is "What makes a writer choose to begin a project?" The second question is "What do writers do once they've started moving toward a writing project?" I am using writing "project" very deliberately here. To take a piece of writing from an idea through to publication is a *project*. When many of us were students in school, the teaching of writing we experienced didn't help us to see this project aspect of writing. We were given a topic on the board and asked either to write about it in that sitting or to work on it at home that night and bring it in the next day. With this kind of teaching, choosing to start a "project" began with being given a topic, and the way we worked on this "project" was to start drafting it. Without instruction, inexperienced writers, even in writing workshops, will continue to work in this way—choose a topic, start a draft; choose another topic, start another draft. But how is the choosing best accomplished, and what happens between the choosing and the drafting?

Many of us have realized the need to have students choose their own topics for writing projects. Many of my preservice teacher education students choose their own topics for the first time in my writing workshops—when they are in *college*. They become so enamored with the idea—being so invested in writing for the first time in their lives—that they make a lifetime commitment to having students choose their own writing projects because it just feels so good to write what they want, to write what they need to write. However, I celebrate this feeling with these future teachers with some caution. I remind them that we don't have students choose their own topics because it feels good—we have them choose their own topics because it matches what real writers do. It is highly theoretical teaching. Real writers have to find their own reasons to write and things to write about. Choosing what writing projects to pursue matches what a writer does in the real world.

So choosing to begin a writing project and knowing how to work on developing that project are far from side issues in a writing workshop, though in many classrooms they are treated as if they were. These two issues represent a major part of what writers have to do. Perhaps we haven't realized in significant ways that there is *curriculum* that goes along with knowing how to choose and develop these topics. The curriculum of *selection and development* is part of the craft of writers' office work. What do our students know about how writers *select* the projects they will work on? What do our students know about how writers *develop* these projects before they ever draft them? Growing writers need to know many things about this part of the process, about the curriculum and craft of selection and development, and the place to learn what they need to know is from studying the office work of writers. So let's consider these two guiding questions now: What makes a writer choose to begin a writing project (selection), and what do writers do once they've started moving toward those projects (development)?

## What Makes a Writer Choose to Begin a Project?

### Inexperienced Writers

Recently I was visiting in a sixth-grade classroom during writing time. As this was an unfamiliar group to me, I began by asking a simple question: "What projects are they working on?" I know from experience that I can learn a lot about what young writers believe about writing by finding out the answer to this question. Here's a representative sampling of what I found them "on about" in their writing that day and in the past from the finished pieces they showed me:

"The day my dog died"

"My first airplane trip"

"When I went to Summer Mind Works" (a camp for kids)

"The time my brother got stung by a jellyfish"

"When I broke my arm riding my horse"

"Our class trip to Ghost Town" (a local amusement park)

"How I won the championship soccer game"

Does this list look familiar to you? It did to me. I had seen many versions of this topic list in very different classrooms, in very different places. And I wasn't altogether disappointed by it. I was pleased that this group had learned to value writing from their own lives. Sometimes children will be unfortunately turned away from personal writing by instruction that forces them, over and over, to write from someone else's topics. Someone had done a good job of convincing these students that their stories mattered. But this sampling also showed me that this group of inexperienced writers held some of the most common but problematic beliefs about writing.

First, these sixth graders seem to believe that the search for a topic is the search for a story that—complete with beginning, middle, and end— already exists and is fully shaped in this predictable, linear structure. Notice that each of these topics exists as a unit of remembered meaning. The act of writing, then, is simply one of faithfully recording these events in the order in which they happened. In a sense, the writers look for topics that are already written. What these writers do not know, it would seem, is that writing can be a process of discovery rather than recording: that a topic often begins just with a writer being drawn toward an idea; that by writing around this idea the writer finds what is important to say; and that the writer then searches for the genre and structure that make the most sense. Katherine Patterson sometimes finds writing projects this way. In the March 1992 issue of *Booklinks* she describes how, after awakening one night, she saw a vision of a boy in her head just briefly. She says, "I was left not knowing who the boy was, what he was looking for, or who was trying to frighten him. I had to write to find out" (22). Writing to find out is something inexperienced writers don't often envision as a possibility for their writing.

Second, this sampling of sixth graders' topics suggests that these writers know only one way to structure non-information-type writing—by the linear sequencing of events. Only certain kinds of topics lend themselves to this structure, and so a writer with a limited structural repertoire is necessarily drawn to the same kinds of topics over and over. In this case we see personal narratives, but you often see the same phenomenon with fantastic or realistic fiction, in which young writers will return again and again to plug some new idea into this formula such as "the giant that ate the kindergarten" or "the girl who found a friend." These writers do not know, it would seem, that a writer can write *about* something, can write just to create an essential image, can write in a series of vignettes, or can write to explain the nature of something. Cynthia Rylant would have had a lot of trouble writing texts like *Scarecrow* (1998), *When I Was Young in the Mountains* (1982), or *Tulip Sees America* (1998) if she had known only the single, plotted, chronological way to structure "story."

Third, though these writers are comfortable writing from their lives, the sample indicates that they believe the life topic must be extraordinary in some way. They do not know that writers of personal narrative (memoirists) often write about the most ordinary aspects of their lives. Sandra Cisneros's writing about "Hairs" in *House on Mango Street* (1991), and Eloise Greenfield writing about "Washing Day" in *Childtimes* (1993) are good examples of this. As a matter of fact, it is the "everyday" quality of so much memoir which attracts readers because they can see themselves in what is being remembered by the writer.

The "once in a lifetime" nature of the topics also suggests that these students likely believe a good topic is what makes for good writing, and that they must find something that is not "boring" to write about—a belief that will shortly lead most of them to say, "I don't have anything to write about." These young writers do not know yet that it's not what a piece of writing is about, but how it's written, that makes good writing *good*. For these inexperienced writers, every new piece begins with a desperate search for a new, exciting idea. Teachers who know writing well, and therefore know that new and exciting topics aren't what makes writing good, will often encourage children to write from the same topics that matter to them over and over again, breaking them of the idea that good topics drive good writing. Good writing will come from finding fresh new things to say about a topic and from knowing how to write about the topic in different ways for different audiences. Patricia MacLachlan says that every piece of writing she writes has the same topic—her love for the prairie. Her experience has shown her she really needs only one good topic to last a *lifetime*.

Finally, this sampling indicates that these writers know of only one way to work with the things they remember and value from their lives—they know to write the story of them. They do not know that writers will often use such memories as parts of works of fiction, or write a larger work of fiction that grows out of a personal event. They do not know that authors will sometimes find what fascinates them about a personal event, and then use that fascination to pursue nonfiction research and writing or works of poetry and lyricism. They do not know that sometimes writers simply "write off" what they remember until it leads them to some unexpected meaning or topic that they didn't know existed. These are the students who need to see texts like Cynthia Rylant's *Tulip Sees America* (1998), for which the writer took a personal event, her move from Ohio to Oregon, and "wrote off that" into a descriptive piece of fiction.

The student-initiated topics in this sixth-grade class suggest that writing instruction has sent them the unspoken but powerful message that *good writing begins at the point of the draft* with a good topic choice. Indeed, our old history of giving students topics had this idea as its underlying assumption, and though we have given up this practice, the message can still come through in other ways. For example, when students make a list of "good topics" they'd like to write about, the message is sent. When writing *begins* with a web or some other outline of what will go into the draft, the message is sent. When the students brainstorm good topics in pairs, the message is sent. In fact, any instruction that leads students to start the writing process by thinking about actual pieces of writing sends the message that writing starts with a draft.

The problem with this message has to do with intentionality. When "writing begins with the draft" is a writer's belief, the topics that are chosen often lack any serious intention beyond making a good piece of writing. Certainly, I think all writers have "making a good piece of writing" in mind as they envision future pieces of writing, and in this general sense, they are intentional in that aim. But experienced writers also know that *any topic* can be written well, so this intention to do good writing is not a significant part of their decision making in *selecting* a topic. For experienced writers, the intention to do good writing is the driving force behind drafting and revision, not behind topic selection. That's worth saying again: *For experienced writers, the intention to do good writing is the driving force behind drafting and revision, not behind topic selection.* This is often just the opposite with inexperienced writers, who believe that the intention to do good writing must begin with the choice of a fantastic topic. What happens when the driving intention in topic selection is to produce good writing? Namely, a writer who believes this will never learn the reasons why experienced writers (who don't believe this) write about certain things in certain ways, and the energy for writing will likely dwindle quickly away as the writer runs out of "good ideas."

## Experienced Writers

So how do experienced writers move toward writing projects? What is the curriculum of selection that is to be garnered from looking at what experienced writers do? The intentions that drive experienced writers toward writing projects are varied, but one characteristic envelops them all. Experienced writers begin moving toward writing projects not because they have great ideas, but because they have *good reasons* to write. With good reasons to write behind them, experienced writers know that any idea can become a good idea. It is the good reason to write that will propel the experienced writer forward through all the processes necessary to move an idea to publication.

After studying for years what experienced writers say about why they pursue projects, I have come to a point where I now group all the reasons I've ever seen into four categories. These categories have been useful in my teaching because they have helped me lead students through a line of thinking that allows them to better envision how to go about selecting writing projects to pursue. These four categories make up my current, best curriculum of selection:

**Good Reasons to Write**

1. Passion or intrigue for a topic or an idea

2. Audience or an occasion

3. Purpose to fulfill

4. Pull of a genre

### Passion or Intrigue for a Topic or an Idea

Sometimes what moves writers toward projects is a passion for a topic in their lives, or an intriguing idea that they cannot shake. Gary Paulsen is an example of an author who writes again and again from a passion in his life. Paulsen loves dogs. He loves dog teams and dog races through the great wilds of the north. He has written fiction, nonfiction, memoir, and poetry about this passion in his life. Two recent additions to my book collection both came from writers following a life passion. Debra Frasier's *Out of the Ocean* (1998) is a project that grew out of her love for Florida beaches, and Jennifer Owings Dewey's *Mud Matters: Stories from a Mud Lover* (1998) grew from her lifelong love affair with mud. Many writing projects grow out of writers' passions for things, passions for families and mountains, children and deserts, animals and sports and one particular stretch of shoreline on the coast of Maine.

Related to this, many writers start projects because they've had some idea they just can't shake, and over time this idea has become very *intriguing*. Perhaps it is the boy Katherine Patterson saw in her dream who left her wondering, or a particularly unusual sky Byrd Baylor saw on a drive through the desert. Maybe it is Patricia Polacco's fascination with a snippet of a family story she remembers from her childhood, or Jerry Spinelli's curiosity about a photograph he saw of a boy's running legs. Because they live their lives as writers and read the world like writers, writers have many ideas that won't leave them alone. They don't allow ideas to leave them alone, and most any old idea can become intriguing if allowed to hang around long enough. James Dickey once said his definition of a poet is someone who notices and is enormously taken by things other people walk right by. Countless writing projects have begun this way, by a writer taking the time to notice life, hatch an idea, and keep the idea burning long enough for it to become intriguing.

Inexperienced writers will often "walk right by" these kinds of ideas because they are so unfinished and so unformed, and in their anxiousness to "start the draft," they just don't see these as possibilities. But the fact is, many, many writing projects start from very small, very contained *ideas,* and often not even ideas for plot lines or poetry or memoir—just ideas, just things a writer finds interesting but has no idea as to where they will lead. Experienced writers know how to write off (often in notebooks or journals) or think off (often on long car rides or sitting under quiet trees) these ideas until they begin to take shape and form, but again, experienced writers know that writing projects don't start at the point of the draft.

This is so critical. When writers believe that writing begins with drafts they hold a huge misconception about prewriting. When we think of "writing process" as a linear process beginning with prewriting *for a draft*, we conceptualize this "stage" as occurring once we know what we are going to write about. Many of us were taught and maybe have taught prewriting this way. Prewriting was an outline or web for a *draft;* meaning, you couldn't start it until you knew exactly what you were writing about. But if we study the lives of authors we realize that we've gotten prewriting all wrong. Writers prewrite all the time, even before they are actually engaged in a draft for a specific purpose. Because they know written products (drafts) will be a part of their future (they *are* writers, after all), they are always on the lookout for ideas. They *live* their lives prewriting, imagining possibilities and seeing potential for writing in the world around them. Patricia MacLachlan has said, "I'm a user. I steal everything. I don't get ideas sitting in a little room. I'll follow people an extra block down the street to hear the end of an interesting conversation if I think I might need it some day." Patricia MacLachlan's writing begins long before she ever starts writing an actual draft or even knows her topic. Great writing begins for her and other authors in how they learn to live their lives as writers.

The extensive work with writers' notebooks carried out by Lucy Calkins and her staff at the Teachers College Reading and Writing Project has probably done more than anything else to further our understanding of the importance of helping children to live writerly lives (Calkins 1991; 1994). The ideas about using writers' notebooks as a classroom structure were developed as Lucy studied alongside professional writers at the Reading and Writing Project. A writer's notebook is a tool for collecting material that can be used in a published writing life. The recognition that writers collect ideas all the time and use a recursive thought process to come to "topics" and begin drafts from these ideas is the driving force behind notebooks. The "already written in their heads" kinds of topics that the group of sixth-grade writers had chosen suggests that what was missing in their writing lives was an alert consciousness that led them to *live like writers* in search of intriguing ideas to write about.

Life passions. Ideas that won't leave them alone. Good reasons to write. Writers follow along behind what interests them, turn those interests into topics, shape them into genres, and move toward writing projects that really matter not just to their writing lives, but to their living lives.

## Audience or an Occasion

Sometimes, however, it isn't a passionate topic or an intriguing idea that pushes a writer toward a draft. Sometimes it is an audience, a feeling of "I know I want to write something for my father." In these cases the writer thinks and writes about the audience at first, eventually making drafting decisions (topic, genre, structure) on the basis of what will work for that audience. "My father loves sailing, so I will try and do some piece connected to sailing," the writer thinks. The project starts with the audience, not with the topic.

Related to this, intention for writing can come from an occasion that presents itself to the writer, and occasions are generally connected to specific audiences as well. A fiftieth anniversary party, a baby shower, or a bar mitzvah celebration are examples of occasions that might be well served by a piece of writing. In this case, decisions about drafts often concern not only audience but also setting, the setting in which the writing will be shared.

My favorite story when I'm helping students understand that writers sometimes move toward projects because of an audience is the story of Cynthia Rylant's book *Dog Heaven* (1995). When I was teaching teachers in Charlotte once, a woman came up to me during a break and we had this conversation:

**Her:** So, you know Cynthia Rylant's work pretty well, huh?

**Me:** Yes, I do, I love it. [I'm thinking, "Is this a test?"]

**Her:** Do you know *Dog Heaven*?

**Me:** Yes, I love it.

**Her:** Do you know it really well?

**Me:** [Oh no, this IS a test!] Well, I think so.

**Her:** Well, I'm Diane.

**Me:** *You're* Diane? [She nods.] Oh my gosh!

She knew I would know. *Dog Heaven* is dedicated "To Diane," and I was speaking to none other than Diane Ward, *the* Diane. It turns out that Diane and Cynthia (she calls her "Cindi") were old friends from West Virginia who first met when Rylant visited the library where Diane worked, and even though Diane is now in Charlotte and Cynthia is in Oregon, they still keep in touch. Cynthia knew Diane's dog, and when that dog passed away, Diane called to tell Cynthia about it and have a friend with whom to share some of the grief. Well, *Dog Heaven* was a writing project that was started by one friend, Cynthia, who wanted to comfort another friend, Diane.

Debra Frasier began *On the Day You Were Born* (1991) for her daughter to celebrate her birth, and Jamie Lee Curtis began *Tell Me Again About the Night I Was Born* (1996) for one of her children. I wrote a seven-chapter novella for my mother for Christmas one summer not long ago, basing the plot on a true story that happened to her when she was a child, a story we used to beg her to tell us again and again when we were growing up. That piece of writing, *The Valley of Snow*, meant a lot to our relationship; it built a bridge between us that helped us find our way back to a friendship. Writing can do that kind of work in our lives, and building a bridge is a very good reason to write.

Having our students think about writing projects they could pursue during the year for specific audiences and occasions is a very good way to help them become planful about their work. I've had fifth-grade boys making ABC books for little sisters, second graders writing poetry for mothers, junior high students writing memoirs for grandparents, and third graders writing descriptive pieces for pen pals living in countries far away. One teacher I know has a big calendar that students can write on to mark deadlines for themselves for the audiences and occasions that they want to write for during the school year. Having an audience or an occasion in mind moves a writer forward because of the anticipation of having that one reader for whom your writing will make all the difference.

## Purpose to Fulfill

Often, intentions toward drafts start with some real-world purpose a writer has, usually to get something done or to have a voice in some matter. The purpose is almost always related to topics and audiences, but in these cases what drives the writer toward a draft is a desire to see something happen because of the writing. A student who feels her rights have been violated writes to plead for justice. A young activist writes editorials designed to get her community involved with social causes. A group of neighborhood kids write and edit a newsletter to let other kids know what's happening. A group of professional writers collaborates on a short-story fiction project designed to build bridges of understanding to young gay and lesbian students. Writers, realizing the power of writing to make things happen in the world, may move toward drafts to see these ends accomplished.

I show students editorials and letters to the editor as a main source for this kind of writing, but I also love to show them books that seem to have been written to fulfill a life purpose an author wanted to address. My favorite example of writing to fulfill a purpose is Jane Yolen's *Welcome to the Green House* (1993). After her stunningly lyrical tribute to the wonderful sights and sounds of the rainforests, Yolen adds a "Did you know?" afterword that explains the horrible destruction of the world's tropical rainforests. She ends by giving an address for the Earth Island Institute, to which readers can write to learn more about how they might get involved with the solution to this problem. "Having our say" is such a good, good reason to write.

### Pull of a Genre

Finally, writers may move toward drafts with another kind of intention, an intention to write in a certain genre. A writer who has written primarily in one genre, say, memoir, may decide to make a move to writing in another genre, say, realistic fiction or poetry. In a case like this, the intention, the drive, really comes from wanting to try another identity as a writer, or to be a particular kind of writer for awhile. In this case the writer "lives like a realistic fiction writer" for a time, collecting character, setting, and plot ideas from his or her world. All drafting decisions (topic, structure, audience, etc.), then, are subsumed within the decision to write in a particular genre—the reason the writer began to write in the first place.

The desire to write in a particular genre was the reason behind Jacqueline Woodson's picture book *We Had a Picnic This Sunday Past* (1997). She says of her decision making: "When I first sat down to write *We Had a Picnic This Sunday Past*, it was because I wanted to write a poem. I wanted to experiment with joy and urgency in tiny spaces. I had done this in other genres and wanted to see how much was possible in this new space." Sometimes writers begin writing projects for the same reason Jacqueline Woodson began—they want to try a new genre on for size. It's a very good reason to write.

To summarize, the curriculum of selection consists of what students know about how experienced writers decide what writing projects they will pursue. Experienced writers make moves toward writing projects because they have found good reasons to write. A good reason to write is what motivates them, what pushes them through to publication. Because experienced writers know that any topic or any idea can be written well, the intention to do good writing is not a part of their selection process. Instead, the intention to do good writing is part of their drafting and revision process. This understanding is very liberating for writers, freeing them to pursue whatever interests them or whatever they need to write for whatever reasons, without fears that "this isn't a good idea."

How are your students going about selecting their writing projects? What kinds of things are they writing about and for what *reasons*? In what ways could they grow toward better understandings in this selection process? The answers to these questions can help you plan the ways you need to let experienced writers help your students. Writing well begins long before drafts. It begins with the craft of knowing how to select writing projects successfully.

# What Do Writers Do Once They Start Moving toward a Writing Project?

## Inexperienced Writers

Inexperienced writers know only one thing to do once the decision to move toward a writing project has been made: They start the draft. If they are particularly savvy, they might first make a web of ideas, but they'll be on that draft in no time at all. School has taught them this. Testing curriculum is teaching this to many of them in extremely detrimental ways. Students in upper grades where writing is tested are being drilled on how to go from a topic they've never seen to the beginning of a draft in ten minutes or less: "Don't spend more than ten minutes planning, or you won't leave yourself any time to revise." I actually overheard this not long ago in a fifth-grade classroom where students were "practicing for the writing test." I might as well have overheard the teacher saying, "2 + 2 = 3" or "Abraham Lincoln was the first president of the United States." "Don't spend more than ten minutes planning" is as misguided as writing curriculum as the other statements are as math and history curriculum, and yet some version of that statement is said thousands of times each year in classrooms nationwide in the name of preparing students for the writing test.

It is so hard to rewrite that understanding in students' minds, to move back and forth between that kind of instruction and a writing workshop where we engage students in learning to write from writers. Very few experienced writers start a draft as soon as they know what they are going to write. Even those who will tell you something they have written "just came out that way" will also tell you, as a matter of course, that it didn't just come out that way until it had been tossed around inside the writer's head over time. It certainly doesn't come out that way for most writers, in ten minutes or less. No, experienced writers typically have a very different way of getting to drafts than inexperienced writers do, so let's think a bit now about their processes.

## Experienced Writers

When we think about how experienced writers get ready to draft, the meaning of "office" gets really very big again. Many people are amazed to find out how active writers really are. I think we have these visions of them sitting alone at desks, draining cups of coffee, speaking to no one for hours on end. And when the drafts actually begin, there *is* a lot of this time put in at the desk. But before the drafts, between the decision to start a writing project and the beginning of the draft, there is a lot of very active work that goes on to get the writer ready to draft. This may be the biggest point of contrast I see between classroom writing and real-world writing. The process of writing that is carried out in many classrooms is often much more passive and quiet than what I know of writing in the real world. Even when we have students staying with an idea in notebooks for a while before they draft, too much of the work they do is at a desk, thinking of more entries to write about their topics. It's not the get-up-and-get-going kind of staying with an idea that many experienced writers engage in.

A few months ago in my writing workshop we spent a few days researching this very question: "What do writers do to develop writing projects before they draft?" Here is the list we made from just reading about a dozen different articles on writers' processes:

### Things Writers Did to Develop Their Writing Projects
- Took photographs of the subject and wrote off these
- Went to a library and did research on a place that interested the writer (for setting)
- Found criminal records of abductions
- Did research on explorations, diaries, logbooks

- Used sounds in a place to generate ideas and memories

- Imagined herself as a person in a certain historical time period

- Visited a museum

- Interviewed family members about a historical event they had experienced

- Immersed herself in a culture she was writing about

- Wrote down a conversation her children were having

- Learned to do something her characters were going to do (work a weaving loom)

Look at how active this list is. For several years I've been keeping a running list in my notebooks like the one above of everything I have read or heard that an experienced writer has done to develop a writing project before it's drafted. Interestingly enough, I have been keeping this list as part of *my* development of *this* writing project. Generalizing my list to turn specific instances into more general possibilities, I came up with the following:

**Developing a Writing Project before It's Drafted**

- Read books on a topic, a time period, a kind of person, making notes and lists of ideas and facts

- Search the Internet for information

- Observe in a setting related to your topic

- Search public documents and records

- Visit a place (like a museum) where there are artifacts of the life and times you will write about

- Learn some skill (like pottery making) your characters will have

- Have an experience (like spending a night in a cave) your characters might have

- Gather artifacts such as photographs and mementos

- Talk to some expert in a field related to your topic

- Talk to other people who remember something you remember

- Talk to people in general about issues related to your topic

- Talk through your ideas and let your listener ask you questions
- Talk to someone "who was there"
- Gather opinions on a subject
- Write questions about your topic and answer them
- Write off words related to your topic and see where your thinking leads you
- Make lists of all kinds of ideas
- Make lists of possible first lines for your piece—in different genres
- Make lists of things about your characters' lives, your settings, your possible plot lines
- Make lists of people and place names
- Make lists of related memories
- Read lots of different texts like a writer, getting ideas for how you might write

When our students envision writers at work, they need to be able to see them doing lots more than just sitting at desks. Active development possibilities like those in the lists above need to be a big part of what our students can envision themselves doing as writers. And this active work is not bound by genres or by the age of our students. Poets do research in the library. Memoirists interview people. Nonfiction writers muse and wonder and think about their topics. Five-year-olds can take a notebook and observe in a setting. Five-year-olds can go to the library and get books on snakes or airplanes or clowns. Five-year-olds can interview a policeman or collect rocks to look at as they write. With any age writers, with any genres or topics the writers are interested in, I try and get them to think about what office work they will do by asking them questions that guide them to the kinds of work listed above:

"Who could you talk to in relation to this topic?"

"What could you read that might help you?"

"Where could you go? What might you do?"

"What things could you collect?"

Questions like these help my inexperienced writers to think more about developing their ideas in the ways that experienced writers do. Basically, what experienced writers know that needs to come between an idea for a writing project and a draft of that project is a period of researching, gathering, thinking, becoming "one"—if you will—with one's topic. If we hope that our students will write well, we need to do more to nurture this part of the process; we need to do a better job of helping our students envision possibilities for this kind of "office work" and to quit sending students the message that the next logical place to go after an idea is nailed down is always a draft.

What do your students do before they draft? What kinds of active work are they already engaged in that supports their writing projects? What else could they envision doing? How are you supporting active work for their writing projects? The answers to these questions will help you plan the ways in which you use experienced writers to help your students understand the curriculum of development. Let experienced writers help your students envision new ways of working behind their drafts.

## STUDYING AUTHORS' PROCESSES

So how do we go about learning the ways in which authors do this active work? As with the study of all craft, the study of the craft of writers' office work is only beneficial if students use what they learn from writers to envision possibilities for themselves. "What is there in this author's process or habits that might work for me?" is the guiding question for this kind of inquiry in the classroom. Studying writers' processes gives us our curriculum of selection and development in the writing workshop.

## Study by Hypothesis

One way to study the craft of an author's office work is to hypothesize about what's behind actual pieces of writing that the author has published. I like to take a text, often a book, and hold it up in front of a group of writers. In a sweeping gesture, I move my hand away from the back of the book as I tell the writers we are going to try and imagine all the life behind this book. I want students to think with me about the writer of this book and what must have happened in his or her life that brought this book from an idea to the published piece we see now. For some students I find that this is a very new kind of thinking. They have read many books and not really thought about the life of the book before it was in Barnes and Noble or the library. "How did this book come to be?" we ask.

One of the simplest guiding questions for hypothetical inquiry is, "I wonder where the author got the idea for this piece of writing?" The piece might be a single poem, a story, a memoir, a nonfiction article—any piece of writing will do. I like to get this question into the room as early as possible in any writing workshop, because if my students are to read like writers throughout the year, this is a question that should be central to that kind of reading. I want this kind of thinking "behind the text" to be a habit of mind for students. When we are first learning to think behind the text, I will introduce the question, think about it with the whole group across a few different, familiar texts, and then usually move students into twos and threes and have them hypothesize about a number of different texts on their own. We then share the possibilities we have generated by following this line of thinking, getting visions into the room of what writers must do behind published texts.

One fifth-grade group of students hypothesized that the idea behind Patricia MacLachlan's novel *Baby* (1993) might have been sparked by something the writer read in a newspaper or saw on a news show, since you often hear or read accounts of abandoned babies in the news. Constructing this hypothesis helped them to envision doing this themselves—searching the news for plots and writing ideas. If they wanted to carry this hypothesizing into actual research, they could try and find out whether this is, indeed, how MacLachlan got the idea for the novel. But it's not necessary to always push on to research. There is value in the act of hypothesizing itself, because it helps writers envision possibilities. Whether or not MacLachlan got the idea from a newspaper, her text moved these writers to envision that as a possibility for themselves. Thinking that she *might* have gotten her idea this way allowed them to think they *might* get an idea in this way. And when this kind of thinking behind texts such as MacLachlan's becomes a habit of mind in the classroom, students will generate all kinds of visions for ways to go about writing as a natural consequence of their reading like writers.

Another good "habit of mind" question, more specific to students who are working with writers' notebooks, is to construct a hypothesis about how a certain writer might use his or her notebook, either generally or in support of a specific piece of writing. The point of this question is to get students to think about the kind of writing an author does behind the drafting of actual texts. When I'm getting this question into the classroom and into students' thinking, I get them to imagine what the notebooks of a familiar author might have in them. We ask, "What do you think we would see if we could look in Cynthia Rylant's notebook?" We also look at specific pieces of writing and imagine what might have been in the notebook that was behind the piece.

A group of second graders looking at Jane Yolen's poem "Bath," in her collection *Water Music* (1995), imagined Yolen using a double-entry format in her notebook. The poem is an extended simile in which Yolen compares the sound of groaning, creaking water pipes with an old woman climbing the stairs with her arms full of groceries. On one side of the page, the students hypothesized, Yolen must really observe things closely and write these descriptions—like the sound of the pipes. On the other side, they decided the poet must come back and think of things that are like the thing she's describing and write them down—in this case, an old woman going up the stairs. Within days, a number of students had tried dividing pages in their own notebooks and writing in this way, collecting observations and then imagining things that were similar. We didn't follow this question into actual research to see whether Yolen really does use a double-entry format in her notebook, but the hypothesis that she did gave these young writers a new vision of what was possible in *their* notebooks.

When a group of students discussed what they thought they would see if they could glimpse inside Shel Silverstein's notebook, they hypothesized that they would see lists of rhyming words and lots of things jotted down that he'd heard people say. They imagined Silverstein spending time around children and taking notes in his notebook since he seems to see so many things like a child. And they all agreed that you wouldn't see many long entries in Silverstein's notebook since he writes "short." Another group of students imagined Eric Carle's notebook would have sketches of animals and facts about them that he had researched. One child added that he thought Carle wrote about feelings in his notebook because all his animals seem to have a lot of feelings. By hypothesizing, the students are creating images of authors at work *before drafts* so that they can better envision their own work.

If I connect this notebook question to genres rather than authors, then we get the question, "How would a poet use a notebook? Or a memoirist, nonfiction writer, fiction writer, playwright, newspaper columnist, and so on?" This question helps students envision different types of writing lives because even though much of their active work is the same—both poets and fiction writers go to the library for research and get ideas from the world—a particular kind of writer engages in these activities in particular ways. Poets are going to need to develop certain kinds of ideas that are different from fiction writers or memoirists. Where a poet will need lots of strong images and connected metaphors, fiction writers will need character sketches and plot possibilities and setting descriptions. Now, many writers publish in multiple genres, as students will, but knowing how to let a certain identity (say, poet) assert itself in a writing life is what will give students dexterity as writers and teach them to be more intentional in their work before their drafts.

I like to follow the hypothesizing we do about particular kinds of writers' notebooks by having students take their notebooks somewhere and collect entries as a poet would, and then a memoirist, and then a nonfiction writer, and then a fiction writer. So if we go and sit in a field of grass, the poet might be writing images of grass, the memoirist might be remembering grass in his life, the nonfiction writer could be asking questions about grass, and the fiction writer could be developing plots and settings and characters related to the field of grass. With this line of thinking we are helping students envision how writers of different genres can go about gathering material and developing it behind their drafts.

One last, fairly sophisticated question in this hypothetical realm which I like to work with involves having students imagine who familiar authors might have had as mentors and what kind of reading they must have done before they started writing themselves. I like this question because it helps students understand that writers stand on each other's shoulders and that all writers were readers first. "What kinds of things do you imagine Gary Paulsen must have read before he started his own writing?" "What authors do you think Mem Fox might have read that influenced her writing?" The hypotheses we make are meant to teach students a way to think as they read like writers—a habit of mind. We want students to think about mentors and about experienced writers' reading lives because we want them mentoring and reading in their own writing lives.

Using these and other questions that lead students to hypothesize about the life behind a text is one of the best ways to help them envision a writer's office work. Thinking about where a text came from and how the writer went about writing it is something that can become a natural part of their reading like writers, teaching them every time they read for the rest of their lives.

## Study through Research

While hypothesizing is taught as a habit of mind, you might also want to take time in a writing workshop to actually organize research into questions related to the craft of writers' office work. Though any type of organized inquiry in a workshop takes time away from students' own work as writers, some time spent in inquiry can be very beneficial. If what you are taking time out to study sends students back to their writing with the energy that comes from new visions of what's possible, then the inquiry is worth the investment of time.

Besides having your students study what writers say about their processes and office work, you, too, as the teacher can rely on no better resource for giving students information in focus lessons and conferences. I must make at least a half dozen references a day in a workshop to things I know that writers have said about the writing process. I research writers' lives and processes because they give me my most essential curriculum; so much of what I say to students about writing is something I've learned from another writer.

To organize inquiry into the craft of writers' office work or to study it for your own teaching, you will need to collect every nugget you can of writers who actually describe the processes behind their work. There are many ways to go about getting such information.

You can invite writers to your school or go and hear them speak at conferences or at bookstores. At NCTE conferences twice a year I map out my days around attending the various author strand sessions. As a writer and teacher of writers, how could I not? I learn more about writing from listening to authors than by any other means. Of course, I've learned *how* to listen to authors. I know how to hear them describe their work and then imagine those habits as part of my own writing life or as part of what I can share

strategically with the young writers I encounter. When I hear Patricia
MacLachlan describe, for example, her process of stripping away all unneces-
sary words as a last revision, I am moved to try this strategy on my own drafts
and see how it works for me. When I hear MacLachlan say that she has hundreds of beginnings and endings with no middles, I tuck that information
away to comfort writers (and their weary teachers) who start many pieces
and finish very few. "You write just like Patricia MacLachlan," I will say.

Of course, we cannot take all our students or even ourselves sometimes
to the places where authors speak about their work, but luckily we don't
have to hear them in person to "hear" them. I buy (or check out) and read
as many books by writers about writing as I can get my hands on, like Anne
Lamott's *Bird by Bird: Some Instructions on Writing and Life* (1994) and
Bill Brown and Michael Glass's *Important Words: A Book for Poets and Writers* (1991). Often, I make copies of parts of these texts for my students to
study as writers. There are many excellent resources that publish interviews
with authors, as well as whole texts devoted to authors talking about their
work, and even audio- and videotapes of various authors. Pamela Lloyd's
*How Writers Write* (1987) is a classic in this genre, but I also really like
*Pauses* (1995) by Lee Bennett Hopkins and Donald Murray's *Shoptalk:
Learning to Write with Writers* (1996). Amy McClure and Janice Kristo's
*Books That Invite Talk, Wonder, and Play* (1996) has a wonderful section of
short articles written by many famous authors about their writing. Many of
the best books on the teaching of writing are filled with writers' voices in
the form of great quotes. Lucy Calkins's *The Art of Teaching Writing*
(1994) and Ralph Fletcher's *What a Writer Needs* (1993) are two of my
favorites. I invite students to study these as well. The World Wide Web is the
latest way to get in touch with writers. Many writers have websites with
information about them and their work, they give you e-mail addresses
where you can contact them, and some will actually go online to chat with
readers about their work.

When we bring these resources into our writing workshops, it is essential
that we teach young writers how to read them like writers. *Readers* are interested in knowing that Cynthia Rylant once had a dog very much like Mudge,
the dog in her Henry and Mudge series. But *writers* are more interested in
knowing how she incorporates tiny snippets of things she remembers from
her own life as details in her works of fiction. "I might try that," a writer

thinks. Writers read what other writers say about their processes because they are trying to get a vision for how this work is accomplished, the work of writing well.

When you get your hands on some information about a writer's process, you'll want some guiding questions to help you read it like a writer. The questions are much like the hypothetical ones above; the difference is that now you don't have to hypothesize—you have some information available to you.

> "What is there in this author's process that might work for me as a writer?"

> "Where does this author get ideas? Could I try this too?"

> "How did this author develop this idea before it was drafted? Could I try this too?"

> "How is this author already like me? How is he or she different from me as a writer?"

> "What authors mentored this writer? Could they be mentors for me as well?"

> "What does this author understand about writing that I had never thought about?"

I tell students as they read to look for action verbs, look for what the writers say they *do* when they write. What you want students to do as they study a writer's process is to imprint the life of the writer onto their own writing lives, to try and see themselves doing what the writer is doing and to figure out if the process might make sense for them as writers. If they envision themselves working like a writer and that vision seems to fit, they can adopt a strategy or an understanding of the experienced writer as their own. There is not always a fit, however. I remember reading about an author who always started fiction with a setting. She had to have a place before she could start, and so she would write and write to try and capture this place first. I tried this, and it was a complete bust. As a fiction writer I'm a people person—I need to start with characters. I discovered this by trying on a strategy that just didn't fit me as a writer, and I now understand well when this same thing happens to students.

As you share information about writers with your students and get conversations going around questions like the ones above, don't be afraid to be intentional in your teaching. If you see a way in which a writer's process is like that used by one of your student's or a way in which it might really help one of your students, point this out.

A good example of this kind of intentional teaching can be illustrated through a short article by Mem Fox in *Booklinks* magazine's May 1993 issue, "On Writing *Wilfrid Gordon McDonald Partridge.*" In the article Fox details how so many of the character names in the book are based on real "characters" she has known throughout her life. Though their lives are fiction, their names are true (31). An alert teacher might connect this to a piece of writing one of his students is doing in which there are a lot of characters who need names and the writer is struggling with what they should all be: "Why not do like Mem Fox and use names you know from different people in your life?" Whether we think Fox's naming strategy is terribly useful, if we can help even one child to think "I'm doing this like Mem Fox did it," we have accomplished some very important teaching. We've helped this student to see that he is part of Fox's club, that he is doing the same thing she's doing as he goes about making decisions for his writing.

## New Visions, New Possibilities

Sam, a five-year-old writer in Lisa Cleaveland's classroom, pointed to a pencil stuck behind his ear one morning and said, "Look Mrs. Cleaveland, I'm a writer, ain't I?" Sam goes to his writing each day with a growing vision of what it means to be a writer because his teacher has helped him mentor himself to experienced writers. He sees his work in the writing workshop as being like the work of the writers he knows from his reading. We want our teaching to help our students envision a whole world of possibilities for their writing lives, from pencils behind their ears all the way to drafting huge, important, life-changing pieces of writing. We want our students to finish each day in our writing workshops saying, "Look, I'm a writer, ain't I." Let Mem Fox and Gary Paulsen and Eloise Greenfield and Walter Dean Myers and all the beloved authors you can find help your students know what it means to say just that.

# References

Brown, Bill, and Michael Glass. 1991. *Important Words: A Book for Poets and Writers.* Portsmouth, NH: Boynton/Cook.

Calkins, Lucy McCormick.1994. *The Art of Teaching Writing.* 2nd ed. Portsmouth, NH: Heinemann.

Calkins, Lucy McCormick, with Shelly Harwayne. 1991. *Living Between the Lines.* Portsmouth, NH: Heinemann.

Fletcher, Ralph. 1993. *What a Writer Needs.* Portsmouth, NH: Heinemann.

Fox, Mem. 1993. "On Writing *Wilfrid Gordon McDonald Partridge.*" *Booklinks* 3.5 (May): 31.

Hopkins, Lee Bennett, ed. 1995. *Pauses: Autobiographical Reflections of 101 Creators of Children's Books.* New York: HarperCollins.

Lamott, Anne. 1994. *Bird by Bird: Some Instructions on Writing and Life.* New York: Anchor.

Lloyd, Pamela.1987. *How Writers Write.* North Ryde, N.S.W.: Methuen; rpt: Portsmouth, NH: Heinemann, 1990.

McClure, Amy A., and Janice V. Kristo. 1996. *Books That Invite Talk, Wonder, and Play.* Urbana, IL: National Council of Teachers of English.

Murray, Donald. 1996. *Shoptalk: Learning to Write with Writers.* 2nd ed. Portsmouth, NH: Boynton/Cook.

Patterson, Katherine. 1992. "On Writing *The Master Puppeteer.*" *Booklinks* 2.4 (Mar.): 22–23.

Woodson, Jacqueline. 1998. "From Jacqueline Woodson . . ." *Language Arts* 75.8 (Sep.): front-piece advertisement.

# A Few Other of My Favorite Books about "Office Work"

Goldberg, Natalie. 1990. *Wild Mind: Living the Writer's Life.* New York: Bantam.

Heard, Georgia. 1995. *Writing Toward Home: Tales and Lessons to Find Your Way.* Portsmouth, NH: Heinemann.

Hemley, Robin. 1994. *Turning Life into Fiction.* Cincinnati, OH: Story.

LeGuin, Ursula. 1998. *Steering the Craft: Exercises and Discussions on Story Writing for the Lone Navigator or the Mutinous Crew*. Portland, OR: Eighth Mountain.

Murray, Donald. 1996. *Crafting a Life in Essay, Story, Poem*. Portsmouth, NH: Boynton/Cook.

Patterson, Katherine. 1995. *A Sense of Wonder: On Reading and Writing Books for Children*. New York: Plume.

# ORGANIZED INQUIRY
## Teaching Students
## to Read Like Writers

A group of third-grade students in Mollie Robinson's class on the Cherokee Indian Reservation in western North Carolina have just finished performing choral readings of their favorite lines from the Cynthia Rylant text *The Whales* (1996). The children gather on the carpet, copies of this beloved text in their hands, with their teacher who is holding the book open so that the children can see the pictures. Everyone knows what will happen next. The class has been working in this way off and on throughout the year. They spend some time getting to know a text really well—Mollie tells them this is "reading like readers"—and then they take that text and study it by "reading like writers," trying to name what they see the author doing and imagine the techniques in use in their own writing. Often, they will begin by doing this in small groups, bringing what they've noticed to the larger group after a while. But they know that the beginning of this study will be the same, whether it is in small groups or with the whole class. The inquiry will start with this question: "So what do you guys notice in the writing that you want to talk about?"

The predictable nature of the study of writing in Mollie's room allows her young writers to live in a way that leads them to understand the craft of writing. As different as the texts these students encounter may be, the way they go about studying craft in these texts doesn't change much. Over time, the students learn to read with that question—"So what do you notice [in the writing] that you want to talk about"—always on the edge of their consciousness. Repeated experience with the question across different texts teaches the students to shift easily between reading like readers and reading like writers. The repeated pattern of inquiry that follows this initial question teaches these children a way of thinking about texts that can become a lifelong habit of mind, helping them learn to write from writers long after they have left Mollie's class.

So how should a text study in the craft of writing best be structured? Through years of working with these kinds of inquiries, I have come to believe there are some predictable ways of working that, when used over time, can help you build an entire year's worth of generated curriculum in the writing workshop that will really help your students write well and learn to read like writers.

## FIRST, READ LIKE READERS

Before you ever begin an organized inquiry into the craft of writing in a text, you and your students should first spend time getting to know the text as readers, if it is a text that is new to most students. You might begin with a read-aloud time that is followed by students sharing in twos and threes about their connections to the text. Often, I will reread the text just after this, inviting students to interact with the reading as we go. If they want to stop me and comment, they do. If they want to whisper to a friend sitting next to them about something in the text, they do. We raise questions and share insights again after the second reading. We almost always do a choral reading (as described in Chapter 4) as a way of beginning to attend to the parts of the text we find striking. Basically, we just engage with the text as we would with any text that was shared as a part of reading, so you can work with whatever reading routines you have already established in your class. For example, you might choose to have students read the chosen text independently, or in pairs or small groups, and discuss the text as readers in this format if that is more the norm in your classroom.

This first encounter with the text might occur on the same day as the organized inquiry, but often I plan on introducing the text (if it is unfamiliar) to the class as readers a day, or even several days, in advance of our studying it as writers. Once in one of my classrooms, we read the same picture book every day for a week before we began our inquiry into its craft. Many teachers are now spending the early weeks of the school year introducing students to texts simply as readers, but with plans for them to return to these texts again and again as writers, later in the year. The bottom line is that students should be quite familiar with a text as readers and have had time to make their natural responses to it in that role before they study it as writers.

## BEGINNING THE ACTUAL INQUIRY

If students are new to the idea of reading as writers, they will need some explanation of the concept. I almost always use the seamstress metaphor explained in Chapter 1 to teach this lesson, as well as sharing with them many of the ideas in that chapter about writing being individual but not unique, about how we will learn to write from writers, and about how we want to describe the ways in which good writing happens in the texts we admire. Along the way I will tell them about Frank Smith, explain envisioning, and just to shake things up a bit, I'll even tell them that the way in which we're learning is based on a socio-psycholinguistic theory of how people learn. I think we need to expose students to our theoretical bases for what we are doing so that they have faith in how we are going about our teaching.

Using the seamstress metaphor as part of the explanation allows me to return to it again and again during the year to explain important concepts about learning to write from writers. I begin the first inquiry into text by saying:

> You will need to read this text the same way my seamstress friend looks at clothes when she goes into a dress shop. You'll need to look and see all you can about how the writing is done. Turn it inside out. Feel free to write all over your copy of the text (or to put Post-It notes everywhere if it's the actual text) as you study how it's done. Nothing you can say about the writing is too small or unimportant. Let's just begin with what you see that we might talk about.

I have to make sure that I really stress the "*how* the writing is done" notion here because we will need the how's in order to have conversations about craft.

As we begin, I have to decide whether I will have students do this initial part of the study with me as a whole group or in smaller groups. I always prefer to start with smaller groups because this structure greatly increases the amount of student engagement with the text. So if students are accustomed to working in small groups, if this is a predictable structure in the room, then I begin this way. I tell them as they go off to work that they'll need to make a list of what they notice (which I call "noticings") about how the text is written, which they'll bring back to the whole group in just a while. I also tell them to talk, talk, talk about what they see.

If I feel for whatever reason I should work with the class as a whole, then together we all begin to generate a list of what the students are noticing about the writing as they look at it, just as the small groups would be doing. On chart paper I record the various aspects of the text that the students want to talk about. This is the same thing I do if I'm using small groups first, only then I do it once we have all reconvened. I'll have each of the groups contribute an item or two from the lists they've made on their own until we have a good collective list in front of us.

To give you an idea of the kinds of lists students generate when they are first learning to read like writers, here's an actual list we made in a fourth-grade classroom where the students were looking at Cynthia Rylant's *The Relatives Came* (1985). You may want to get this book and look at the text as you consider these.

### Structure

- She writes it so that it makes a circle (*leaving Virginia, returning to Virginia*).

### Ways with Words

- She uses commas a lot.
- She puts periods at the ends of words that aren't sentences (*Missing them.*).
- She uses "funny" words together like *hugging time*.

- She uses dashes.
- She uses the same words a lot (*hugging, breathing,* etc.).

Notice the labels above the two sections of the list. As I am compiling the whole-class list, I always divide the students' insights into those that relate to "structure" and those that relate to "ways with words." Remember that structural crafts are ways in which parts of the text work together; ways-with-words crafts are instances of crafting that stand alone. I find that before long, this division will become a part of students' thinking about craft, and they will start to offer things they notice to me as, "This is something we noticed about the structure." You will almost always have a lot more things listed under "ways with words" because these crafts run throughout the text, where the structure is often a single, crafted element or two. Sometimes, if there is not a very obvious structure to the text, you won't have any comments at all in the structure column.

Once we have a number of possibilities to explore, like the ones on this list, then it is time for me to lead students in a conversation that teaches them how to think like writers about what they have noticed. This part will be the hardest if you are new to studying writing in this way. First of all, you have no idea ahead of time what will show up on the list the students generate, so you can't plan ahead for what you might say in the discussion. This, of course, is true of any inquiry you lead that is student generated. Early on, many of the things that students notice will be those which you most likely will not have discussed as crafts of writing. You won't have names for much of what they'll see. Some of what they'll notice will contradict assumptions you hold about writing. Considering all of this, you'll need a spirit of adventure about these discussions to really make them work. Consider your teaching to be an inquiry as well and just jump in and try it. Use all you do know in an exploratory kind of talk with your students.

I always use a predictable line of thinking when I read like a writer, and it's this line of thinking (outlined below) that I teach students in these conversations about what they have noticed. My hope is that after a number of experiences with organized inquiry, students will come to own this line of thinking and be able to engage in it independently as a habit of mind.

There are five parts to this line of thinking, and when you first begin studying craft, you'll have to go through them rather deliberately, one by one. As you and your students get experience and the line of thinking becomes more a habit of mind, you will move around in the different parts much more recursively. I have really paid attention to this line of thinking, and I have noticed that, even when I'm not teaching, even when I'm just reading on my own like a writer, I find myself going through this line of thinking in a fairly predictable, linear fashion *when I am noticing a crafting technique I have never studied before*. But I've studied craft a lot, and so I see lots of things I already know about. The fascination for me is to keep seeing them in different kinds of texts. But the point is this: Once you get a history of studying craft behind you, you won't need to go through all the parts in the line of thinking because you will already have "been down the line" with many of the crafting techniques you see as you read like a writer. The teaching challenge will be for you, when you get lots of experience, to be able to return to the deliberate "down the line" kind of thinking necessary to teach new students how to study craft. So these are parts, in a line of thinking, for you to *start with* in your organized inquiry.

### The Five Parts to Reading Like a Writer

1. *Notice* something about the craft of the text.

2. *Talk* about it and *make a theory* about why a writer might use this craft.

3. Give the craft a *name*.

4. Think of *other texts* you know. Have you seen this craft before?

5. Try and *envision* using this crafting in your own writing.

Now let's look more closely at the parts of this line of thinking.

## Notice

The first step—noticing things about the craft of the text—is what we have already described students as doing in the previous section. The list from *The Relatives Came* (1985) is an example of this step in action within an actual classroom. Noticing things as these fourth graders did is definitely more challenging when you first start reading like a writer. You will see so much more once you develop a history of reading in this way. However, as I mention here and there throughout this book, children are often better at the noticing part than adults are.

The one thing you will have to be alert to during the noticing phase of the inquiry is a tendency for students to "notice" things that aren't really specifically about the craft of the writing. I call noticings that are specific to the craft of writing *writerly* things. But students often offer more general responses, based on general feelings about the text that the words have evoked in them as readers. I call these noticings *readerly* things. You may struggle some with this distinction yourself. We all have a lot more experience responding to texts as readers than we do as writers.

For example, one thing students often say in an inquiry is some version of "It [the text] just makes pictures in my mind. I can really see it." This, as it is stated, is a reader's response to the writing, not a specific comment about the craft. Readerly comments like this one do not get very close to the actual text. These comments sort of hover above the text as general impressions, and they can't help us much like that as writers. All we can envision doing as writers from a comment like this one is "to write so it makes pictures in someone's mind." But what does that mean? Comments on the craft of writing have to get right on top of either the words, the way the words are put together (often including marks of punctuation), or the structure of the text if writers are to envision the craft in their own writing.

When the preceding list from *The Relatives Came* (1985) was generated by the fourth graders, I am certain there were readerly responses which were offered as possibilities; they just didn't end up on the list I recorded. What do you do when students give you a more readerly insight during the inquiry? Don't get frustrated, and don't treat it like a wrong answer. Readerly responses aren't wrong; they are simply different than writerly responses. You cannot learn about the craft of writing, however, without learning to see writerly things in the text. So honor the response by naming it for the student as a readerly insight. The only way students will ever learn the difference between the two kinds of noticings is for you to name what they have said as "readerly." You might, however, help the students to transform a noticing like this into a writerly comment. If I think there is a crafting technique behind the readerly insight, which I often do, I will ask the student to show me the actual place in the text where this feeling of "making pictures" (or whatever) is true.

Here are some other kinds of comments which I often hear that are really too readerly, as they are stated, to teach us much about writing. Below them is a question meant to direct these responses to a more writerly kind of noticing:

He writes it so it has a lot of action in it. The whole thing is just action.
(How is this "action feel" accomplished?)

The text just flows. It flows so beautifully from one part to the next.
(What does "flow" mean?)

The text is very descriptive. Everything is described well.
(Where, exactly, is a great descriptive place?)

The ending is so perfect. It just brings everything together.

The beginning is so perfect. It just kind of draws you into the text.
(What words accomplish this perfection?)

By the time you finish this book, and especially the chapters on structures and ways with words, you will have a very clear sense of the kinds of things in a text that would qualify as writerly. Your students will learn these over time as you help them make the distinction between readerly and writerly during inquiry, and through experience with your mini-lessons and conferences that show them specific writerly crafts.

## Talk/Make a Theory

As noticings are "taken down" from the list, one at a time, and discussed, the next step in the line of thinking is to talk about each one, as it is in its place in the text, constructing a theory about why a writer might choose to have the text work in just this way. You will want to go for a real richness of discussion here. Feel free to let the talk wander through all sorts of possibilities the students might suggest. Before long you will learn to trust this rich talk to lead you to very interesting places and to show you exactly what curriculum makes sense for your students at a given time. Remember the two stories at the end of Chapter 1 that describe incidents in which conversations during inquiry generated the need for curriculum about pronouns and verbs? The "need to know" during these conversations will provide you with many opportunities to explain usage and grammar concepts to students within (con)texts that make sense.

As we go through the rest of the steps, let's work with one of the fourth grader's noticings from *The Relatives Came* (1985). To explore the "talk about it and make a theory"step, let's take from the list "she uses the same words a lot." The first thing we would need to do is to get right on top of this: "What, exactly, are the words that are repeated? How many times? Where? How are they used? Always in the same form, or different forms of the same words?" Questions like these nudge us to a more specific level of inquiry.

Once we've answered questions like these, we must begin to think about "why." Why would a writer like Cynthia Rylant not go and get her thesaurus, find comparable words, and get some more variety in her word choices? Adults might ask this question more strongly than children because many of us were so discouraged from using the same words too many times that we wrote everything with a trusty thesaurus at our side. After some talk, the students in this class decided that a writer might often repeat the same forms of words because he or she wants readers to know these were the main things happening in the text; for example, in Rylant's text when the relatives were visiting, lots of hugging and breathing were going on, so she kept repeating these words in various forms throughout the text to remind readers of this.

Now, here's an important point about making these kinds of theories about an author's crafting decisions. What if our theory is incorrect? What if Cynthia Rylant was not even intentional about repeating those words? What if the text just came out that way? Or, what if she did decide to use repetition, but for different reasons than we think? Making an incorrect theory about why a writer did something a certain way in a particular text is always a possibility, but it's not really a problem. We are trying to understand what we see in an author's text for *ourselves*. We are trying to generate curriculum, to know things to do with writing for *ourselves*. Though this process might feel a lot like the literary critique we engaged in in high school and college, it is not literary critique, and our goal is not to figure out the exact mysteries of Rylant's intentions. We are simply looking at her well-written text and wondering about why *a writer* (like Rylant, but more important, like ourselves) might choose to craft it that way. The general wording *a writer* is important because it lets us off the hook in feeling we have to know *this writer's* exact intentions.

You see, what we want is for students to understand their own writing as a process of decision making. We want them to write with a strong sense of "I could write it this way, or I could write it that way, or even that way." This is what writers do as they craft during drafting and revision: They make decisions about how it will all go, and so theorizing about a writer's decision-making process really helps students return to their own writing understanding this decisive process of crafting a text. I want students envisioning a writer like Rylant sitting at a desk, trying to decide whether to say "hugging" again or to look for something different. If students can picture Rylant doing this, they can more easily envision themselves being engaged in the heavy decision-making processes of writers.

## Name

Once you feel like you've got a good handle on why a writer might craft in a certain way, the next thing to do is to name the technique you are discussing, if it doesn't already have a name that you know. The purpose of this is to create a language of craft in your classroom that allows you and your students to talk easily about various techniques. If you or one of your students wants to suggest a technique to someone else, it makes it much easier if that technique has a name in the room. Names also make it easier for individual writers to access crafting techniques in their thinking as they write. In a way, the names act as labels for what's in a writer's head about craft. The names help to organize the information in a writer's thinking in the same way labels might help you to organize your files in a file cabinet. Does it matter if no one else in the world calls a certain technique by the same name that you and your students do? Not really. The main thing that matters is that you and your students have access to it when you write.

You'll want to choose a name for the technique that captures the essence of how that technique is used. The names are often short phrases, and you need not put pressure on yourself to make them cute or clever. We might call the one we have been discussing "repeating key words" or "sprinkling key words everywhere." This second one would soon come to be called simply *sprinkling*, I'm sure. In a room filled with a largely invented language of craft, it doesn't take long for nicknames to replace original names for often-used crafts. This won't happen until everyone is very familiar with a technique and how it works, so by that time it won't matter if the nickname loses the essence of how the craft works.

If students are describing a crafting technique that has a name—personification, alliteration, metaphor, etc.—then we use this name for that technique. This happens a lot. Students will notice these, say things like, "It says 'he jumps like a cat,'" but they don't know that this is called "simile." Their noticings provide me with the perfect opportunity to teach them what these devices are called and how they work for writers in natural contexts. So, if a technique has a name, we use it, but if it doesn't, we don't hesitate to make up our own.

## Other Texts

Next in the line of thinking is to connect what you are discussing to other texts you know. Have you ever seen this writer (in a different text) or another writer use this same technique before? This step is a very important one, and one that will get easier and easier as you and your students get more and more experience reading like writers. This step in the line of thinking is the same in principle as one of my criteria for selecting books for craft study. When we can connect crafting techniques to other texts, it helps us broaden our understanding of their use, and it teaches us that these techniques are not owned in the same ways that ideas are owned. Experienced writers use the same kinds of crafting techniques to write well, so our students have a right to use those crafts too.

Are there other texts that use the "sprinkling key words" technique? There certainly are. Take a look at Jane Yolen's *Welcome to the Green House* (1993). Over and over in this text Yolen uses the word *green*. She doesn't even attempt to vary its use in any way. She just uses *green* attached to all sorts of nouns. You could say it is her adjective of choice in this text. And my theory is that she does it for the same reason Rylant repeats words in her text. In the rain forest, it is green. Green dominates everything. Everything is wrapped in green in the rain forest, and so it is in this text. Repeating the word adds a layer of meaning to the text about the dominance of green in the same way that Rylant adds a layer that shows the dominance of the close family encounters.

You will find that you and your students may add many other text examples to a crafting technique long after an organized inquiry is over. Throughout the year, you will want everyone to be on the lookout in new texts for crafting techniques that they already know. This is the one step that will become the most absorbed into the others as you know more and more texts and more and more crafting techniques. Connecting a familiar crafting technique that you see in a new text to another text you know will become almost automatic and will be the first thing you do when you become proficient at reading like a writer.

## Envision

As is so often the case with last parts of things, the last part of this line of thinking—envisioning the crafting technique on a piece of your writing—is the most important one. None of the other steps are worth the effort if they don't end with writers being able to take the crafting techniques back to their own writing when they need them. Interestingly, I was a couple of years into studying the craft of writing before I really added this step to my thinking (and teaching) in any deliberate way. Early on in studying craft I just hoped our learning from the texts would have an osmosis-type effect on our writing—I hoped something would sink in. Now, we rely on more than just "sinking." Now, we spend time really envisioning what a crafting technique would look like if we tried it in our own writing. This step assumes, of course, that students have ongoing drafts and ideas for drafts focused around topics of their choosing.

As developed in Chapter 3, the word "envision" is chosen carefully. It is important to me that students are able to envision using various crafting techniques in their own writing. If they can envision them, then they can have more power as writers because they have more choices about how they will write something. It is not at all important to me whether all students go stick a crafting technique that we are discussing into their drafts. I would not make it a requirement that students must choose to use a craft we have envisioned for their writing. I simply want students to be going through the thinking process of envisioning what a technique would sound and look like *if* they used it on some topic of their own.

To get at this envisioning, you will need to begin by helping students to make a general statement about the crafting technique under discussion that is some version of this:

So, if I am writing and I want to _____, then I can use this technique.

The "I want to" part of that statement and what follows it are critical because they assert the deliberate choosing of the craft for a writer's purpose. Writers craft words in specific ways for specific reasons, and so it is not enough for students to just know what a crafting technique looks like in text; they need to understand why a writer might choose to use that technique. Writers choose crafting techniques to match the meanings they have in their minds about their topics; writers do not choose crafting techniques and then match their meanings to fit the techniques. Writing always starts with meaning and purpose, and the form follows this function.

In the sprinkling-key-phrases example we have been using, the key statement might go like this:

So, if I am writing and I have one or two really important details I want to be strong all throughout the text, then I can use this technique of just finding places to keep repeating key words or forms of key words.

Notice that, in this statement, there is no trace left of the text in which this crafting technique was first identified. For these statements to be useful to writers, they must be made in a way that is untied from any particular text. The statement is no longer about Rylant's *The Relatives Came* (1985)—now it is about writing in general, about a general meaning of "important details and repetition," not about "hugging and breathing" anymore.

Defining crafting techniques so that they are accessible to other writers and other topics is an important step toward helping students own the techniques in their own writing. But good definitions by themselves often aren't enough to really help students envision them in use, especially when the students are new to the study of craft. You will need to give examples of what crafting techniques might sound like if students tried them in their own writing. So when we get to this step in our inquiry, I begin my practice of leading students to do what I call "writing in the air."

I haven't always had students write in the air during my teaching career. As a matter of fact, it's another one of those practices that I've grown into over time in my studies of craft alongside students. Writing in the air is a way of envisioning a crafting technique quickly and efficiently without any commitment to using it in a draft. Basically, writing in the air requires us to take a technique we are discussing, either a structural technique or a ways-with-words technique, and "write" (in the air) using that technique with a topic that belongs to someone in the class. I begin writing these examples in the air to help students envision how a technique might work in a piece of their writing. I always begin by explaining why a certain technique might work for the writer whose topic I've chosen to use as a demonstration.

For example, with the sprinkling-key-words technique, my writing in the air demonstration for students might go something like this:

> Let's see. Roger, you know that entry you let me read in your notebook about being at your grandmother's in Mississippi? You know how you said to me that I just couldn't imagine how hot it was down there? I'm thinking that if you ever decided to write a published piece from that seed idea, this technique might be a good one for you to use, so you could just get that big idea across about the heat. You could just sprinkle the words *heat* and *hot* all through the text. Let me see if I can remember some of the details you had in there. OK, you might have lines like *"My feet burned on the hot pavement"* and *"Our clothes stuck to the hot back seat of the car"* and *"We ate pancakes in the hot oven that was the kitchen."*

Notice that I actually mean that I *write* some of it in the air. Before I became comfortable with giving examples, I would always stop little demonstrations like the one above at the point where I suggest that Roger might sprinkle the words *hot* and *heat* throughout. Now, however, I go on and say, "It might go something like this if you actually tried it. . .", and I write a little bit of it. If it's a structural technique I'm working with, I'll say something like "If you used this structure your chunks of it might be something like . . .", and then I'll give an actual example or two of how the structure might work. If, for example, I was helping students imagine the technique they noticed in

Rylant of "she writes it so it makes a circle," I might use Roger's topic again. This time I would offer something like this:

> If Roger were going to do that piece on Mississippi summers, I can see him maybe trying this technique. If he decided on that, he would need a scene that would both open and close the piece. Let's see—it could be anything. He might start with a scene where he is loading his camera before he makes the trip, and then come back to that scene at the end and show himself unloading the film. Or he might start with a scene where he is sitting down to breakfast on his first morning there, and then end the piece at the breakfast table again, on his last day. He might start with something like a telephone conversation to his grandmother before he goes to her house, and close with a similar conversation after he's been and returned home. Anything like these would work. If anyone decides to use this structure, just remember that you'll need the same scene at the beginning and end, but at the end something in the scene will be a little different because of what's happened in the story in the middle.

As we discuss a particular crafting technique, I usually play with several ideas for using the technique with different students' topics as I demonstrate this thinking. For me to lead this, of course, I need to have a handle on the kinds of things my students are writing about. When working with the whole class in this way, I might write in the air from an entry I know of in someone's notebook, from someone's draft I know is in progress, from a topic I know is a favorite of some student, from an idea I know a student has for a draft, or sometimes even from a piece a student has already published. No matter what, I want to demonstrate writing in the air off my students' writing because this is what will make the crafting techniques seem like real possibilities to them. I do not try and use every student's writing as an example every time; I select just a few that I can imagine easily to get the sound of the technique in the room.

You will need to give yourself time to become skilled at helping students envision crafting techniques being used in other pieces of writing. It will be hard at first because it is so unlike how we are accustomed to thinking about writing, but experience will help. You will need to know how to envision crafting techniques in other pieces of writing because, over time in your classroom, you will want your demonstrations of this to be teaching students how to envision on their own.

You may be wondering if students ever go back to drafts and use verbatim the lines I've written in the air. Sometimes this happens, if they like the way something sounded. I don't see this as problematic. I make sure from the start that students understand what I am doing when I demonstrate writing in the air. "I'm just playing around with ideas," I tell them. "I want to help you guys envision what this stuff could be like if you tried it in your own writing." I have found that envisioning what's possible with their ideas gives the writing workshop a sort of playful energy that makes students want to try things. I don't mind if students try something I've helped them to envision. I never write the ideas down; I only write them in the air, so if students want to go back and grab a crafting idea out of the air to use with their topics, I let them go for it. I believe in letting students stand on my shoulders if they want to while they are learning something.

After a few demonstrations, it never takes long for students to get quite adept at writing in the air right along with me, especially if we have gotten a good handle on how a crafting technique works and seen that technique used in several different texts. When we get to this part of an organized inquiry, if I know that students understand how writing in the air works, I'll often ask if anyone wants to have a go at envisioning the technique in their own or in someone else's writing. I often hear students writing in the air for and with each other during regular writing workshop time when they are working on their individual pieces. I love the sound of this collaborative talk in the room—it's the sound of "possibility," and it gives the writers so much energy when they can envision in this way.

When students actually choose a crafting technique that we have learned in our organized inquiry to use in a real draft—in other words, when they "write it on the paper instead of in the air," I ask them to please let me know so that we can add their examples to our collection of examples of the various techniques. This will happen, of course, after the organized inquiry is over and will continue throughout the year as students return to techniques we have discovered together.

You might want to use some version of the chart on the facing page for you and your students to make records of your craft inquiry. Notice that the questions that head each column represent the five parts of the line of thinking for the inquiry.

| What is the author doing? (example) | Why is the author doing this? | What can I call this crafting technique? | Have I ever seen another author craft this way? | Examples of this technique in my writing. |
|---|---|---|---|---|
| So they drank up all their pop and ate up all their crackers and traveled up all those miles until finally they pulled into our yard. | Try to make time move quickly in the story—letting a lot happen in one sentence | Making a long story short | Yes. Rylant in I Had Seen Castles. "After the war ended, America made Germany its friend, Russia its enemy, and it helped rebuild Japan." (whole outcome of war in one sentence) | Writing about my baseball game: "Innings came and went, runs were scored, and then we found ourselves with one last out left." |
| We were so busy hugging and eating and breathing together. | Not using any comma, only "ands." Makes them seem like things that all run together, rather than separate | Connecting And's | Yes. Rylant in Night in the Country. ". . . the groans and thumps and squeaks that houses make when . . ." | Writing about my sister's playroom: "I made my way through Legos and Barbies and baseball cards spread out everywhere." |
| It was in the summer of the year when the relatives came. | Using "the" instead of "my" to make it a more general memoir, not so personal | Intentional Vagueness | Yes. Rylant in The Whales. "They are floating like feathers in a sky." (more general than "the sky") | Writing about my little brother: "The little brother was coming to live with us any day now." |

Inquiry chart for The Relatives Came by Cynthia Rylant

## MOVING OUT TO OTHER TEXTS

As you can imagine, using this line of thinking for each crafting technique that the students notice will take some time. I have on occasion spent two or three days on one text in a classroom if the students and I are really into it. Sometimes, however, we don't even get to everything on the list as a whole group. I might have students work in small groups after we've been through the line of thinking with a few noticings on our list. How do I decide which noticings we should discuss? Usually I just ask someone to suggest one that looks especially interesting. It really doesn't matter where you start, or in what order you consider the various noticings. Remember that your primary goal in organized inquiry is to teach students how to read like writers, not to deliver a specific body of content from the texts. If there is something specific you want students to learn from a writer, save that for a focus lesson—don't force it into an inquiry if it's not what your students are interested in.

Once you have finished an organized inquiry of one text, you will have some decisions to make about what should happen next in your class. The following outline lists some possibilities for you to think about as you plan for studying craft in your writing workshop:

- You will need to decide where to keep a record of your inquiry. You might keep the insights on the chart paper you use in the inquiry. You might make a class book and keep the various crafting techniques you discover in it, adding to it as the year goes on. You might have students record the techniques they want to remember in their notebooks.

- You will need to decide whether to go straight into an inquiry of another text or to wait awhile.

- When you do get ready to study in an organized way again, you will need to decide what your next text will be. You might let students help you select. You might choose another text by the same author. You might choose a similar kind of text. You might just choose a very different but equally well-crafted text. Whatever you decide, you will want to talk comparatively across the texts about the crafts whenever possible.

- You will need to decide when and how you can begin giving up more and more of the responsibility for the inquiry to the students. As you notice them getting better at reading like writers, think about letting them do more of the inquiry in small groups, teaching the whole group from what they have learned. Think about letting students choose the texts they will study, sharing with them your criteria for selection of these texts and letting them develop some criteria on their own.

- Once you have students working independently in the organized inquiry, you might think about studying an author or a kind of writing as a class, rather than everyone studying the same text. Students can work on studying different texts by the same author or of the same kind.

- You will need to decide how much time you will spend on organized inquiry. This possibility leads us to our next section.

## WHEN ARE INQUIRY STRUCTURES APPROPRIATE?

I think it would be very interesting to use writing workshop time again and again to engage in inquiry about the craft of writing in many different texts. Without a doubt, everyone in a workshop like this would know a great deal about how writers accomplish the brilliant texts they create. The only problem is that no one in the classroom would ever have time to write if this was the norm in the writing workshop. Studying the craft of writing through inquiry is time-consuming, and it doesn't make sense to engage in it at all if no one is writing around the study. The whole purpose of craft study is to make the writing in the room better.

So when is it best to take the time to engage in a study of craft with your students? I can make a few recommendations. First, you will need to pay deliberate attention to organized craft study in your workshop if students are new to the concept of reading like writers. If you find that they have never studied writing in this way, then you will need to teach them what reading like writers means and how it is a way of looking at texts. The best way to accomplish this is to plan for several organized inquiries into texts, early in the year. The time will not be wasted since you will be setting up a way of looking at texts that will permeate all their work, all year long.

When you engage in organized craft study because students are new to the concept of reading like writers, it is important to remember that the point of this instruction is to teach students *how to read like writers*. The crafting techniques you discover in the inquiry are really secondary in importance to this goal. Keeping this in mind will help you orchestrate your moves in the inquiry. Try not to take it over if the students don't see everything that you do in the texts while they are learning. So that students can get the feel of generating the insights on their own, let some things go if they miss seeing them and come back to them later in focus lessons.

If you as the teacher are very new to studying writing in this way, then you will benefit greatly from repeated experience in organized craft inquiry. It will take time for you to learn how to talk with students about the various crafts they see, since many of them will be unnamed and new to you too as a writer. You will need time to learn how to help students envision what they are seeing on another piece of writing, and the best way to get experience like this is to engage in the inquiry. So, early on, you might engage in more of this kind of work in the room simply because *you* need it. Your students will understand. Share with them that you are learning too, and it will be one of the best lessons you will ever teach them.

After organized inquiry has made you and your students comfortable with what it means to read like writers, you'll want to think of structures that encourage students to notice craft independently and spend a lot less time on organized inquiry as a whole class. You might get lucky enough to have students who come to you at the beginning of the year quite comfortable with this kind of inquiry and this habit of reading like writers. But be it at the beginning of the year or in late spring, when everyone knows how it works, don't spend as much workshop time on organized inquiry as a whole-class engagement. At this point I would recommend that you organize studies (as described in this chapter) only when you encounter a text that is very interesting in some way and worthy of a closer look by all writers.

Here are a few ideas for how you might set up independent structures that encourage the study of craft outside of whole-class inquiry:

- You might have students volunteer and sign up to teach focus lessons on crafting techniques that they have noticed on their own. They could show examples of the technique and examples of how someone in the room might try the craft in his or her own writing.

- You might have open-group share times for students to share interesting crafting techniques that they have seen on their own.

- A friend of mine, Kevin Tallat-Kelpsa, had a basket in his third-grade classroom, into which students put any texts they wanted him to copy so that they could study them more closely as writers. The basket made a profound statement about the kinds of reading and writing lives Kevin expected them to be leading in his room and how he was willing to support his students in those lives.

- Students might be asked to have a portion of their portfolios represent their own study of the craft of writing and the impact that study has had on their writing.

- You might just stop routinely after some sort of shared reading, especially in the lower grades, and ask the question, "Did you guys notice any crafting you want to talk about?"

- You might start a class handbook on the craft of writing which students could add to whenever they encounter new bits of craft or new examples of craft that you have already identified as a class.

## ORGANIZED INQUIRY: A SUMMARY

The organization of the inquiry is important because it represents a line of thinking that is characteristic of studying the craft of anything, not just writing. I often have my student teachers use this same line of thinking to study the craft of teaching. As they observe in classrooms they will *notice* some move a teacher makes, *talk* (or write) about that move and try to *make a theory* about why the teacher is doing this particular thing. They will *name* the teacher's action in a way that captures the essence of the theory about that action, try and think of *other* teaching *moves* they've seen like this before, and finally, *envision* themselves making this same move in various teaching contexts.

By engaging students in this line of thinking, you are actually teaching them a way of learning in the world that is much bigger than just learning better ways to write. Anytime we want to study how something is done, using this line of thinking will help us access the craft of the person doing whatever it is we want to learn. This is why the investment of time in organized inquiry of this type is so essential in the classroom—learning to learn in this way permeates the whole curriculum, the whole day.

Related to this, we often forget that writing is something you do, not something you know. There are things to know about how it's done, but the doing is what's critical. Studying writing in this way teaches students to study writing as something someone does, not just something that happens. This has huge curricular implications. When we understand writing as a series of intentional, decisive moves that a craftsperson makes in the pursuit of a final product, then we can better understand the need to study writing in this way, just as we might study the work of anyone doing anything.

Let's summarize now the critical points about organizing a study of craft in your classroom:

- Use criteria related to excellence in craft in writing to select a text for study.

- Spend time becoming comfortable with the text and responding to it first as readers.

- Find a way to give students close access to the text so they can really study it.

- Help students to begin looking at the *writing* with some engagement (like choral readings) that really focuses their attention on the words.

- Follow a predictable line of thinking to read like writers and study the text:

  1. *Notice* something about the craft of the text.

  2. *Talk* about it and *make a theory* about why the author used that craft.

  3. Give the craft a *name*.

  4. Think of *other texts* you know. Have you seen this craft before?

  5. Try and *envision* using this crafting in your own writing.

- Make it your goal to move students as quickly as possible into reading like writers independent of whole-class inquiries.

- Watch the balance of time. If you are having many wonderful discussions about writers' craft in your class, but none of your students are ever getting to their own writing, it's time to rethink your time issues.

# A QUICK REFLECTION

I would be remiss if I didn't say that, as I think back over the years of studying writing in this way with my students, I realize I have needed the deep inquiry into texts as much, if not more, than any of my students have ever needed it. As a teacher I needed a new way to think and talk about writing, and over the years it is the inquiry that has given me both. Though at times I have been shaken by the enormous task of relearning everything I thought I knew about good writing, more often than not I have tremendous energy for the task. There is nothing I love more than breaking out a new text I've just encountered with a group of writers and asking that trusty question, "So, let's see what we could talk about here." Beloved authors who care enough to write the very best keep giving and giving and giving.

If you work with a group of colleagues who are interested in teaching students how to read like writers, my suggestion would be that you take some time to study texts together in these ways. Building your own knowledge base about craft will give you more confidence in working with students on building theirs. At the end of Chapter 8 I have included a list of my favorite "ways with words" texts. You might select a few of these to start your inquiry together.

# AN INVITATION TO MY LIBRARY
## The Craft of Text Structure

*I would like to invite you into my library. It's kind of crowded in here—more bookshelves than open space—but I'll try and make room for us. You should know that you being here makes me a little nervous because I know you will be able to tell all about me by my books. I feel a little* exposed, *but come on in anyway. I know, I know, there* are *a lot of Cynthia Rylant books, but I really* like *her. . . .*

So many times, as I have worked alongside teachers in their classrooms, they have said to me, "I just wish you would tell me what books you have and how they help you teach." And I have been reluctant just to hand out a list and say, "Here, have at it." I am reluctant because there is so much to understand behind a list like that. It has taken years of thinking and inquiry alongside students and teachers for me to understand, as a teacher of writing, what's in my library. And when it comes to teaching, the understandings are as important as the books themselves. So it's not that I haven't wanted to share my books—it's just that I have wanted to share *a lot more* than my books. Now that *Wondrous Words* is written, now that I have been able to lay out some understandings about learning to write from writers, I am finally free to say, "Here are the books I have, and here are some ways the authors of them help me teach."

As I've pointed out several times throughout *Wondrous Words*, there are two primary ways in which writers help me to teach students about texts: They offer possibilities for ways to structure texts, and they offer possibilities for ways with words. I can show you my library using either one of these as a focus, and I will pull my books in different ways, depending on the focus we choose. In this chapter I will use the first focal point—the craft of text structures. When I want to offer students curriculum about structural possibilities, I organize my library by gathering stacks of similarly structured texts. As I assemble the stacks, I am looking for writers who have made similar structural decisions.

When I organize my entire library in this manner I have more than thirty stacks. Try and imagine that you really are in my crowded, tiny library and that I really am sitting there with all these stacks around me. I want to show them all to you, talk you through each stack one at a time and tell you what each one means. But first, let me tell you a little about what you will see.

## TYPES OF TEXTS

In my stacks assembled by structure, you will see mostly picture books, with a few chapter books scattered throughout. The reason for this is simple. Picture book texts are *short*, and so considering a structure at work in a shorter text is much easier than in a longer text. But remember—that doesn't mean that understanding these structures will only help you if you plan to write picture books. As I've mentioned again and again in this book, craft crosses all genres, all types of texts, and writing for all kinds of audiences. On top of the stack of picture books that are structured with repeating lines you might find I've stuck John Grisham's mystery *The Partner* (1997). The beginning paragraphs of this novel all start with a repeating phrase: "They found him. . .", just as Cynthia Rylant structures her picture book text *When I Was Young in the Mountains* (1982) by repeating and completing the same phrase eight times. And many, many essays and editorials and newspaper articles will use this same technique to structure a series of related sentences or paragraphs within a longer text.

So I pull a lot of picture books when I organize my library by structure because they provide easily accessible examples of crafted structures in use.

The accessibility of these texts to those just beginning to learn to write from writers makes them very useful to my teaching. Once writers get an initial understanding of a certain crafted text structure, they will recognize the structure in many other texts. I fully expect that as I show you my stacks and explain them to you, you will quickly think of other texts that are already in your library which you could add to my stacks.

Finding and making your own text stacks will be important to your teaching. The bigger you can make a "stack" of texts in which writers are using similar craft structures—adding in examples from genres such as magazines, newspapers, and novels—the more easily your students will understand the structures as separate from the topics of particular texts, and the better they will be able to envision using the structures someday in their own writing with their own topics. To make my stacks even bigger I keep newspaper clippings and copies from magazine articles and novels tucked inside many of my picture books; items I've selected because I find writing in them that matches the writing in the picture book. In any given stack of texts using the same structural crafting technique, students will see writing about different topics and in different genres, and seeing this they will continue to develop their very sophisticated understanding of writing being individual but not unique, an understanding so critical to their being able to learn to write from writers.

## BOOKS THAT BELONG IN MORE THAN ONE STACK

As I show you my stacks I will, from time to time, have to move a book from one stack to another because it is an example of several crafted structures. This shouldn't be surprising. Many well-written texts have several structures working in them at once. *Raven and River* (1997), by Nancy White Carlstrom, will have to go in four different stacks, and of course one of the great beauties of this short text is the way in which all the parts of it work so well together structurally. These "multistack" books are so important to my library. Writers who have crafted short texts with such a strong sense of structure help to lead my students' development into more and more sophisticated kinds of texts for which they will need to manage several structures at once.

This is a good place to remind ourselves again that many of the structures that govern all of a short-text picture book can be used to write a single paragraph, or a single series of paragraphs in a longer text such as an article, an essay, or a novel. Here's another good example. During the 1997 football season, an article by Keith Jarrett appeared in our local paper, *The Asheville Citizen-Times*. The article was about Florida State quarterback Thad Busby. The article begins with a framing question, "What are you looking for in a quarterback?" just as the picture book *I Want to Be* (1993), by Thylias Moss, is organized out of a framing question. Then the next six paragraphs of the article are written in a question-and-answer, seesaw fashion with questions such as "Wins?" and "Production?" and answers such as "Wins? Thad Busby is 18–1 as a starter for Florida State and hasn't lost a regular-season game the past two years" (D-1). This seesaw of questions and answers is the same structure Harley Jessup uses in the picture book *What's Alice Up To?* (1997). Only the beginning paragraphs of Jarrett's article use this structural device, creating an attention-getting lead-in for his editorial. So keep in mind as I show you my stacks of different structural possibilities the potentials they have not just for whole texts, but for writing well in small portions of longer texts.

## ENVISIONING NEW TEXTS

I'm almost ready to show you my stacks of books, but first I need to tell you about one more thing. It's an invisible thing, so you'll have to use your imagination to see it. Sitting on top of each of these stacks of similarly structured texts is another, much taller, invisible stack of texts that reaches almost to the ceiling. I can't put the texts in this stack into your hands. I can't let you touch them, but I can describe them to you. The texts in this stack are the ones I can *envision* my students and myself writing. You see, it doesn't help me in my teaching to know five different real texts that use the same crafted structure if I can't envision that structure as a possibility for other pieces of writing. I have to lead my students in coming to know more than structural possibilities. I have to lead them in thinking about how they might use these possibilities in their own writing.

So for every stack of real texts I assemble from my library, I take the time to make another invisible stack to go with each one. It's an invisible stack of texts I've written in my mind that helps me make sure I know the structure as a writing possibility for my students and me. It's a stack that transforms the real texts underneath it into curriculum I can offer my students. Let me show you an example.

One of the stacks I will show you has books in it structured according to time being constant but settings changing continuously. There are three books in this stack, all of them picture books:

*Somewhere in the World Right Now* (1995) by Stacy Shuett

*Your First Step* (1996) by Henry Sorensen

*On the Day You Were Born* (1991) by Debra Frasier

Each of these writers holds still a moment or a period in time, using a repeating line to anchor the time, and then they move about in various locations to see what is happening at that specific time in different places. This structure can be used to show contrasts in place or to show many different things happening at once. On top of these three books I can envision other texts that my students might write and structure in similar ways. Let me describe three texts for you from this "invisible" stack:

• Robert, a fourth grader, is writing about his mother's sadness that his large family will be scattered in different parts of the country during the Thanksgiving holidays. Brothers and sisters at far-off colleges, aunts and uncles in distant towns, a grandfather who has to work. Robert could write a piece using this structure in which he captures each family member in his or her activities in all their various locations at the moment the Thanksgiving meal is served. Robert could write it so that in the descriptions of the family members' activities at that moment, each one sends special thoughts to his mother, whom they are missing as well. One piece of it might go something like this: "And at the same time that we sat down to have our Thanksgiving meal, my sister Sara was meeting her fiancee's parents for the very first time. Smiling and telling them how glad she was to be there, and she was glad, but a part of her wished to be with her own parents, at her own table, at this moment."

• Marinel, a high school sophomore, is writing a piece about the injustices she sees in the ways schools are funded. Marinel might write the opening for this piece using this structure. She could hold time constant at 8:30 in the morning, say, and show students entering different schools in many different locations, contrasting the differences in the schools as she moves to each new location. She would show how the ritual of going to school is common to all the situations, but the experience once you get at each location can be quite different. She might use a repeating line like: "And at 8:30 the school day begins for students in . . .", weaving in her place descriptors to make the location changes quite obvious.

• Alex, a seventh grader, has been studying what happens to living things when the first signs of spring appear and wants to write about what he has learned. One way he might do this is to use this structure. He might have a framing line that holds time in its place, something like: "On a Tuesday afternoon in March, when the temperature has climbed past 60 for the fourth straight day, tiny leaves and tiny buds begin to take notice. . . ." And then he could move from living thing to living thing, telling how each one responds to that Tuesday afternoon temperature at the same time.

Now this might seem like some fairly elaborate thinking by someone who leads a fairly active fantasy life, but the fact of the matter is that if I can't push my thinking to this point, if I can't actually "write" some actual text using a structure I've seen, then I don't really know for sure whether I own an understanding of that structure. I can see a structure used in several different texts, understand it as separate from any one of the topics in those texts, but until I write a little bit of it myself, I only know it as a reader. I haven't pushed myself to know it as a writer. So for every stack of texts with similar structures I have in my library, I have taken the time to push myself as a writer, to make another invisible stack of texts I can envision which use that structure.

I make these stacks because I know I will need to demonstrate this kind of thinking again and again to my students. I want them to see the techniques we find as possibilities for their own writing, so we will all have to develop the ability to see what hasn't been written yet. Let me encourage you to envision your own possibilities for other writing as I show you my stacks of texts.

So here we go. I'll show you now the writers and texts I use to help me teach writing. Remember that these stacks of texts represent only the books I am lucky enough to have in my library and only the text structures I am lucky enough to know. I hope that they will help you *define* some crafted text structures, but they are by no means *definitive* lists:

### Circular Texts

*Night of the Gargoyles* (1994) by Eve Bunting

*House on Mango Street* (1991) by Sandra Cisneros

*My Mama Had a Dancing Heart* (1995) by Libba Moore Gray

*What's Alice Up To?* (1997) by Harley Jessup

*The Sunsets of Miss Olivia Wiggins* (1998) by Lester L. Laminack

*The Relatives Came* (1985) by Cynthia Rylant

*Grandpa Was a Cowboy* (1996) by Silky Sullivan

*Miz Berlin Walks* (1997) by Jane Yolen

*Home Run* (1998) by Robert Burleigh

These circular texts have beginnings and endings that match. Typically, many of the same words are used to make this match with some small change to the ending which shows that the text has progressed. Some young students I once worked with called this "going out the same door you came in."

### Texts with Thread-backs

*Raven and River* (1997) by Nancy White Carlstrom

*On the Day You Were Born* (1991) by Debra Frasier

*The Squiggle* (1996) by Carol Lexa Schaefer

*Your First Step* (1996) by Henry Sorensen

These texts use a structural technique near their endings that threads back through many of the details of the text, mentioning them again in a very compressed fashion, often in a single sentence.

### Seesaw Texts

*It's Going to Be Perfect* (1998) by Nancy L. Carlson

*No One Told the Aardvark* (1997) by Deborah Eaton and Susan Halter

*Tough Boris* (1994) by Mem Fox

*The Seasons and Someone* (1994) by Virginia Kroll

*Say Something* (1993) by Mary Stolz

*Do Cowboys Ride Bikes?* (1997) by Kathy Tucker

*The World Is Full of Babies* (1996) by Mick Manning and Brita Granstorm

*When I Was Little Like You* (1997) by Jill Payton Walsh and Stephen Lambert

*Lost* (1996) by Paul Brett Johnson and Celeste Lewis

*What's Alice Up To?* (1997) by Harley Jessup

*Grandad Bill's Song* (1994) by Jane Yolen

The seesaw structure is one that sets up a predictable balance of information that moves back and forth, back and forth, between chunks that work together in some way. The back-and-forth pieces have some kind of relationship, and what's key is, when you get one side of the relationship, you come to expect that the other side will follow directly. The pairs might be comparisons, questions and answers, statements and generalizations, commands and responses—any kind of back-and-forth relationship. Often, even the sentence structures of the corresponding pieces are similar, signaling the back-and-forth movement. The structure can be used for a whole text, short or long, or for a paragraph or section within a longer text.

### Framing-Question Texts

*The Moon Was the Best* (1993) by Charlotte Zolotow

*I Want to Be* (1993) by Thylias Moss

*The Other Way to Listen* (1978) by Byrd Baylor and Peter Parnell

*The Seashore Book* (1992) by Charlotte Zolotow

*Cat's Colors* (1997) by Jane Cabrera

With this text structure, writers work off a central question at the beginning of the text and then make the rest of the text a series of responses to that question. Often, there is some scene that is set up at the beginning in which the framing question is situated. The main body of the text is written as a succession of responses, all of which answer the question in another way, revealing another facet of the information, description, or storyline being presented. Often, when this text structure is used you will see that the responses will include the repetition of key words from the framing question. The length of the responses may vary significantly, from one word to several paragraphs, but keep in mind that the more structurally similar the responses are, the better the text works together. The structure can be used for a whole text, short or long, or for a paragraph or section within a longer text.

### Conversation Texts

*Yo! Yes?* (1993) by Chris Rashka

*What Is the Sun?* (1996) by Reeve Lindbergh

*I Am the Dog, I Am the Cat* (1994) by Donald Hall

In a conversation text structure there is no commentary and no narrative. The entire text is fashioned as a conversation. Usually, the text moves back and forth between just two characters or speakers, and the conversation tells the story or conveys the information. The conversation may happen through actual spoken words, or may be captured in a series of letters. This is typically a whole-text structure and can be used for short or long texts.

### Texts Embedded with Quotations or Song Lyrics

*But I'll Be Back Again* (1989) by Cynthia Rylant (Beatles' songs)

*Silent Night* (1997) by Will Moses (famous Christmas carol)

*The Tent* (1995) by Gary Paulsen (quotes from the Bible)

Writers will sometimes create an organizing thread in a text by embedding quotations or song lyrics between sections of the text. The embedded quotations are connected in some way to the text or illuminate the story or ideas presented in the text.

### Texts Embedded with Response

*Nappy Hair* (1997) by Carolivia Herron

*Cinderelli* (1994) by Frances Minters

In these types of texts writers will surround the story or the information with characters' comments and responses on what is happening or being presented in the text. The comments are like asides, and they create an interactive, parallel text. Essentially, writers create a character to read along with you, the reader, and converse with you about the text, adding additional perspective. In nonpicture-book texts you will often see the responses in parentheses.

### Time Flies Texts

*Homeplace* (1995) by Ann Shelby

*In My Own Backyard* (1993) by Judy Kurijan

*The Blue and the Gray* (1996) by Eve Bunting

*The Rifle* (1995) by Gary Paulsen

*This Is the Bird* (1997) by George Shannon

In this text structure writers use one setting or one object as a focal point and have a great deal of time pass while this focal point remains constant. In other words, time moves while place stands still. Often, this structure is used to show changes occurring in the place that are brought on by the natural movement and changes of time. Throughout the text the writer brings you back again and again to the focal point. This is often achieved by also focusing the details and keeping them of one kind. For example, in *Homeplace* Ann Shelby looks specifically at the daily activities people are doing as each period of time passes, and so the sections of new time are matched in this way as they pass across the backdrop of the family "homeplace." Sometimes this structure is used to simply move time back and forth in a particular place, as Eve Bunting does in *The Blue and the Gray*, moving between contemporary time and the era of the American Civil War.

### Texts Where Time Is Constant, but Settings Change

*Somewhere in the World Right Now* (1995) by Stacy Shuett

*Your First Step* (1996) by Henry Sorensen

*On the Day You Were Born* (1991) by Debra Frasier

This type of text is a reverse of the "time flies text." Using this text structure, writers will hold a moment or a period of time still, often using a repeating line to do so, and will move about in various locations to see what is happening at that specific time in different places. This structure can be used to show contrasts in place or to show many different things happening at the same moment.

**Narrative Poem Texts**

*Mississippi Mud: Three Prairie Journals* (1997) by Ann Turner

*Been to Yesterdays* (1995) by Lee Bennett Hopkins

*Soda Jerk* (1990) by Cynthia Rylant

*Nathaniel Talking* (1988) by Eloise Greenfield

*Meet Danitra Brown* (1994) by Nikki Grimes

*Out of the Dust* (1997) by Karen Hesse (chapter book)

*Santa's Time Off* (1997) by Bill Maynard

*Family Reunion* (1994) by Marilyn Singer

These texts are actually structured as a series of separate poems that can be read individually, but when they are read together they have narrative or expository elements that tie them together—characters, setting, plot, information. Basically this is a cross-genre text structure where poetry is used to write memoir, fiction, nonfiction, or any other genre.

**Thematic Poem Texts**

*That Sweet Diamond* (1998) by Paul B. Janeczko

*It's Raining Laughter* (1997) by Nikki Grimes

*Sky Words* (1994) by Marilyn Singer

*This Big Sky* (1998) by Pat Mora

*Cactus Poems* (1998) by Frank Asch and Ted Levin

*Water Music* (1995) by Jane Yolen

*Sacred Places* (1996) by Jane Yolen

*Come Sunday* (1996) by Nikki Grimes

*Lunch Money and Other Poems About School* (1995) by Carol Diggory Shields

*Insectlopedia* (1998) by Douglas Florian

These texts are written as a series of poems about a single topic. Significantly, each of these texts is by a single poet (or in one case, two poets). They are not collections of poems by various poets writing on the same topic. The reason this is significant is that these texts can show writers a way of using poetry to write about many aspects of a single topic, as a single author.

**Lyrical Fact Texts**

*On the Day You Were Born* (1991) by Debra Frasier

*Out of the Ocean* (1998) by Debra Frasier

*Cactus Poems* (1998) by Frank Asch and Ted Levin

*Moonflower* (1997) by Peter and Jean Loewer

*All Pigs Are Beautiful* (1993) by Dick King-Smith

*Big Blue Whale* (1997) by Nicola Davies

*The World Is Full of Babies* (1996) by Mick Manning and Brita Granstorm

*Sky Tree* (1995) by Thomas Locker

*Welcome to the Ice House* (1998) by Jane Yolen

*Where Once There Was a Wood* (1996) by Denise Fleming

*Dream Weaver* (1998) by Jonathan London

*Lewis and Papa: Adventure on the Sante Fe Trail* (1998) by Barbara Joosse

In these texts writers pay some sort of lyrical tribute to their subjects, either through story or poetry or beautiful description, and then somewhere in the text (often at the end, but sometimes to the side or in the pictures) facts that support the tribute are pulled out and explained, much as they might be in an encyclopedia or reference book. Writers of these texts are able to address nonfiction subjects in compelling ways for readers.

**Alphabet Texts**

*A Is for Africa* (1993) by Ifeoma Onyefulu

*A Mountain Alphabet* (1996) by Margriet Ruurs

*Autumn Acrostics* (1997) by Steven Schnur

*ABC I Like Me!* (1997) by Nancy L. Carlson

*The Desert Alphabet Book* (1994) by Jerry Pallotta

*Many Nations: An Alphabet of Native America* (1997) by Joseph Bruchac

*On the River ABC* (1993) by Caroline Stutson

Alphabetical structure is no longer reserved just for label books that teach the alphabet. Writers are using alphabet structures to write nonfiction, fiction, poetry, description, memoir. Basically any genre can adopt this structure. You will find great variety in the different ways writers incorporate the letters into the twenty-six text sections, ranging from the simple label format to more sophisticated weaving of letters into sentences or longer narrative passages.

### Vignette Texts with Repeating Lines or Phrases

*I Love Animals* (1994) by Flora McDonnell

*I Love Boats* (1995) by Flora McDonnell

*The Someday House* (1996) by Anne Shelby

*When I Was Young in the Mountains* (1982) by Cynthia Rylant

*When I Was Little* (1993) by Jamie Lee Curtis

*Nocturne* (1997) by Jane Yolen

*The World Is Full of Babies* (1996) by Mick Manning and Brita Granstorm

*When Hunger Calls* (1994) by Bert Kitchen

*Somewhere Today* (1992) by Bert Kitchen

*The Sunsets of Miss Olivia Wiggins* (1998) by Lester L. Laminack

*High in the Mountains* (1989) by Ruth Yaffe Radin

This is a very common text structure, appearing as a whole-text structure in many short texts and as a section structure in many long texts. The text moves from vignette to vignette with the help of a repeating line or phrase that either begins or ends each vignette. The vignettes may be chunks of information, description, or narration. The repeating line or phrase is generally a statement that captures the connection common to all the vignettes.

## Texts Fashioned as a Series of Short Memoirs

*Childtimes* (1993) by Eloise Greenfield

*Walking the Log: Memories of a Southern Childhood* (1994) by
Bessie Nickens

*House on Mango Street* (1991) by Sandra Cisneros

Writers of memoir sometimes structure their texts by writing a series of
short memoir pieces that can each stand alone as single narrative units. The
short pieces appear essentially without transitions between them, just as a
collection of short stories would be assembled, with titles between each
story. The difference in the structure of a short story collection and in this
memoir structure, however, is that characters, settings, and some plots travel
across the stories as they are written to illuminate a specific life.

## Journal or Diary Texts

*Mississippi Mud: Three Prairie Journals* (1997) by Ann Turner

*Starry Messenger* (1996) by Peter Sis

*Searching for Laura Ingalls* (1995) by Kathryn Lasky and
Meribah Knight

*Catherine, Called Birdy* (1994) by Karen Cushman

*Celia's Island Journal* (1992) by Loretta Krupinski

Sometimes writers will structure a text around diary or journal entries.
The text may be made up of *only* the entries in the journal or diary, without
any parallel text. In these cases the entries are usually dated, and sometimes
they may be titled or sectioned off as well. A variation of this structure is to
weave together journal or diary entries with commentary or narration, creating parallel or interactive texts. The journal/diary entries may have the same
speaker as the accompanying text, or the speakers may be different. In either
case the journal/diary entries may be excerpts from journals and diaries of
real people, but writers may, for a variety of purposes, also create entries for
fictional characters to either tell a story or present nonfictional information
through a character.

**Letter Texts**

*Dear Mr. Blueberry* (1991) by Simon James

*Dear Rebecca, Winter Is Here* (1993) by Jean Craighead George

*Nettie's Trip South* (1987) by Ann Turner

*The Gardener* (1997) by Sarah Stewart

Writers will sometimes choose to structure a text as a letter (when it is actually not a letter, of course). The text might be a single letter, or a series of letters either back and forth among two or more characters or over time from only one character. While maintaining all the genre aspects of letter writing, the content of the letter(s) can help writers with almost any purpose, from telling a fictional story to conveying important information in a professional nonfiction article. The letters may be embedded in commentary or narration, or they may stand alone in the text.

**Two-Part Texts—Changing Situation**

*Night in the Country* (1986) by Cynthia Rylant

*Rainflowers* (1992) by Ann Turner

*Sophie* (1994) by Mem Fox

*Underground Train* (1997) by Mary Quattlebaum

*Raven and River* (1997) by Nancy White Carlstrom

When you read a text structured in this way, you feel as if the text clearly has two parts to it. Writers write the first part of the text with the content strongly influenced by some situational factor, and then in the second part of the text that factor changes and its influence on the text is clear. Everything is one way, and then it changes and everything is another way. For example, in *Sophie*, the grandfather first takes care of Sophie, and then as he ages, Sophie takes care of him. In *Rainflowers*, in the first half of the text a storm is building, and in the second half the sun returns and the storm goes away. Generally, this type of text is used to show some kind of contrast, and it is a common paragraph or section structure used in longer texts. The shift doesn't have to come in the middle of the text; it can come at any point.

### Two-Part Texts—Shifting Focus or Perspective

*For the Love of the Game: Michael Jordan and Me* (1997) by Eloise Greenfield

*Whoever You Are* (1997) by Mem Fox

This structure is quite similar to the preceding one. Just as with changing situations, there is a clear place in the text where the second half of the content is contrasted to the first half. The difference is that in these texts, the contrast comes about not because of a changed situation that is part of the narrative, but because the writer simply shifts the focus or perspective and takes the reader in another direction. In other words, the shift is not embedded in a situation in a story—it simply happens. Often, in this text structure writers will bring the two parts of the text together in some way as an ending.

### Story within a Story

*We Got Here Together* (1994) by Kim Stafford

*Knots on a Counting Rope* (1987) by Bill Martin Jr. and John Archambault

*Everglades* (1995) by Jean Craighead George

*The Seashore Book* (1992) by Charlotte Zolotow

*The First Song Ever Sung* (1993) by Laura Krauss Melmed

When writers use this structure, they use one story to tell another story or to present information, memoir, or description. The structure has a framing story which generally has some sort of "trigger" in it that moves the text to the inside story. The trigger may be another character asking a question, or some other stimulus in the frame story's setting that takes the text to the inside story. Often, the text moves between the two stories as characters from the frame story interact by commenting on the inside story being revealed.

### Inanimate Voice Text

*Cry Me a River* (1991) by Rodney McRae

*Mojave* (1988) by Diane Seibert

*Water Dance* (1997) by Thomas Locker

*North Country Spring* (1997) by Reeve Lindbergh

In this way of writing a text, an inanimate "character" has the speaking role that narrates the text. The decision to fashion a text in this way allows the writer to shift readers' attention to an unusual, unexpected perspective. The effect is surprising because it truly "brings to life" something that is lifeless, something that we do not expect to speak.

### Photo-Poetry

*Brown Angels* (1993) by Walter Dean Myers

*Something Permanent* (1994) by Cynthia Rylant and Walker Evans

*Water Music* (1995) by Jane Yolen

Sometimes writers will structure a text as a series of poems that accompany photographs which interest them. Usually the photos are connected to a central idea, making the collection thematic rather than random.

### Photo-Narratives

*In My Family/En Mi Familia* (1996) by Carmen Lomas Garza

*Snapshots from the Wedding* (1997) by Gary Soto

Texts written in this way are fashioned to sound like someone is showing the reader a photo album and narrating the story of each picture. As each new page is turned and a new photo or picture is revealed, it is accompanied by narration such as, "This is my sister Mary Jane's birthday party" (*In My Family*); again, so it sounds like someone showing the reader a photo album. In the case of *In My Family*, Carmen Lomas Garza actually was telling Harriet Rohmer the story of each picture, and they decided to retain that show-the-picture, tell-the-story voice rather than change it. Gary Soto uses the same voice—only fictionalized—in *Snapshots*.

### Narratives Sequenced by a Series of Objects, People, or Animals

*We Had a Picnic This Sunday Past* (1997) by Jacqueline Woodson

*Aunt Flossie's Hats (and Crabcakes Later)* (1991) by Elizabeth F. Howard

*So Much* (1994) by Trish Cooke

*Wilford Gordon McDonald Partridge* (1985) by Mem Fox

*All the Places to Love* (1994) by Patricia MacLachlan

*A Street Called Home* (1997) by Aminah Brenda Lynn Robinson

*The Very Hungry Caterpillar* (1987) by Eric Carle

*Raven and River* (1997) by Nancy White Carlstrom

*Grandad Bill's Song* (1994) by Jane Yolen

Texts structured in this way tell stories that are sequenced primarily by moving through various objects, people, or animals, rather than the more traditional event sequencing of many narrative texts. These texts move the narrative along by moving from object to object, person to person, or animal to animal and the reader comes to expect that the next part of the story will be connected to the next object, animal, or person.

### Idea Texts Sequenced by a Series of Objects, People, Animals, or Concepts

*In the Wild* (1997) by Nora Leigh Ryder

*Do They Scare You?* (1992) by Sneed B. Collard

*If You Want to Find Golden* (1993) by Eileen Spinelli

*Families of the Deep Blue Sea* (1995) by Kenneth Mallory

*Water Dance* (1997) by Thomas Locker

*Rough Sketch Beginning* (1996) by James Berry

*Chidi Only Likes Blue* (1997) by Ifeoma Onyefulu

These texts are very similar to those above, the difference being that these texts are not storytelling narratives, so the movement through the series of objects, people, animals, or concepts doesn't work to tell a single story. Instead, these texts follow an idea through these various things. For example, *Do They Scare You?* looks at the idea of very unusual, some might say scary, animals and why they look the way they do. This structure is quite common and very useful for many types of informational writing, but can also be used for descriptive texts.

**Handbook or Guide Texts**

*Tomorrow on Rocky Pond* (1993) by Lynn Reiser

*The Pirate's Handbook* (1995) by Margaret Lincoln

*The Knight's Handbook* (1997) by Christopher Gravett

These texts, which aren't really intended as real handbooks or guides, use this familiar structure to tell a story or present information. The texts have sections of explanations, lists of advice, diagrams on how to do things, and so forth, just as a real handbook or guide would, but they are actually parodies of that genre, using it to achieve some other purpose.

**Cumulative Texts**

*Here Is the Southwestern Desert* (1995) by Madeleine Dunphy

*Bringing the Rain to Kipiti Plain* (1981) by Verna Aardema

*This Is the Bird* (1997) by George Shannon

*This Is the Star* (1996) by Joyce Dunbar and Gary Blythe

These are "The house that Jack built" texts, very complicated structurally. Using lots of repetition, they add layers of new details to previous ones, and each text section repeats all the previous details. Often, the texts turn in the middle and take layers away until the text is stripped back to the original, single detail. This is not a text structure you will find often in writing for adults, unless it is used as parody. You might be surprised, however, that the structure is used in some texts such as *Here is the Southwestern Desert* and *Bringing the Rain to Kipiti Plain*, that are not simply fun, silly texts. Each of these conveys a lot of nonfiction information using the cumulative structure. For a writer to choose this text structure, he or she needs to be working with information or a storyline that is clearly cause-effect in nature, and to be writing for an audience who will not be distracted by the excessive repetition in the text.

**Multigenre Texts**

*Our House: Stories of Levittown* (1995) by Pam Conrad

*Tears of a Tiger* (1996) by Sharon Draper

*Katja's Book of Mushrooms* (1997) by Katja Arnold with Sam Swope

These texts are structured in sections written in different genres. In a single text, writers may combine sections written as letters, journal entries, interview transcripts, memoirs, phone conversation transcripts, homework assignments, encyclopedia entries, newspaper articles, refrigerator notes, poems, short stories, etc., etc. These texts read like a menagerie of writing, but together the various genres tell a single story or build a single idea.

### Participation Texts

*Shark in the Sea* (1997) by Joanne Ryder

*Winter Whale* (1991) by Joanne Ryder

*Families of the Deep Blue Sea* (1995) by Kenneth Mallory

*The Seashore Book* (1992) by Charlotte Zolotow

These texts use a second-person "you" to address readers directly and invite them to participate in the text. The effect of this is that it makes readers feel as if they are experiencing what the "characters" are experiencing.

### Geographical Texts

*Tulip Sees America* (1998) by Cynthia Rylant

*How to Make an Apple Pie and See the World* (1994) by Marjorie Priceman

These texts borrow specific geographical structures to help them move their narratives along. The pieces of text work together to create a story that follows a real map from place to place. Often, each "stop" on the map in the text will be written in a similar way, with corresponding kinds of details and sometimes even similar sentence structures.

### Texts That Borrow a Structure from Nature

*My Mama Had a Dancing Heart* (1995) by Libba Moore Gray

*Pond Year* (1995) by Kathryn Lasky

*Let's Eat* (1996) by Ana Zamorano

*Trevor's Wiggly Wobbly Tooth* (1998) by Lester L. Laminack

*Water Dance* (1997) by Thomas Locker

*Look to the North: A Wolf Pup Diary* (1997) by Jean Craighead George

*Snow Toward Evening* (1990) by Thomas Locker

*Moonstick: The Seasons of the Sioux* (1997) by Eve Bunting

Texts like these are written to follow some natural structure that exists in the universe. Often, these universal structures are chronological in nature, so they help establish time movement in the texts—days of the week, months of the year, seasons, etc.—but not always. Writers may also borrow stages of a cycle for text structures, as Locker did in *Water Dance*.

**Repeated, Wraparound Paragraph Structure**

*Tulip Sees America* (1998) by Cynthia Rylant

*The Important Book* (1949) by Margaret Wise Brown

*If You're Not From the Prairie* (1995) by David Bouchard

*Raven and River* (1997) by Nancy White Carlstrom

Sometimes writers will construct a very sophisticated text in which a long series of paragraphs (sometimes the whole text) is structured repeatedly in the same exact way. In the four example texts above, each writer uses a similar wraparound structure for paragraphs in which a beginning and an ending sentence, the first a statement, the last a clarification of that statement, wrap themselves around a body of details in the middle sentences.

# References

Grisham, John. 1997. *The Partner*. New York: Doubleday.

Jarrett, Keith, "He's lost just once, but Busby still criticized," *Asheville Citizen-Times*, 6 November 1997, D-1.

# ANOTHER INVITATION TO MY LIBRARY
## Ways with Words

In this chapter, as in the previous one, I would like to invite you into my library once again. This time, however, I am going to take you on a different kind of tour. We will see some of the same books we saw before, but this time we'll be looking at them with a different focus. This time I want to show you, between the covers of my beloved books, some wondrous ways with words.

I have loved the sound of wondrous words since I was child. At weddings, I was more taken with words than wedding gowns, waiting throughout the ceremony to hear the seesawing rhythm of "For better or worse, for richer or poorer, in sickness and in health. . . ." I would let the sound of those beautiful, loving words ring in my ears for days after I had attended a marriage service. I would wait all year for that great Biblical passage, heard only at Christmas in my church, that began, "And it came to pass in those days that a decree went out from Caesar Augustus that all should be taxed. . . ." And on the police shows—so popular when I was growing up—I found myself waiting anxiously to be satisfied, when they got their villain, for those somber, serious words, "You have the right to remain silent. Anything you say can and will be used against you in a court of law. . . ." I love the sound of words, well-chosen and well-placed.

Through inquiry, my students and I during the past few years have tried to find out how wondrous words happen, how they are chosen and placed together on the page in ways that *sound good*. We have turned our attention to how things are written because we have believed there are things to know about how wondrous words come to be, things beyond "they just come out that way." We have searched for patterns of language use, trying to understand what wondrous words have in common across many different, beautiful texts. We have listened as Gary Paulsen has said of his writing, "Language, really, is a dance for me and I'll do anything with it, including getting fast and loose with grammar, to make a story work right" (McClure and Kristo 1996, 276). Oh, show us your dance moves, Gary Paulsen, we have pleaded.

The writers we admire (like Paulsen) have not let us down. They have shown us their moves again and again. By focusing on the small moves writers make to get to wondrous words in their beautiful texts, we have developed a repertoire of understandings about writing well that crosses all genres, all topics, and all audiences. We have tried stripping writing down to its bare bones, down past elements of genre and topic and audience, to study texts at the word, phrase, and sentence level. What we have wanted to know has gone beyond how to develop a good character for fiction, a compelling point of view for persuasive writing, or a focus for memoir. What we have wanted to know is, "Within these larger issues of writing, how do we write this sentence well, this phrase, that last paragraph?" What we have found is that the craft of good writing is more alike than it is different, and seeing the likenesses across texts has helped us as growing writers to come to own good writing techniques for ourselves more easily.

So this tour of my library will be organized around the many, varied ways with words writers use as they craft. Along the way, I will open several different texts for you and show you where writers are using words in similar ways. I hope that what we see will delight you, but I also know that some of what we see may surprise and even challenge you.

You will see that some of the things you were taught as never being a part of good writing are actually quite common and are used in texts in fairly consistent and very meaningful and effective ways—things like artful sentence fragments or "ands" at the beginning of sentences. The ways-with-words techniques will also challenge us to look at familiar language concepts—such as parts-of-speech names—in new ways. When we consider parts of speech or marks of punctuation as crafting techniques, we think about them in terms of what work they can do for us as writers. As writers we don't need to know some chalkboard definition of an adjective—we need to know what adjectives can do in texts to make them wondrous.

Transforming our existing parts-of-speech knowledge into crafting knowledge is often quite a challenge because we just don't have experience in thinking this way about what we know. But recasting what we know is so important to our teaching. In inquiry we need to become adept at naming and defining for children the wondrous words they discover as they read like writers. A student may know that "waiting cotton-quiet until she cleared her throat" (in *Miz Berlin Walks* by Jane Yolen) is some wondrous language, but not know that the unusual "cotton-quiet" serves as an adverb. As teachers, we give students these labels for what they are seeing as they see them, matching real-world language learning that has worked so efficiently for them throughout their lives.

I hope that, during this library tour of wondrous ways with words, you will begin to transform your existing knowledge about our language into explicit curriculum for how to write well, curriculum you can share with students again and again in conferences and focus lessons. Many of the issues that were relevant the last time I showed you my library of text structures hold true here as well. Once again, I will show you many of my picture books as example texts, as well as a few chapter books. Remember that the choice of these books has to do with their ease and accessibility for classroom study, not because these ways with words are found only in picture books. You will again see books listed several times as example texts for different ways-with-words techniques, indicating that some texts have a lot to offer as mentors for young writers. And just as with learning about new text structures, you will again find it helpful to try envisioning ways-with-words techniques by writing examples of your own "in the air" to go with each set of examples I show you. Write your own examples using different topics and envisioning writers of all ages trying the techniques.

And finally, just as with the listing of stacks of text structures, this outline of ways-with-words techniques is limited to my own library and my own knowledge base of these techniques. In some ways it is even more limited because I have only included a few defining examples of each technique. These are the crafting techniques I am using in my teaching right now, and these are some of the writers who are helping me to show students how to use them. To really understand the techniques I highlight here, you will need to go and find these books and see the larger contexts in which the crafting is found. And, as before, this outline is meant to be defining, but not definitive. My hope is that it will show you just enough to start you on your way toward looking closely at the writing in the texts you admire.

# WONDROUS REPETITION

## Close-Echo Effect

A writer will often repeat words or phrases very close together when it is not necessary to do so, creating an echo effect in the text. Often, you will see these repetitions in places where a conjunction could easily be used to tie text elements to one key word or phrase, but instead the keys words are repeated. This lets the writer both call attention to words and repeat text rhythms because the number of syllables is repeated.

- *Night in the Country* (1986) by Cynthia Rylant: "There is no night *so* dark, *so* black as night in the country" (n.p.).

- *The Whales* (1996) by Cynthia Rylant: ". . . someone is standing on a shore and his heart is *filling up. Filling up* and ready to burst. Whales do not know *how they* change people, *how they make* them better, *how they make* them kind" (n.p.).

- *Water Dance* (1997) by Thomas Locker: "I wind through broad, golden valleys *joined by* streams, *joined by* creeks" (n.p.).

- *Miz Berlin Walks* (1997) by Jane Yolen: "*Without missing* a step, *without missing* a word . . ." (n.p.).

- *Dreamplace* (1993) by George Ella Lyon: ". . . and see for the first time across the trees: *like a* dream, *like a* sandcastle this city the Pueblo people built under a cliff" (n.p.).

## Repeating Details

Sometimes writers will take specific details and repeat them at different points in a text, creating a thread of continuity through the artful repetition of detail. Sometimes the details are repeated using the exact same words, but not always. Sometimes just the detail will come up again and some small aspect of it has changed.

- *Roxaboxen* (1991) by Alice McLerran. The colors of the desert glass—"amethyst, amber, and sea-green"—are mentioned twice in the text (n.p.).

- *The Relatives Came* (1985) by Cynthia Rylant. Grapes are the repeating detail. They are "nearly purple enough to pick, but not quite" and "almost purple grapes," and finally, at the end, they are "dark purple grapes" (n.p.).

- *Miz Berlin Walks* (1997) by Jane Yolen. A paper fan and a shiny black umbrella are details mentioned here and there throughout the text (n.p.).

## Repeating Sentence Structures

In just one place in a text, writers will sometimes repeat a sentence structure or a series of sentence structures for effect. This is a repetition not of *words,* but of *kinds of words,* and how they are put together. These sophisticated repetitions tie the sentences together in a rhythmic way, adding an interesting sound to the text.

- *Secret Place* (1996) by Eve Bunting: "The growl of traffic, the snort of trains, the *beep-beep* of a backing truck. The secret place has its own noise: The cackle of coots, the quack of teals, the *rah-rah* of the mallards that ring the sky" (n.p.).

- *Night in the Country* (1986) by Cynthia Rylant: "There are owls. Great owls with marble eyes who swoop among the trees and are not afraid of night in the country. Night birds. There are frogs. Night frogs who sing songs for you every night: *reek reek reek reek*. Night songs" (n.p.).

## Re-Say

The re-say is the repetition of an *idea* which comes immediately after the idea has been presented. The re-say is the stopping to say something again, another way, right away. Much like a close echo, a word or two are often repeated in the re-say.

- *Dreamplace* (1993) by George Ella Lyon: ". . . and see for the first time across the trees: like a *dream*, like a *sandcastle*, this city the Pueblo people built under a cliff" (n.p.).
- *Baby* (1993) by Patricia MacLachlan: "Only Byrd looked happily satisfied, as if something *wonderful*, something *wished for*, had happened" (18).

# WONDROUS WORD CHOICES

## Striking Adjectives

Writers will sometimes describe a noun using an adjective that is unusual or unexpected in some way. Sometimes the effect is achieved because of crossed parts of speech—a word that is usually not an adjective is used as an adjective—but often it's simply an adjective we don't think of as a "normal" modifier for a particular noun. This craft makes the writing lively because it catches the reader's eye—it's surprising.

- *Letting Swift River Go* (1992) by Jane Yolen: "Then I heard my mother's voice coming to me over the *drowned* years" (n.p.). We don't think of "years" as something that would be "drowned."
- *The Relatives Came* (1985) by Cynthia Rylant: "Then it was *hugging* time" (n.p.). In this case we just think of "hugging" more as a verb, and so we are surprised to see it used as an adjective.
- *Miz Berlin Walks* (1997) by Jane Yolen: "And if you listen real hard, you might even hear a *block-long* tale" (n.p.). An unexpected adjective, very specific to the content of the story.

## Out-of-Place Adjectives

In English, adjectives typically come before the nouns they modify. With this crafting technique, a writer will place an adjective after the noun it modifies or in some other unexpected place. Doing this draws attention to both the adjective and the noun because of the unexpected language.

- *My Mama Had a Dancing Heart* (1995) by Libba Moore Gray: ". . . and drink lemonade *cold*" and "drink hot tea *spiced*" (n.p.). We expect "cold" and "spiced" to come before their nouns.
- *Baby* (1993) by Patricia MacLachlan: "My mother stood with her hands up to her face, *shocked*" (18).

Writers who use this technique are playing with our ears, playing with what we expect to hear. In the example below, Jane Yolen moves an adjective after an adverb phrase that modifies it, causing readers to hear something quite unexpected.

- *Miz Berlin Walks* (1997) by Jane Yolen: "But one [feather] rained into my hand, and it was all over *gold*" (n.p.). Our ears expect "gold" to come before "all over."

## Striking Verbs

This crafting technique involves the very careful selection of striking verbs that catch a reader's attention. Like other striking parts-of-speech uses, striking verbs work out of some unexpected quality. Writers will choose verbs that readers don't expect to see with their subjects. Sometimes the verbs very subtly personify something in the text, but just as often they are just plain surprising with their subjects.

- *My Great-Aunt Arizona* (1992) by Gloria Houston: "For fifty-seven years my great-aunt Arizona *hugged* her students" (n.p.). We just don't expect this verb in this text about someone who teaches for a long, long time. Hugging hasn't been mentioned at this point in the text, only teaching, and so its appearance in this important, summarizing sentence is unexpected and delightfully surprising.

• *The Whales* (1996) by Cynthia Rylant: "In the blackness of the Black sea, the whales are *thinking* today" (n.p.). In this first line of text, we are caught by surprise because we expect whales to be "swimming" or "fishing" or "hunting" or something we associate more with these creatures. But "thinking" personifies them at the outset and sets the gentle tone for the entire text—all with one carefully chosen verb.

• *Maniac Magee* (1990) by Jerry Spinelli: ". . . especially when he got a load of the kid *drowning* in his clothes" (85). This verb creates so much visual imagery it seems to be fighting to be an adjective. We just don't expect "drowning" to be used in this context, and so its use here is truly stunning.

• *Secret Place* (1996) by Eve Bunting: "There are warehouses with windows *blinded* by dust and names *paint-scrawled* on their brick walls" (n.p.), and "The phone wires *rocked* the moon in their cradle of lines" (n.p.). Two verbs that personify, one created by an unexpected combination of words.

• *Miz Berlin Walks* (1997) by Jane Yolen: "I ran up and touched her hands and we *knitted* our fingers" (n.p.). "Knitting" is usually done with needles, not hands, making it an unexpected choice for this wondrous sentence.

## Striking Adverbs

Writers also use adverbs in unexpected ways to create striking textual effects. They can achieve an unexpected quality in adverbs in a number of ways, by creating words to make new adverbs, using another part of speech as an adverb, putting two adverbs unexpectedly together, or just choosing one we'd never think of putting with a particular verb.

• *Miz Berlin Walks* (1997) by Jane Yolen: "I'd walk with Miz Berlin, side by side, step by step, waiting *cotton-quiet* till she cleared her throat" (n.p.). Not only is it an interesting way to wait, Yolen makes up this adverb with a noun-adjective phrase, choosing not to change "quiet" to its adverbial *-ly* form.

- *The Lost and Found House* (1997) by Michael Cadnum: "All night trucks rumble past. But I *hardly really* sleep" (n.p.). A very unusual combination of two adverbs.

- *Nocturne* (1997) by Jane Yolen: ". . . a big moon balloon floats *silent* over trees" (n.p.). Another example of Yolen making an effective decision to use an adverb in adjective form. Crossing the parts of speech makes the language lively and interesting.

## Intentional Vagueness

Sometimes writers will be intentionally vague for effect in their texts. This is often achieved by manipulating pronouns and adjectives that modify nouns, making them nonspecific when we expect them to be more specific.

- *The Relatives Came* (1985) by Cynthia Rylant. Rylant brilliantly makes this every reader's story by choosing not to use a possessive pronoun in front of "relatives." Throughout the text they are referred to as "*The* relatives" lending an anyone's-story appeal to the text.

- *The Whales* (1996) by Cynthia Rylant: "They are floating like feathers in *a* sky" (n.p.). The choice of "a" to modify "sky" instead of "*the* sky" (which we expect) is intentionally vague, leaving open the possibility that there are more "skies" than just the one above us and adding a setting to the simile of the whales "floating like feathers."

- *The Aunt in Our House* (1996) by Angela Johnson. In this story about an aunt who comes to visit, Johnson always refers to her as "the aunt," in an intentionally vague usage like Rylant's "the relatives." the aunt is never named or claimed by a possessive pronoun.

## Proper Nouns

Writers know the power of names. Name dropping in texts does so much work for writers: brand names, people names, place names. Using proper nouns gives writing a specificity that makes readers trust the authority of the narrator. Proper nouns, especially in the form of brand names, can almost take on the role of adjectives because, in their specificity, they call up so many sensory images for readers.

- *Missing May* (1992) by Cynthia Rylant: "Before she died, I know my mother must have loved to comb my shiny hair and rub that *Johnson's* baby lotion up and down my arms and wrap me up and hold and hold me all night long" (4). Can't you just smell that lotion?

- *Missing May* (1992) by Cynthia Rylant: "My eyes went over May's wildly colorful cabinets, and I was free again. I saw *Oreos* and *Ruffles* and big bags of *Snickers*" (8). She could have just said "cookies and chips and candy" but it wouldn't have had the same specific, sensual detail that the proper nouns have for readers.

- *Baby* (1993) by Patricia MacLachlan: "He danced every evening before dinner, after his six crackers (*Ritz*) with cheddar cheese (extra sharp), between the first glass of whiskey that made him happy and the second that made him sad" (5).

## Make-Your-Own Words

Sometimes writers can't find just the right words they need, but they are not distracted by this. They just make up words! By combining words or word parts that are familiar to readers, writers don't shy away from making new words that fit most perfectly with their meanings. Often, these new words are hyphenated, but not always. Often, you will see they are adjectives trying to describe the indescribable, but not always.

- *Maniac Magee* (1990) by Jerry Spinelli: "That's why his front steps were the only *un-sat-on* front steps in town" (17) and ". . . and— *unbefroggable!*—the "ball" was heading back home too!" (27).

- *Home Run* (1998) by Robert Burleigh: "Then there is only the *echoey, nothing-quite-like-it* sound" (n.p.).

- *An Angel for Solomon Singer* (1992) by Cynthia Rylant: "and the *smiling-eyed* waiter told Solomon Singer to come back again to the Westway Cafe" (n.p.).

- *Nocturne* (1997) by Jane Yolen: "in the wraparound *blacksurround* velvet night" (n.p.).

# Wondrous Sentences

## Artful Use of "And"

Many authors start sentences with "and." As a matter of fact, it is so common that it almost doesn't warrant being listed as a crafting technique. I list it because it is something most adults were warned not to do in school but also because there is an art to its use. You and your students will need to collect many examples of this crafting technique to really understand it in use.

Often, you might notice that sentences starting with "and" do not stand alone well, away from the surrounding sentences in the text, thus hinting at the function of the conjunction. Starting a sentence with "and" lets the writer set a part of something off by itself—showing it's still tied to the rest (by the "and") but giving it its own sentence significance. Sometimes sentences starting with "and" are meant to show a narrator's afterthought. Interestingly, writers will often end entire texts with a sentence that begins with "and," capitalizing on the archetypal feeling and sound all readers know: "And they all lived happily ever after."

Again, this "technique" is so common that I could have gotten examples of it from almost any text. Here are just a few for your consideration.

- *Missing May* (1992) by Cynthia Rylant: "And then a big wind came and set everything free" (89). Last sentence.
- *When I Was Young in the Mountains* (1982) by Cynthia Rylant: "And that was always enough" (n.p.). Last sentence.
- *What You Know First* (1995) by Patricia MacLachlan: "And so I can remember, too" (n.p.). Last sentence.

## Runaway Sentences

To convey a sense of franticness, of desperation, excitement, or being carried away with something, writers will sometimes craft a very long, winding runaway sentence. Taken out of the texts they're found in, these kinds of sentences are awkward, but it is their awkwardness that makes them *work* in context. The winding length of these seemingly out-of-control sentences matches their meaning in some way.

Sometimes runaway sentences are actually textbook run-on sentences, but often they are not; they are just very long. Runaway sentences are often filled with marks of punctuation, especially commas, that slow and quicken the pace as you read through them.

• *House on Mango Street* (1991) by Sandra Cisneros: "But my mother's hair, my mother's hair, like little rosettes, like little candy circles all curly and pretty because she pinned it in pincurls all day, sweet to put your nose into when she is holding you, holding you and you feel safe, is the smell of bread before you bake it, is the smell when she makes room for you on her side of the bed still warm with her skin and you sleep near her, the rain outside falling and Papa snoring. The snoring, the rain, and Mama's hair that smells like bread" (6–7). The sentence conveys a sense of being carried away with the beauty. Notice the thread-back, textbook fragment that follows the runaway sentence.

• *Missing May* (1992) by Cynthia Rylant: "I searched for topics that had generally interested both of us before, like whether or not we should get a dog and did we think that young guy at the hardware store was drunk or just had a speech problem and maybe this spring we ought to buy one of those Weed Eaters so we could clean out that mess around the old Chevy" (48). Sense of desperation—she can't get Ob to talk.

• *Amazing Grace* (1995) by Jonathan Kozol: "All the strategies and agencies and institutions needed to contain, control, and normalize a social plague—some of them severe, others exploitative, and some benign—are, it seems, being assembled: defensible stores, defensible parks, defensible entrances to housing projects, defensible schools where weapons-detectors are installed at the front doors and guards are posted, 'drug-free zones' in front of the schools, 'safety corridors' between the schools and nearby subway stations, 'grieving rooms' in some of the schools where students have a place to mourn the friends who do not make it safely thorough the 'safety corridors,' a large and crowded criminal court and the enormous new court complex now under construction, an old reform school (Spofford) and the new, much larger juvenile prison being built on St. Anne's Avenue, an adult prison, a prison barge, a projected kitchen to prepackage prison meals, a projected high school to train kids to work in prisons and in other crime-related areas, the two symmetrical prostitute strolls, one to the east, one to the west, and counseling and condom distribution to protect the prostitutes from spreading or contracting AIDS, services for grown-ups who already have contracted AIDS, services for children who have AIDS, services for children who have seen their mothers die of AIDS, services for men and women coming out of prison, services for children of the men and women who are still in prison, a welfare office for determining who is eligible for checks and check-cashing stores where residents can cash the checks, food stamp distribution and bodegas that accept the stamps at discount to enable mothers to buy cigarettes or diapers, 13 shelters, 12 soup kitchens, 11 free food pantries, perhaps someday an 'empowerment zone,' or 'enterprise zone,' or some other kind of business zone to generate some jobs for a small fraction of the people who reside here: all the pieces of the perfectible ghetto, the modernized and sometimes even well-served urban lazaretto, with civic-minded CEOs who come up from Manhattan maybe once a week to serve as mentors or 'role models' to the children in the schools while some of their spouses organize benefit balls to pay for dinners in the shelters" (135–36). A single, amazing run-away sentence—more than 350 words—meant to convey a sense of desperateness about life in the South Bronx. I believe this is one of the most amazing sentences I've ever read.

## Artful Sentence Fragments

In all kinds of writing, good writers will craft sentence fragments for effect. If you take these sentence fragments out of context and place them on a classroom chalkboard, they do appear to be incomplete thoughts. But inside the texts in which they are found they are always quite complete.

We have the grammatical concept of an "understood" part of a sentence. We say that the subject of a command is an understood "you." And if we look closely at writing in the real world, we see that writers frequently rely on understood parts of sentences to make thoughts complete.

Artful sentence fragments are just that, *artful*, not arbitrary or by accident, and they do fairly consistent work in texts. Most commonly, you will see artful fragments that clarify, reiterate, exclaim, or list. They are certainly not the leave-you-hanging or chopped-off kinds of fragments that inexperienced writers sometimes write without realizing it. Here are just a few examples I really like.

- *Maniac Magee* (1990) by Jerry Spinelli: "For instance, he would eat dinner with Aunt Dot on Monday, with Uncle Dan on Tuesday, and so on. Eight years of that" (6).

- *I Had Seen Castles* (1993) by Cynthia Rylant: "The mills were fed coal and men so Pittsburgh might live. And it did. Very well" (2). And just a page over in the text: "Evidence of the father's taste lies behind glass doors of a bookcase. Theory. Darwin. Empiricism. Words to bind you to this room, this house, this planet. Words to make sense of everything" (3).

- *Woodsong* (1990) by Gary Paulsen: "Largely because of Disney and posed 'natural' wildlife films and television programs I had preconceived ideas about wolves, about what wolves should be and do. They never really spoke to the killing. Spoke to the blood" (6). The fragment here— "Spoke to the blood"—is actually its own paragraph in *Woodsong*, a feature found in lots of Paulsen's writing.

- *Baby* (1993) by Patricia MacLachlan: "Mama was covered with flecks and smears of paint, and I could tell by the colors what she was working on. The island" (7).

- *Home Run* (1998) by Robert Burleigh: "Then it is as it should be. Smooth as silk. Easy as air on the face. Right as falling water" (n.p.). He is describing the "one-ness" of Babe Ruth and the ball when Babe hits it.

## One-Sentence Paragraphs

Defying the school adage that every paragraph must have five sentences, writers will often set off a sentence as its own paragraph for emphasis. These are not sentences with quotations in them (which are often their own paragraphs). These are simple sentences set off by themselves for effect. When you look at these sentences in relation to the other sentences around them, you see that by giving them their own paragraphs, writers have used the white space around them as a mark of exclamation.

- *Little by Little* (1987) by Jean Little:

  Since Jamie had gotten that Robin Hood book for Christmas, acting out Robin's adventures had become our favorite game. Eight-year-old Jamie was Robin, of course, since he was the oldest and could read the book. Ronnie and Hugh, who was only three, were Will Scarlet, Little John and the Sheriff of Nottingham. I was graciously permitted to be Friar Tuck and the entire outlaw band. But Marilyn was chosen to play Maid Marian every single time.

  "Why do you always pick her?" I had asked. Jamie had shown me the illustrations.

  "Maid Marian has to have curly hair," he said. "Yours is straight. Besides, Marilyn sounds like Marian."

  I was getting sick of Sherwood Forest. (2)

In this case, I think that making "I was getting sick of Sherwood Forest" its own paragraph does more than give it emphasis, I think it gives it tone as well. I can't help but read it and hear a very dead-pan voice, fed up with the turn of events.

- *Baby* (1993) by Patricia MacLachlan:

  My mother stood with her hands up to her face, shocked. My father's face was dark and still and bewildered. Only Byrd looked happily satisfied, as if something wonderful, something wished for, had happened.

  And it had.

  Her excitement was here. (18)

## Direct-Contact Sentence

These are sentences—often commands, but they can be of any sentence type—in which the writer interrupts the narrative to speak directly to the reader or to comment on what's happening in the text. These sentences invite readers to be active participants with the writer, either by following the writer's instructions or by listening to the writer's commentary.

- *But I'll Be Back Again* (1989) by Cynthia Rylant. In her memoir chapter on kissing, Rylant is telling the story of one of the most powerful kisses she had ever received as a teenager:

> It was like sitting with Tom Cruise, so strong was Robert's manly aura. We had talked for some time, with quite a bit of space between us, when suddenly he asked if he could kiss me.
>
> Well, would you refuse Tom Cruise? (42)

No, I guess I wouldn't—and I love that my favorite author stepped outside her text for a moment and shared this little revelation with me directly.

- *Night in the Country* (1986) by Cynthia Rylant: She interrupts her description of night in the country and suddenly tells the reader, "Listen:" (n.p.). And then we hear an apple fall from the tree.

## Seesaw Sentences

Seesaw sentences are crafted with predictable pairs of information or detail, just like seesaw text structures, but on a smaller, one- or two-sentence scale. The pairing effect gives these sentences a two-part rhythm.

- *An Angel for Solomon Singer* (1992) by Cynthia Rylant: "So much of Indiana was mixed into his blood that even now, fifty-odd years later, he could not give up being a boy in Indiana and at night he journeyed the streets, wishing they were fields, gazed at lighted windows, wishing they were stars, and listened to the voices of all who passed, wishing for the conversations of crickets" (n.p.).

- *Whoever You Are* (1997) by Mem Fox: "Joys are the same, and love is the same. Pain is the same, and blood is the same. Smiles are the same, and hearts are just the same" (n.p.).

## Taffy Sentences

These sentences begin with a central idea and then pull that idea out a little bit, and then a little bit more, and maybe even a little bit more. Each time the sentence is stretched, a little more detail is added and the original detail is repeated.

- *Nocturne* (1997) by Jane Yolen: "In the night, in the velvet night, in the brushstroked bluecoat velvet night . . ." (n.p.).

## Short, Short, Long Sentences

In a move seemingly borrowed from musicians, writers will often craft a series of three sentences in a rhythmic "duh, duh, duh-duh-duh" three-part rhythm.

- *Welcome to the Green House* (1993) by Jane Yolen: "Welcome to the green house. Welcome to the hot house. Welcome to the land of the warm, wet days" (n.p.).
- *An Angel for Solomon Singer* (1992) by Cynthia Rylant: "He could not have a cat. He could not have a dog. He could not even paint his walls a different color. . ." (n.p.).

## Sentences That Make a Long Story Short

Sometimes when writers want to move in a hurry through a lot of time or activity in a text, they will write one sentence that covers lots of ground fast. These sentences compress time and detail and are the opposite of the crafting technique in which writers will stretch a moment out, sometimes making a single action last several pages. Techniques like making a long story short clearly show that writers are in control of time in their texts.

- *The Relatives Came* (1985) by Cynthia Rylant: "So they drank up all their pop and ate up all their crackers and traveled up all those miles until finally they pulled into our yard" (n.p.). She makes the traveling part of the trip pass by very quickly.
- *I Had Seen Castles* (1993) by Cynthia Rylant: "After the war ended, America made Germany its friend, Russia its enemy, and it helped

rebuild Japan" (90). Sums up the entire outcome of the war in one sentence.

# WONDROUS MARKS OF PUNCTUATION

## Whispering Parentheses

Writers use this technique to communicate directly with readers, stepping "outside" the regular text for a moment to whisper something in the reader's ear. These are usually asides of explanation that are more characteristic of spoken language than written language, but the form they take in texts is often parenthetical. Whispering parentheses give texts a conversational tone, making readers feel like insiders with an author. Cynthia Rylant is obviously a writer who likes to pull her readers close and make them feel like insiders. Here are three examples of her using this technique in different texts.

- *An Angel for Solomon Singer* (1992) by Cynthia Rylant: "When he reached the end of his list of dreams (the end was a purple wall), he simply started all over again and ordered up a balcony (but he didn't say the balcony out loud)" (n.p.).

- *Missing May* (1992) by Cynthia Rylant: "May started talking about where they'd hang the swing as soon as she hoisted herself out of the front seat (May was a big woman), and Ob . . ." (5).

- *But I'll Be Back Again* (1989) by Cynthia Rylant: "When the Beatles came to America in 1964 the boys lost most of us girls to either John Lennon, Paul McCartney, George Harrison, or Ringo Starr (not many to Ringo)" (15).

## Commentary Dashes

You will see that another way writers add layers of commentary to a text is to set extra, "by-the-way" details off with dashes. You may have been accustomed to using dashes in journals and notebooks, but didn't realize they were appropriate for many types of published writing as well. Writers use "commentary dashes" not just to expand an idea, but to do so with *voice*. They sound like an additional thing the narrator has just thought to tell you. An interesting study is to look at parenthetical asides (like those in the examples above) and compare them to the asides set off by dashes.

- *Missing May* (1992) by Cynthia Rylant: "Ob was an artist—I could tell that the minute I saw them—though *artist* isn't the word I could have used back then, so young" (6).
- *Canyons* (1990) by Gary Paulsen: "He lived alone with his mother and when he was home—which was less and less as he approached fifteen and his mother spent more and more time working to live, working to be, working to feed and clothe her only son—the two of them existed in a kind of quiet tolerance" (9–10). Notice also the lovely repetition in this stunning sentence.

## Items in a Series

If you run for a usage manual every time you write items in a series, trying to remember whether there is a comma after that last "and" or not, you may want to investigate a little more how writers handle such instances. I was always taught that you just followed the "rule" when you needed to list things, but studying the craft of writing has shown me that you have a lot more options with this usage than just one rule provides. And that's how "items in a series" ended up as a crafting technique, because when you really look at texts, you see that writers often make very deliberate decisions about how a list will be punctuated.

When you look at items in a series in texts, you will see some that are punctuated with all commas and no conjunctions; some that use all conjunctions and no commas; some that place periods between the items in the series, making each one its own sentence; and some that are punctuated following the more traditional "rule" for items in a series.

Toying with how items in a series are punctuated lets the writer play with rhythm and with meaning. Read some of the examples below as if they were punctuated another way and listen to the difference in rhythm it makes. Also, think about how the listed items *mean* what they mean through their listing. Items separated by conjunctions only, with no marks of punctuation, are items that run more together, as if they are separate parts of one thing, whereas commas or periods between items make them seem like very separate things.

This is another crafting technique for which there are examples in almost every text you encounter. Here are just a few of my favorites.

- *The Relatives Came* (1985) by Cynthia Rylant: "We were so busy hugging and eating and breathing together" (n.p.).

- *Night in the Country* (1986) by Cynthia Rylant: ". . . the groans and thumps and squeaks that houses make when they like you are trying to sleep" (n.p.).

- *The Whales* (1996) by Cynthia Rylant: "Thinking of those things that matter most to them: friends, family, supper. A song they used to know" (n.p.). A combination of commas and a period.

- *Welcome to the Green House* (1993) by Jane Yolen: "If we do not do something soon, there will be no more green house, not for the monkeys and fish and birds and bees and beetles and wild pigs and bats and kinkajous and all the hundreds of thousands of flowers and fruits and trees. And not for us either" (n.p.).

- *Scarecrow* (1998) by Cynthia Rylant: "The earth has rained and snowed and blossomed and wilted and yellowed and greened and vined itself all around him" (n.p.).

## Super Colons

Colons are something we never learned much about in school. They were always sort of the last mark of punctuation in the grammar book, and sometimes we didn't even get to them before the school year was up (probably because we'd spent so much time on all those comma rules). But studying the craft of writing has made me very interested in colons. Writers use them to do lots and lots of artful work in texts (and they are way more fashionable than semicolons!). Colons can set an idea off from others, show that someone is thinking or talking, or serve as markers that something big is about to follow (my students came to call these "on-your-mark, get-set, go colons").

- *Tulip Sees America* (1998) by Cynthia Rylant: "And we left Ohio and went across America. This is what we saw:"—this colon sets up the entire rest of the text (n.p.). From later in the same text: "You drive between a stand of firs and you think: no ocean. Then you blink, and there it is:"—a description of the ocean scene follows this colon (n.p.).

- *Dreamplace* (1993) by George Ella Lyon: ". . . till we come around a bend and see for the first time across the trees: like a dream, like a sandcastle, this city the Pueblo people built under a cliff" (n.p.).

- *Scarecrow* (1998) by Cynthia Rylant: "They ignore the pie-pan hands and the button eyes and see instead the scarecrow's best gift: his gentleness" (n.p.).

## Super Ellipses

Like colons, those three little periods in a row—known as "ellipses"—do a lot of artful work for writers too. Ellipses can show that an action is continuing, transition from one action to another or from one idea to another, move time or place, or show that there just are not words for something.

- *Dog Heaven* (1995) by Cynthia Rylant: "They turn around and around in the cloud . . . until it feels just right, and then they curl up and sleep" (n.p.).

- *On the Day You Were Born* (1991) by Debra Frasier: "a rising tide washed the beaches clean for your footprints . . . while far out at sea clouds swelled with water drops" (n.p.).

- *The Whales* (1996) by Cynthia Rylant: "There are not enough poems in the world to tell. . ." (n.p.). There is nothing that follows these ellipses in the text that completes them. They show a speechless narrator.

- *Down the Road* (1995) by Alice Schertle: "Then she continued down the road . . . through a meadow . . . across a stream . . . past a house or two . . . down a street . . . around a corner . . . up some steps . . . and into the cool shadows of Mr. Birdie's Emporium and Dry Goods Store" (n.p.). Those are some real traveling ellipses!

- *Madelia* (1997) by Jan Spivey Gilchrist. Gilchrist uses ellipses again and again across several pages to mark pauses in a long, flowing sermon: "'There is a place . . . a place,' Daddy sang out, 'Oh, yeah . . . a place far away . . . a beautiful place . . . yes, Lord . . . where the streets glisten in the sunlight . . . and shimmer in the moonlight . . . we will go there one day . . . we'll ride on high . . . we'll sail through the sky . . . with a host of many'" (n.p.).

## Quotation Mark-less Quotations

You may not have realized that quotation marks are not the only method of setting off direct quotations in texts. Writers will sometimes choose to represent speech in other ways for various meaning-making reasons.

- *All the Places to Love* (1994) by Patricia MacLachlan. Quotations in this text are written in italics and not enclosed within quotation marks. This decision might have been made because each quotation in the book is something someone has said in the past about why he or she loves a certain place above all others. The atypical direct speech is therefore marked in an atypical way.

- *House on Mango Street* (1991) by Sandra Cisneros. There are no marks for direct speech of any kind in this text, though the text is full of direct speech that follows traditional markers such as, "He says" and "She says." Here's an example:

  Where do you live? she asked.

  There, I said pointing up to the third floor.

  You live *there*? (5).

The only place in the entire chapter book text where quotation marks *are* used is near the end in this context:

  I make a story for my life, for each step my brown shoe takes. I say, "And so she trudged up the wooden stairs, her sad brown shoes taking her to the house she never liked" (109).

By using quotation marks only here, Cisneros seems to be making a statement about the permanence or superiority of story language over spoken language.

- *We Had a Picnic This Sunday Past* (1997) by Jacqueline Woodson. This author uses bold print to mark direct quotations: "**The tooth fairy bring you anything?** Paulette wanted to know. **Got a quarter for them,** Astrid said, and held out his hand to show us the shiny quarter there" (n.p.).

## WONDROUS PRINT

### Interesting Italics

Writers use italics in many interesting ways that add layers of meaning to any text. You will see italics that make noise, give emphasis, distinguish present from past, match speech patterns, show that someone is remembering, and do all kinds of other work in texts. Readers use the context to figure out what that meaning is, and writers make sure the context supports the italicized meaning.

- *Baby* (1993) by Patricia MacLachlan. Italics are used throughout the text in many interesting ways, but especially to set apart Sophie's memories from the rest of the text.
- *Night in the Country* (1986) by Cynthia Rylant: "Night frogs who sing songs for you every night: *reek reek reek reek*. Night songs" (n.p.). Italics that make noise.
- *Maniac Magee* (1990) by Jerry Spinelli: "You *have* eaten pizza before, haven't you?" (49). Italics are frequently used to match speech patterns in the text.
- *Water Dance* (1997) by Thomas Locker: "I fill and overflow. *I am the lake*" (n.p.). Italics are used each time the water identifies itself.

### Text Shaped to Match Meanings

Sometimes writers will lay out text or the print of a single word on the page in a way that matches the meaning of the text in that place. While this is a very common technique in picture books and in poetry, you will also occasionally see it in other genres.

• *Dreamplace* (1993) by George Ella Lyon. Lyon writes the part of the text where she describes the Anasazi climbing to their homes in the cliffs this way:

> hands
>    and
> feet
>    finding
> slots
>    in the
> stone (n.p.)

• *Canyons* (1990) by Gary Paulsen: "It was going to be a long, loong night" (41).

## MY WAYS WITH WORDS BOOKLIST

I would like to offer a booklist here of the books in my library that seem to be just filled with interesting ways with words. These are the books I pull out again and again as I teach, and they are the books I use for inquiry when I am teaching students to read like writers for the first time. I am keeping the list short, only including what I consider the best in my private collection.

Robert Burleigh
   *Home Run* (1998)
Nancy White Carlstrom
   *Raven and River* (1997)
Sandra Cisneros
   *House on Mango Street* (1991; chapter book)
Ralph Fletcher
   *Twilight Comes Twice* (1997)
Debra Frasier
   *On the Day You Were Born* (1991)
Libba Moore Gray
   *My Mama Had a Dancing Heart* (1995)

Eloise Greenfield
  *For the Love of the Game: Michael Jordan and Me* (1997)

Thomas Locker
  *Snow Toward Evening* (1990; poetry collection)
  *Water Dance* (1997)
  *Home* (1998)

George Ella Lyon
  *Dreamplace* (1993)

Patricia MacLachlan
  *Baby* (1993; chapter book)
  *All the Places to Love* (1994)
  *What You Know First* (1995)

Thylias Moss
  *I Want to Be* (1993)

Gary Paulsen
  *Woodsong* (1990; chapter book)
  *Dogteam* (1993)

Ruth Yaffe Radin
  *A Winter Place* (1982)
  *High in the Mountains* (1989)

Mary Lyn Ray
  *Mud* (1996)

Cynthia Rylant
  *When I Was Young in the Mountains* (1982)
  *This Year's Garden* (1984)
  *The Relatives Came* (1985)
  *Night in the Country* (1986)
  *But I'll Be Back Again* (1989; chapter book)
  *Missing May* (1992; chapter book)
  *I Had Seen Castles* (1993; chapter book)
  *Dog Heaven* (1995)
  *The Whales* (1996)
  *Scarecrow* (1998)
  *Tulip Sees America* (1998)

Cynthia Rylant and Walker Evans
  *Something Permanent* (1994; poetry and photography collection)

Jane Yolen
  *Nocturne* (1997)
  *Welcome to the Green House* (1993)
  *Miz Berlin Walks* (1997)
  *Welcome to the Ice House* (1998)

# References

Kozol, Jonathan. 1995. *Amazing Grace: The Lives of Children and the Conscience of a Nation*. New York: Crown.

McClure, Amy A., and Janice V. Kristo. 1996. *Books That Invite Talk, Wonder, and Play*. Urbana, IL: National Council of Teachers of English.

# SELECTING BOOKS FOR CRAFT STUDY

Not long ago, Ellen Best Lamit, the principal of a school I was consulting at, hired me to go with her to a bookstore and, as I looked at books, just talk out loud about what would make me want a particular book for the teaching of writing. Ellen wanted to get inside my head and know what it was that I was looking for as I browsed. So we pulled books out from the shelves, one after another after another. Some were quickly returned to their places; others we talked excitedly about for a long time. After several hours we had spent a lot of money on books for her school (Yeah!)—and the experience had forced me to really, specifically articulate how I choose books or any texts for my craft-study collection.

I realized after this experience that the ability to select texts effectively for the teaching of writing comes from having a solid understanding of the craft of writing. I recently led an advanced day of study for teachers on the craft of writing through the Teachers College Reading and Writing Project in New York City. We spent a good part of the day thinking about how teachers read like writers to select texts for their teaching of writing. Some of those involved may have been surprised that text selection was part of an advanced day, but I really believe that this is an advanced concept. In teaching students to learn to write from writers, a good place to start is to get someone else's booklist and teach effectively from it in your classroom. But to really advance your own knowledge base, eventually you need to be able to look through stacks of texts and assemble your own booklist, knowing specifically why you selected each text on that list.

Knowing why a new text that you've encountered can help you with your teaching of writing really means two main things. First, it means you really know how to read like a writer yourself, because to select a text you will have to see not just what it's about but also how it is written. The better you are able to read like a writer, the better you will be able to lead your students in doing so themselves. And second, if you know why you need a particular text for your teaching of writing, it means you have some sense of your students as writers—it means you are able to see into the future of your students' writing lives.

You see, envisioning, an important writing concept we have developed throughout *Wondrous Words*, is also an important teaching concept. In order to select texts effectively for your teaching of writing, you need to be able to envision what that text offers your students as writers. The bottom line for why I select a text is that I see something in *how that text is written* which would be useful for my students to also see. I see something about the text that holds potential for my students' learning. I am looking for texts that have something in them or about them that can add to my students' knowledge base of how to write well. I need to try and envision what my students will know and what they will be able to do as writers after encountering the text I am considering adding to my collection.

At the advanced day of study at Teachers College, one of the participants asked a very good question. She said, "What about a book that just really evokes in me a very deep response? Would that be a good book for the teaching of writing?" I was hesitant to answer because I never want to send the message that this kind of book is not a good book to have in your classroom. I so believe that students need to see significant adults who are moved by what they read that I would never, ever want to send that message. But whether a book like this would be good for the teaching of writing *depends*. To figure this out, this teacher will need to sit down with this book and try to look at how it is written. I told her that one good rule of thumb is to ask yourself,

"Can I imagine pulling this book off the shelf during a writing conference to show a child some writing move?" If not, it may be that the story moves her so because of something in its meaning that she really has a personal connection to and not because of any specific ways in which it is written. Such books can be important to writers in helping them see the impact that texts can have on readers, helping them to anticipate audience in a powerful way, but they just aren't the texts that give us the most mileage when we are teaching students the craft of good writing. The "high-mileage" texts are those that demonstrate writing moves (crafting techniques) that stand apart from the text itself, available for use across a wide range of topics and types of writing. These are the texts we will reach for again and again as we teach writing.

So, can you envision pulling this text off the shelf or out of a folder during a writing conference to show some child a writing move? Can you envision the difference this text might make in your students' understandings about writing well? With these as our benchmark questions, let's explore some lines of thinking that can help us select texts with lots of potential for helping our students learn to write well.

## TEXTS THAT SHOW STUDENTS WRITING POTENTIALS

### Texts That Have Background Information Included

One of the things that will cause me to select a text for the teaching of writing is good background information. I like books or articles that have opening notes or endnotes or back flaps that tell something about how the writer went about writing the text. Texts like these help me when I am teaching students about the craft of writers' office work. I want students to envision where writers get their ideas, how writers often research before they write, and how writers go about taking an idea to publication. Many writers will include notes about this in the published form of the text.

Several books on my shelf are there at least partly for this reason. *Man on the Moon* (1997), with text by Anastasia Suen, is a good example. The writer has an author's note that tells about watching moon missions as a child and how this grew into a fascination as an adult with all things moon related. *The Hired Hand* (1997), with text by Robert D. San Souci, has a good author's note that tells how the writer based the book on a folk tale he had heard in his community while growing up, and the note explains how he did research to flesh out the details of the story. *Baby in a Basket* (1997), with text by Gloria Rand, has an author's note that tells how this writer based the story on an actual historical event that happened in Alaska in 1917. Each short story or poem in Jane Yolen's collection *Here There Be Witches* (1995) has an introductory note telling where the idea for the story or poem came from, making it a goldmine text for learning about where writers get ideas. One of my favorites is a note that explains a childhood fascination with the witches scene from Shakespeare's *Macbeth*. Yolen bases a poem in the book on these witches.

What's important in each of these books is not the moon or a hired hand or a baby in Alaska or witches. What's important are fascination, folk tales, historical events, and beloved literature. A student might get an idea from Jane Yolen for basing a story on a favorite scene not from *Macbeth* but, say, from the Broadway production of *Cats*. A student might get an idea to write from his fascination not with the moon, but with his own fascination with all he has heard and seen about the ozone layer. Another student might dig out old newspapers her grandfather has saved from his life in Dallas, Texas, looking for ideas for stories in the events recounted there, the way Gloria Rand did. Remember, we are trying to envision *how* the writers went about finding their ideas, not specifically the topics of the ideas themselves.

Sometimes just a small bit of information in "about the author" flaps can be significant in this teaching. The flap of *Tulip Sees America* (1998) by Cynthia Rylant explains that she "packed up her station wagon in 1983 and drove with her son and two dogs from Ohio to their new home in Oregon." This bit of information could be very significant in helping students understand the idea of *basing a story* on something that really happened to them. Many students only know how to tell the story of something that happened as it actually happened. The concept of basing a work of fiction on something real is a sophisticated understanding, and when I saw that flap on Rylant's book I thought, "This could help me explain this to students."

So I check for "author's notes" and good book flap information when I shop for books. I can envision pulling books like these off the shelf when students struggle with where to get ideas for writing and how to develop those ideas. In these texts writers share information that demystifies this part of the process for students.

## Texts in Which the Concept of the Writing Is Interesting

Some texts I select because the concept of the writing in them is interesting to me. I select these because I think that the *way the author went about the writing* is interesting, and I see in that way potentials for my students' writing. These concepts are bigger than anything specific about the writing, the structure, or any of the ways with words. These concepts are more the approach to the writing than the writing itself.

*The Divide* (1997), with text by Michael Bedard, is a good example. I chose this book because I liked what Bedard was doing with his obviously biographical research. He wrote a fictional story about the author Willa Cather that is based, not on any single event from her life, but on what he learned about what her life was like. I thought about my students who are fascinated with people, historical and contemporary people, and how so often they can't see anything to do with their fascinations except write "reports" on these people. I can envision pulling Bedard's book to give these students an idea for another kind of writing they might do that's based on what they know of a person's life.

I recently chose a collection of poems because I saw potential in the concept of the book. Bill Maynard's *Santa's Time Off: Poems by Santa as Told to Bill Maynard* (1997) is a very interesting book conceptually. What Maynard has done is to set up a situation in which he claims that his writing is "as told to me" by someone else—in this case Santa. I like that, and I could envision students trying out this technique. A student might write poems "as told to me by my cat" or a story about a yet-to-be-born baby in the family "as told to me by the baby." One of my college students who's training to be a teacher might write a piece "as told to me by my future students." The concept of "as told to me by" is a very neat one, and its use is the main reason I chose Maynard's text for my teaching of writing collection.

Another example that can help make clear what we mean by interesting concepts are Sharon Draper's chapter book *Tears of a Tiger* (1996) and Pam

Conrad's book *Our House: Stories of Levittown* (1995). Both of these books are written as a combination of several genres in one. Draper uses kinds of writing such as homework assignments, newspaper clippings, and transcripts of telephone conversations to tell her story of a tragedy in a high school. And Conrad uses a combination of writing like journal entries, memoirs, and interviews to tell the story of Levittown. I like the idea of what these two writers are doing. The concept of mixing a number of different genres, some of them written genres and some of them spoken genres written down, is one I could envision students trying in their own writing. I can see myself pulling these books off my shelf to help a writer who is struggling with how to go about writing something in an interesting way.

One of my college students did mentor these books as he wrote a piece about his girlfriend this past semester. After looking at *Tears of a Tiger* he decided to write about his relationship with his girlfriend in all newspaper genres. He had a piece written like a horoscope, a piece like a sports report article, an advertisement, a want ad, and he ended with—you guessed it—an engagement notice. These books helped him envision a new possibility for his writing.

Sometimes a text added for an interesting concept has just one thing in it that helps me envision an interesting potential for my students. I selected Paul Erickson's *Daily Life in a Covered Wagon* (1997) because I liked the way he embedded quotes from actual diaries of wagon train survivors throughout the text. I can envision my students embedding quotes from their own diaries in memoirs, or making up diary-like entries for pieces of fiction, or writing historical-type pieces with real diary entries they've found through research. I liked Erickson's book because I liked the idea of embedding diary entries. I wanted my writers to see this.

Similarly, I chose Tres Seymour's book *The Gulls of the Edmund Fitzgerald* (1996) for just one reason. At the beginning of the book he has the text of the actual, official government document from the United States Department of Transportation reporting that there is no known cause for the wreck of the Edmund Fitzgerald. I thought, "What a neat idea" to put that document in there. I could envision students embedding similar official documents in and around texts, such as marriage licenses or birth certificates or copies of speeding tickets or ticket stubs. The book had an interesting concept of what to include in the text which I wanted my students to see.

So, to summarize, a text with an interesting concept can help my students envision possibilities for how they might go about writing something in an interesting way. The concept is larger than any particular crafting technique; it is more a way of going about writing about something. I reach for these texts when students are in search of ideas for how to write about something in an interesting way.

## Texts That Remind Me of Other Texts

Many texts I select for my collection because something about the way they are written reminds me of another text I know. For my students to understand that craft is not a matter of ownership and not tied to content, they need to see several authors using the same sort of crafting techniques in very different kinds of texts. Just one strong craft connection to another text is enough to make me buy a book or to cut out an article without further question, though in most of these examples the texts had a lot more to offer than just that connection.

Sometimes the connection is one of structure. I bought Bert Kitchen's book *When Hunger Calls* (1994) for this reason. Its collection of vignettes tied together with a repeating line reminded me of Cynthia Rylant's book *When I Was Young in the Mountains* (1982). A recent purchase, *Dinosaur Ghosts: The Mystery of Coelophysis* (1997), with text by J. Lynett Gillette, was made because it has a three-tiered structure holding the ending of the book together that reminds me very much of the three-tiered structure in Jean Craighead George's book *Look to the North: A Wolf Pup's Diary* (1997). Both books use three layers of text—label, story, and information—to structure the writing.

Sometimes the connection is one of concept. When I first looked at Nikki Grimes poetry collection *Meet Danitra Brown* (1994), I knew it was the same kind of text as Eloise Greenfield's *Nathaniel Talking* (1988), so I bought it. Both texts use a series of poems that have character and setting and, taken together, tell the story of someone's life.

I cut an editorial out of the newspaper last Christmas because it reminded me so much of Carolivia Herron's book *Nappy Hair* (1997). Donald Kaul, at Tribune Media Services in Chicago, wrote a piece entitled "House divided against itself cannot stand . . ." that was published in my home paper in December of 1997. In this piece, Kaul rails against the super-ficiality and commercialism of the Christmas season with lines like "people exhausting themselves buying presents they can't afford for people who don't need them" (A-7), while throughout the article Kaul's wife comments parenthetically on all he's saying. In response to the above statement, she says, in parentheses: "(Ha! Once, just once, I'd like him to buy me a present he can't afford. Last year I got Donna Karan sweat socks.)" This technique of embedding outside commentary around your text is the same thing Her-ron does in *Nappy Hair* when she has various members of the family com-ment on the story Uncle Mordecai tells at the family picnic.

Sometimes the connection is one very small crafting technique. I cut out an Associated Press news bulletin in our paper a few years ago because it had a sentence fragment that reminded me, exactly, of one I know in Jane Yolen's *Welcome to the Green House* (1993). The news article reads: "The O.J. Simp-son civil trial is on such a brisk pace that the plaintiffs could reasonably finish their case around Thanksgiving. This Thanksgiving" (A-5). And Jane Yolen's text in the afterword reads: "Today we are destroying fifty acres a minute. Every minute" (n.p.). Two writers crafting exactly the same way—I HAD to have these!

I reach for a stack of books in which writers are crafting in similar ways anytime I can when I am showing a student how to make some type of writerly move. If I can show that student more than one example of this technique in very different kinds of texts, then it helps the student to under-stand the craft as separate from topic so much more easily, and it makes it easier for that student to envision the craft in his or her own writing. Con-nected texts are worth the investment in time and money to assemble them for our teaching of writing.

## Texts Crafted with Interesting Structures

Many texts have been added to my collection because their structure is strik-ing in some way. How to make a text work together in interesting, efficient ways is a challenge all writers face, including my students. Too often in school we try to oversimplify this aspect of writing, teaching students to write everything either as a story with a chronological beginning, middle, and end, or as an essay with three to five paragraphs. We know that we do this because structure matters in the pursuit of good writing, but I believe that for students to write well, they need a repertoire of structural under-standings that go beyond these two basic forms. So I am always on the look-out for texts that are held together by interesting structures. Since we mentioned many of these text structures in Chapter 7, I'll mention just a few examples here to reinforce the importance of these texts.

Jean Craighead George's book *Look to the North: A Wolf Pup's Diary* (1997), mentioned earlier in the section on connections, was added to my col-lection because of its amazing structure. *Look to the North* has three tiers of structure operating at once. These tiers consist of a time frame, a partially repetitive line of lyrical text about where the wolf pups are in their growing, and then a longer section of narration that tells about the lives of an actual wolf family. The three-tiered format is repeated fifteen times in the text structure as the pups go from one day old to ten and a half months old. Here's a short sam-ple of the writing which shows the three tiers at work together:

> *9 Weeks Old.*
>
> When firecrackers shoot skyward, look to the north. Wolf pups are learning wolf talk.
>
> Boulder, Scree, and Talus can lower their ears to say to their father and mother, "You are the beloved leaders of our pack." They can spank the ground with their front paws to say, "Come play with me," and they can scent mark bones and pretty stones to say, "This is mine." (n.p.)

The "look to the north" phrase is the one that is repeated at each of the sec-ond tiers. For my students to envision writing that is well-structured, they need to see a text that works as well together as this one does. Texts like these can help my students envision all sorts of possibilities for ways to bal-ance pieces of text in their own writing.

Often, the structures of texts are very sound but much simpler than *Look to the North*, and these are especially important to my youngest writers for their whole texts, and my older writers for parts of their more intricate, longer texts. The book *Cat's Colors* (1997) by Jane Cabrera is an example of such a text. It is structured by setting up one central question—"What is my favorite color?"—and then moves through a series of questions and answers about a cat's life: "Is it brown? Brown is the earth where I dig my holes" (n.p.). This is a simple text structure for a beginning writer, but also a nice organizational structure for a more advanced writer. You may remember that the Keith Jarrett piece discussed on page 142 used this same framing-question structure as an interesting lead for a feature article.

If my students are to learn how to structure their own texts in interesting ways, they will need to be able to envision possibilities for this. I will need to be able to reach for texts with striking structures again and again to help them gain this vision.

## Texts Full of Crafted Ways with Words

This reason for selecting a text is also similar to the earlier craft-connections reason. The reason for this is that, of course, I will recognize many crafting techniques in a new text because I've seen them before in other places. But in these texts it is not a strong connection to another text that makes me choose them necessarily; it is the sheer number of things to learn about writing well that are found in the text that matters. These are texts that can give me lots of mileage because they have so much to offer. These are the texts that I often use in inquiry when I am teaching students what it means to read like writers because I know they have lots of things in them for my students to discover. These are texts where the writing is stunning, rereadable, read-aloudable.

In terms of reaching for these texts in my teaching, the texts full of crafted ways with words are the ones I reach for most often. For example, while it is important for me to have Bert Kitchen's *When Hunger Calls* (1994) because of the way it is connected structurally to other texts with repeating lines, for the most part this is a book that I find myself reaching for only for that reason—to show another example of a repeating line. Texts like Thomas Locker's *Water Dance* (1997) or Nancy White Carlstrom's *Raven and River* (1997), on the other hand, are texts I can reach for in many different situations because they have so much to offer in their ways with words. The ability to look at a text and say "Now that is full of neat crafting techniques" comes with experience studying craft. One hope I have for this book is that it will teach those of you new to writer's craft enough about what it is so that you can see it in many texts.

Cynthia Rylant's book *The Whales* (1996) is one that was added to my collection because it is full of interesting ways with words. The text has many crafting techniques I know and love, such as close echoes, re-says, fabulous repetitions, artful "ands," interesting ellipses, personification, and intentional vagueness. Like many of the books that are full of interesting ways with words, *The Whales* is not a storybook. It's a piece of descriptive writing that is image driven rather than plot driven. What makes you want to read this book is the beautiful writing in it, not the appeal of its story.

I often find that some of my best storybooks don't stand up as well when we are studying the craft of the writing because the writer hasn't had to attend to craft in the same way to make the reader interested. The story is so interesting that the writer can rely on the reader's interest in plot development to maintain attention. Texts which aren't plot driven don't have this going for them, however, and this is why you so often find them full of very well-crafted text. The same is true in reading the newspaper. The general news stories are not usually written with much attention to craft because they don't *have* to be. Readers will read about a hostage crisis or a plane crash, even if it's poorly written, because they want to know about it. Editorialists and feature writers, on the other hand, don't have the draw of the big news going for them, and so they have a greater challenge to make readers interested. This is why you often find very well-crafted texts in these sections of the daily paper. I often tell my students that it's the writers who can write about such ordinary things as hair (Sandra Cisneros's "Hairs" in *House on Mango Street* [1991]) or relatives coming for a visit (Cynthia Rylant's *The Relatives Came* [1985]) and make them interesting that are the really great writers.

This isn't to say, of course, that a text with a good story in it will not be well crafted. Many chapter books have fabulous stories and fabulous craft in them. I'd put any chapter book by Gary Paulsen, Jerry Spinelli, Patricia MacLachlan, or Cynthia Rylant in this "full of crafted ways with words" category. Jane Yolen's picture book *Miz Berlin Walks* (1997) is a fine example of a story-driven book that is particularly well crafted. She has a beginning and ending that match, a thread-back line at the end, recurring details, close echoes, unexpected adjectives, great verbs and adverbs, and many other interesting crafting techniques. No, what's necessary to know is just that a book with a great story in it, or a book that, as my friend at Teachers College said, "evokes a deep response in you," does not automatically qualify it as a book that's full of crafted ways with words—it may be full of fabulous story instead.

You must look at the words closely to see if they are well crafted. Ask yourself, "Can the way these words are written stand apart from what this book is about? Can I talk about what this writer is doing in this text in a way that makes it available as technique for my students' writing?" If the answer to these two questions is "yes," then you are likely to have a text in your hands that is full of crafted ways with words. Hold onto it. You will find yourself reaching for it again and again.

A note here about these texts for our youngest writers. If you teach the little guys, the five- and six- and seven-year-old writers, you will want texts that, in particular, have many crafted ways with words found in the print of the writing. Our youngest writers are quite in tune with print and how it looks because they are still figuring so much out about how it works. For this reason I like to find texts for them that craft a lot through the print. I recently added three books to my collection for this reason. *How the Snake Got His Hiss* (1996) by Marguerite W. Davol, *Underground Train* (1997) by Mary Quattlebaum, and *In the Driver's Seat* (1997) by Max Haynes all make meaning by crafting the print in the text to match the meaning. For example, in Haynes's book, he writes: "B-b-b-boy, this mountain trail sure is b-b-b-bumpy" and the "b's" are spaced up and down like bumps. Though experienced writers can craft print to make meaning too—remember Gary Smith's "rightthisveryminute"—it is an especially good way of crafting for our youngest writers to play around with in their texts.

## Texts in Which Writers Take Risks with Language

I often find myself selecting books for my students in which the writers have taken risks to use language in interesting, usually unconventional ways. Though many teachers may not share my enthusiasm for this, I want my students to see language as something that they control as writers. I want them to see that language is meant to be used, not only to make writing understandable, but to make writing come alive, and that the two are not mutually exclusive. As you might imagine, many of the texts that fall into this category also belong in the preceding category—they are full of crafted ways with words. I like to discuss risky language separately, though, because it's a very specific kind of language use I'm looking for.

My studies of craft have led me to believe that all language is, in fact, is *use*. Its use defines it. Language doesn't really exist except in actual exchanges between human beings, and I want students to see it in all its complex uses in these exchanges, so I choose texts in which writers have taken risks with language use because I envision my students as bold, brave writers.

I have chosen many Gary Paulsen texts for my craft-study collection for just this reason. Remember the quote from him in the last chapter, in which he said he will do anything with language to "make a story work right." Well, he will. *Dogteam* (1993) is a good example. This text is full of interesting uses of language, but the one that caught my eye first and made this a "must have" in my collection was what I call the "framing fragments," a technique that is actually a Paulsen hallmark. The text is full of sentences like these: "The dance." "Into the night." "A lake." "Wolves." Paulsen uses these almost like titles of sections, though they aren't. After each one he opens the text up and details the short fragment. The fragments frame these detailed sections. Here's an example from that text:

> Wolves.
>
> They come alongside in the moonlight, moonwolves, snowwolves, night-wolves, they run with us, pace the dogs, pace our hearts and our lives and then turn, turn away in the blue dark. (n.p.)

With passages like these, Paulsen sets a panting, dogteam-running pace throughout the text. You've probably noticed that, in addition to the framing fragment, the whole excerpt is crafted in an interesting way, with a layered noun effect and subtle repetition. What he is doing is not unlike what Jane Yolen does in *Welcome to the Green House* (1993). Yes, your beloved author of *Owl Moon* (1987) can also get pretty risky with her language use. Look at this example, in which she describes the green house:

> This is a loud house. A bright house. A day house. A night house. A wet house. A warm house. A single and a swarm house. A monkey house. A tree house. A fish and bird and bee house. (n.p.)

Yolen chooses to punctuate this very long set of items in a series as individual sentences. Can she do that? Well, she did, and isn't it lovely? The whole text of *Welcome to the Green House* is a study in using language in risky, interesting ways.

I pull texts like Yolen's and Paulsen's to help my students envision how to exploit language for their own purposes as writers. If I see students doing a particular kind of writing for which this kind of language might work, I don't hesitate to show them how these mentor writers are "dancing with words" in their texts.

To summarize, we've outlined six ways in which texts can be selected to help you in your teaching of writing:

1. Texts that have background information included
2. Texts in which the concept of the writing is interesting
3. Texts that remind you of another text
4. Texts crafted with interesting structures
5. Texts full of crafted ways with words
6. Texts in which writers take risks with language

While keeping these in mind, it is important not to forget the rule-of-thumb question we started with: "Can I envision pulling this text out during a writing conference to show a student some writing move?" If the answer to this is "yes," then you must know what the move is, and you probably need to add this text to your collection.

## RELATED ISSUES IN SELECTING TEXTS FOR THE TEACHING OF WRITING

It is useful now to think back through what we've said about selecting texts for the teaching of writing and to look at some issues related to this discussion.

## Age and Grade Levels

You might have noticed that I hardly ever mentioned, in any of this discussion, that certain texts were more or less appropriate for various grades and ages of writers. This is significant. I hope that in Chapter 2, as we defined craft by looking at Gary Smith's article, it became clear to you that craft—particular ways of using words—is not bound by genre, kind of text, or intended audience. We see similar craft techniques across all types of texts intended for all types of audiences. For example, having a text's ending and beginning match is a common crafting technique found in picture books for children and in human interest articles in magazines for adults. I want them both to aid my teaching of writing at any level if I can find them. I don't hesitate to use picture-book texts in adult writing workshops, and I don't hesitate to show children excerpts from adult writing that match the writing they see in their own texts. Even the one time I mentioned thinking about our youngest writers during the discussion above, looking for texts where lots of the craft is in the print, I could have just as easily been talking about showing those texts to adult writers. Remember in Chapter 2, when we looked at Gary Smith writing "rightthisveryminute"? That's crafting through the print as well.

Well-crafted writing is well-crafted writing is well-crafted writing. As long as the content is appropriate (I wouldn't read first graders a really well-crafted sex scene, no matter how many close echoes it had in it!), you can use any text to help your writers understand how to write well.

## Why the Word "Text"?

You may have noticed that I've relentlessly held onto the word "text," even when many of the texts I was mentioning were books, especially picture books. I held onto that word because some of them were not books. I do use a lot of books in my teaching of writing, but I know that craft can be found not just in books, but also in newspaper articles, love notes, billboards, advertisements— any kind of writing intended for an audience and designed to get that audience's attention through writing. So when I talk about finding craft to study as writers, I don't want to send the message that it's only found in books.

Also, though we often study craft in books in my classrooms, many of my students aren't writing books per se, and especially, many of them aren't writing picture books. Using the word "text" in my teaching serves as a constant reminder to my students that what we are looking at as craft is not tied to writing in books—it is tied to writing in *texts*. The word "text" widens the playing field, so to speak, of students' understanding that craft is transferable across all sorts of writing.

# Why, So Often, Picture Books?

We have addressed this issue several times in *Wondrous Words*, but I believe it bears repeating as it relates to this discussion. Because crafting techniques are absolutely generalizable across all kinds of texts, unless I'm in a specific genre study, it doesn't matter much what kind of texts I choose for my craft studies. I choose picture books frequently for several reasons. One is that they're pretty. I like pretty things. Another reason is that they aren't very big, so they aren't very heavy. When I think of lugging them with me here and there as I teach, trust me, that matters.

Another reason I like picture books is that they're short. This makes it easy to consider the writing in them as a single unit, and this really helps, especially when looking at the craft of the structure of the text. Also, I can find things more quickly in a shorter text than I can in a longer text—though I have to confess that my long chapter books are full of Post-It notes marking pages where I often show students some writerly move. Still, I can go more quickly to the parts of shorter texts that I need. Sometimes I really think the writing in picture books is better too *because* they're short. In many ways it's harder to write short than it is to write long, because every word *matters so much* when there aren't as many of them.

The other thing that having picture books around ensures is that I've always got an appropriate text—reading level and content appropriate—available. While I can move all the way up to writers at the senior citizens' home with picture-book texts, I can't always move down to my first graders with a really great John Grisham novel. I need the content to be appropriate, of course, but I also like the students to be able to linger with a well-crafted text on their own without me standing over them, so having books somewhere close to the independent reading levels I've got in my room does matter. So picture books give me a wider teaching range in that respect than does any other type of text.

You may be wondering if it isn't a little irreverent to study primarily the written text in a picture book, leaving the pictures out of most conversations. Isn't a picture book, by definition, a collaboration in meaning between texts and pictures? It most certainly is, though you may be interested to know that if a picture book has a separate author and illustrator, there is often very little (if any) collaboration between them on the final product. The author does the text work and then, finished, hands the manuscript to the publisher who takes care of getting an illustrator. So, though the written text and the pictures collaborate to create meaning in the finished product, the writer and the artist who created them often don't collaborate.

Still, considering the written text separately from the pictures changes the meaning of them both as they are in the picture book. If I were studying picture books as *a genre* because my students were going to write and illustrate picture books, then I wouldn't separate text and pictures in this genre study. But if I am simply studying the craft of good writing in a way that crosses all genres, then I am just looking for examples of very well-crafted texts, and I find them in the richly crafted, easily accessible form of picture-book texts. My students and I enjoy the books as readers first, pictures and written text fully intact. But when it's time for us to study the craft of good writing, I have no reservations about pulling those words out and really looking at them.

So, I love picture-book texts for studies in the craft of writing, but I also frequently use articles from magazines and newspapers, short stories from collections, and single chapters from longer novels in my teaching. Once you've learned to read like a writer, you may decide that you like studying a very different kind of text in your teaching. That's OK. Remember, you can find good crafting anywhere, and good crafting always leads to more good crafting, even in very different kinds of texts.

## Knowing Your Students

Throughout the discussion of selecting texts, I hope you noticed a number of references I made to the students I teach. I am always thinking about them as I look at texts and envision possibilities—the students are a big part of the vision I have for what could come of having a particular text in my collection.

When I envision possibilities for students, I think about two main things. One is, "What do many of my students struggle with as writers?" I know that almost any struggle they face can be matched with learning from writers—struggles finding topics, struggles knowing how to revise, struggles getting ideas for how to structure a text. I am always on the lookout for texts that can demonstrate something to my students that will help them see their way through their struggles as writers.

But I am also thinking about more than just students' struggles; I am also thinking as I look at texts, "What might my students be excited to see as writers? What might they want to try?" I love having a writing workshop full of possibilities for things that students might try. As students go about choosing what they want to try and do as writers, I like for them to be able to choose from a smorgasbord of writing possibilities, so as I look at a text I think, "Hey, someone might want to try this." I think of my collection of texts I use in the teaching of writing almost like a huge box of Legos. Think about how a child goes to a box of Legos thinking, "I'm going to build a city," and he looks at that box of Legos as if every piece is a possibility. I want my students to take their writing ideas to my collection of texts and look at them with the same eyes of possibility.

So think about your students as you think about selecting texts for your teaching of writing. Think about their "reading like writers" eyes that will look over what you've got. What will they see there that will help them as writers? What will they see there that will *excite* them as writers?

## Start Your Own Collection

What books line the shelves in your classroom right now? How did they get there? If you selected them, what criteria did you use? You may or may not have used the criteria I've suggested for selecting craft-study books, but more than likely you already have some books that meet these criteria and will go in this specific collection. No doubt, however, you will want some new books for your teaching after thinking through these teaching issues.

If money in your school is tight, think about assembling a part of your collection in the school library. Most librarians welcome recommendations for book purchases that will aid in instruction. Though I have a large collection of texts for the teaching of writing, the truth is that it's a small number of them which are essential in my day-to-day teaching. Those are the ones I need on hand all the time—I call them my "short stack"—and whatever books become a part of your short stack are the ones you'll need to have in your personal classroom collection. The others you want but will need less frequently, however, could be housed in the school library.

If money is tight, you might also think about really scouring magazines and newspapers for well-crafted texts to add to your collection. You can make a classroom copy of texts you find and use them again and again. *Sports Illustrated for Kids, National Geographic World,* and *Ranger Rick* (to name a very few) all have very good writing for children in them, and if you teach older students, the adult versions of these magazines are also full of good writing. I cut about one article a week out of the local paper which has some kind of interesting writing in it, and I save these with connected texts in folders for my teaching. You don't have to lay out sixteen or more dollars a pop for a picture or chapter book every time you want a new text for your teaching of writing—remember, think *text.*

So, with some criteria in mind to guide you, you can start your own collection of texts for craft study in your classroom. You will need to spend lots and lots of time just looking at texts. I routinely set aside a whole afternoon to go to a bookstore or a library and look through books, and I get impatient with teachers who aren't willing to do this, those who just want someone else's booklist to go by. The books are important, but your learning to look at books and choose texts for your teaching of writing is just as important, and the only way to learn to do this is to put the time in, on your fanny (excuse my bluntness), in a bookstore or library. The time will not be wasted. Not only will your ability to read like a writer grow exponentially, you can stand years' worth of writing curriculum for many, many students on a good collection of well-crafted texts.

# References

Associated Press, "Speed marks Simpson trial second time," *Asheville Citizen-Times,* 3 November 1997, A-5.

Jarrett, Keith, "He's lost just once, but Busby still criticized," *Asheville Citizen-Times,* 6 November 1997, D-1.

Kaul, Donald, "House divided against itself cannot stand," *Asheville Citizen-Times,* 24 December 1997, A-7.

# 10

# GROWING TALLER IN OUR TEACHING

*"I can't believe how much I have learned. I mean, in two weeks it's like a whole new world has been opened to me. I'm really excited, but I'm going to have to rethink everything I'm doing in my writing workshop."*

Not long ago, a teacher said this to me after spending three weeks in an intensive course on learning to write from writers. This teacher had learned to look at texts with completely new writer's eyes—seeing past what they were about into how they were written—and what she saw amazed and delighted her. During the three weeks she had studied dozens of texts like a writer and began to shape for herself, for the first time in her life, definitions of good writing techniques. She had read countless pages in which writers talk about their writing processes—from ideas to publication—and had collected more than fifty wonderful quotes from writers about their office work and drafting processes. She had been to the bookstore and made some initial purchases of books she just *had* to have. In casual conversation, she was throwing around first names of writers like she knew them, like they were close friends. And in her notebook, she had begun to draft her own memoir, poetry, and essays on politics. She dreamed of fiction. . . .

Now what was she supposed to do?

Sometimes, maybe we can learn too much too fast. Sometimes, we can learn so much—all at once—that it *changes who we are*. When this happens, the idea of returning to our day-to-day selves is scary. We don't recognize ourselves anymore, and as teachers it can knock us flat off balance in our classrooms. We are unsure of how to act in a place that was once so comfortable and so familiar.

During the past few years I have seen this happen a lot. Learning to read like a writer *really* changes, quite dramatically, what we see. And this subtle shift into looking at how things are written doesn't stay subtle for long. It wrenches us into so much new seeing and learning, so fast. Reading like writers opens new worlds to us, worlds that have always been there, as long as we've been reading—we just haven't noticed them before.

And then there's just the whole idea of it, of learning to write from writers. An idea so simple and so sensible. An idea that we might have said we had all along. "*Of course* we learn to write from writers. How else?" we would have said, before.

But now we are saying, "Oh my gosh, we *do* learn to write from writers. How do I make this happen?"

One teacher who was reading Randy Bomer's book *A Time for Meaning* (1995) wrote in the margin of that book, "He's messing with what I thought I knew." Really good learning does that for us—it messes with what we think we know, creating a tension in our lives that can be uncomfortable. When we begin to feel this discomfort our only choice seems to be to quit learning and wait for the "pain" to go away, or to rethink what we know and muck around a bit in stuff that's really hard for us. I'm partial to mucking around a bit myself, and I have in fact made peace with the idea that there will always be some new hard thing for me to think about in my teaching. There will always be some part of my teaching that, when I think about it, causes me discomfort because I don't feel as sure about it.

My learning to write from writers during the past few years has caused me to rethink so much of what I thought I knew. Beyond the inquiry into the craft of office work and the craft of texts, beyond inquiry into the nuts and bolts of teaching writing, I have had to figure out how to make my new knowledge base fit with my day-to-day teaching acts. "Now that I know what I know," I have asked, "how do I plan, present lessons, confer, assess, and respond differently? How do I teach in ways that cause my students to directly apprentice themselves to other writers?" The answers to these questions will be a career-long quest, I know, but together with the teachers and students I have encountered during the past few years, I am now thinking about teaching issues in significantly new ways. I would like to consider some of these issues in the next few chapters. While any one of them—planning, focus lessons, conferring, and assessment—is big enough to be its own book topic, I will consider each one in this single, focused light: learning to write from writers. What do we do with each of these when that is our classroom goal?

## Reference

Bomer, Randy. 1995. *Time for Meaning.* Portsmouth, NH: Heinemann.

# 11

# PLANNING FOR THE WORKSHOP
## Writers Learn from Writers

In our conversations as a profession about the teaching of writing, perhaps the place where we are outgrowing ourselves the most is in our thinking about planning for the writing workshop. More and more teachers are realizing the need to map out a year of thoughtful study in the workshop by focusing writers' attention for days or weeks on issues that will really help them to grow as writers.

## PLANNING STARTS WITH PREDICTABILITY

The beauty of the writing workshop lies in its predictability. Students come to know very quickly how the workshop works and what its components are. They know that there will be some time when they will meet as whole group, a larger block of time when they can work on their own writing, either alone or with a group of peers. They know that during this time their teacher will be moving about conferring with various ones of them. They know that near the end of the block of time known as writing workshop, they will probably meet back together as a whole group, either to share from the day's work or to get one more bit of writing advice from their teacher. In the best writing work-shops students know what is expected of them in terms of maintaining their writing—expectations about managing materials, supporting other writers, generating ideas, drafting, and publishing. Writing workshops need to be pre-dictable places so that wonderful, unpredictable things can happen in them.

The time that we spend up-front, at the beginning of the year, teaching our students how the workshop "works" is an investment for our teaching during the rest of the year. Setting up the management structures and rou-tines buys us quality teaching time for later. We do not have to invent ways of working over and over for our students, directing every move they make dur-ing the block of time we have set aside. So in that sense, planning for a writ-ing workshop looks very different than traditional planning has looked, where each segment of time, each day, is accounted for with a "plan."

But there are ways in which planning for the writing workshop should look very much like traditional planning. Namely, we need to know what it is we are "working on" with students at any given time in the workshop. We need *units of study* where our focus lessons over a period of time work together to build big, important understandings about writing. Without units of study our focus lessons become a hit-and-miss series of bits of teaching, isolated sound bytes that don't come together into larger, more lasting understandings.

For a long time I think we resisted thinking of writing workshops as places that needed curriculum organized into units of study. "Don't they just learn what they need to know from the experience of writing?" Well, yes. Our students learn many, many things about writing and about themselves from engaging in daily work as writers. We hold onto this time for our students like it was sacred for just this reason. But if we accept that we need instruction around this, and if we accept that some of this will be *whole-class* instruction, then we need a way of planning for that instruction that is meaningful beyond single lessons. We need big answers to the question, "Why am I going to teach this lesson?" Big answers to "What am I trying to accomplish here?"

## PLANNING BEGINS WITH VISION

Planning for the writing workshop begins with us as teachers thinking about our vision for our teaching. We must ask ourselves, "After spending a year in my writing workshop, how do I hope my students will *be* as writers?" Notice the phrasing of this question. I didn't ask, "What do I hope they will know?" I asked how I hoped they would *be*. The object of the verb "teach" in our writing workshops is "writers." We teach writers, not writing. We teach writers things about writing, but the point of those things always leads us back to writers. We can't know what we want them to know until we know how we want them to be.

So before we can begin to think about planning we have to answer this question: "After spending a year in my writing workshop, how do I hope my students will be as writers?" It is a question that many groups of teachers in schools, across grade levels, have been working together to answer. I spent an entire school year with teachers at P.S. 7 in the Bronx, working to formulate an answer to this question that was big enough to shape curriculum, instruction, and assessment in writing for the entire school. I continue to shape my own teaching by the vision we developed that year. Here's what we came to as we answered the question of how we hoped our students would be:

**Over Time in a Writing Workshop, We Hope to See Students Developing . . .**

- a sense of self as writers and personal writing processes that work for them;

- ways of reading the world like writers, collecting ideas with variety, volume, and thoughtfulness;

- a sense of thoughtful, deliberate purpose about their work as writers, and a willingness to linger with those purposes;

- as members of a responsive, literate community;

- ways of reading texts like writers, developing a sense of craft and genre in writing;

- a sense of audience and an understanding of how to prepare writing to go into the world.

And that's it. We believe that everything we can imagine teaching students can and should help them grow in one or more of these ways. Notice that the vision is big enough to go across all grades, ages, and abilities of writers, *if* we think about how it will manifest itself in developmentally appropriate ways. For example, the manifestation of "thoughtful, deliberate purpose" will look very different in a six-year-old than it does a twelve-year-old. I won't expect a typical six-year-old to collect lots of entries around a topic before he or she writes it, or to draft a piece several times before publishing. Growing toward "thoughtful, deliberate purpose" in a six-year-old might be as simple as staying on a piece of writing for more than a day! But that is still growth toward this goal for that child. So all the teachers in a school might be working on the same goals across all grade levels in writing—they will just have different curriculum that students will need in order to move toward those goals and different ways of seeing that growth in the work of a variety of children.

If there were no whole-class direct instruction, there would still be many ways that the writing workshop could, by itself, support students' growth in these areas. For example, a child who writes every day can't help but develop some sense of himself as a writer. If he is allowed to talk to others about his writing or their writing, he will develop more of his sense of self and also develop as a member of a responsive, literate community. If that student gets to read aloud something he has written, he comes to understand something of audience. So in the very ways in which we set up the writing workshop, we need to keep in mind how our structures and routines are supporting students' growth as writers.

## POSSIBILITIES FOR FOCUSED UNITS OF STUDY

Beyond the growth that we know will happen in the natural course of the workshop, we need to use the vision we have to help us plan units of study for our whole-class instruction. A unit of study in the writing workshop is a period of time, from a few days to several weeks, when the community of writers turns its attention in a single, focused direction. All of the whole-class focus lessons will center around the topic in the unit of study, and many of the conferences and class sharing times will bring the topic side by side with the work of individual students. Sometimes the direction of the study will impact *what* students write during independent writing time, as in a genre study for which they write pieces in that genre, but often the study simply supports their learning around all their self-selected pursuits as writers.

When we teach our students to learn to write from writers, we plan these units of study in ways that consistently turn students' attention to what real writers in the real world do. We bring these writers who are "out there" into our classrooms and let them serve as mentors for our students' growth. Let's look now at just a few possibilities for units of study that would support various aspects of the vision outlined above.

### A Sense of Self as Writers and Personal Writing Processes That Work for Them

- A study of writers' lives and what they say about their writing processes
- A study of writing in other professional lives (other than professional writers)
- A study of our own lives and histories as writers

### Ways of Reading the World like Writers, Collecting Ideas with Variety, Volume, and Thoughtfulness

- A study of what writers need to gather from the world to sustain a published writing life
- A study of the gathering-from-the-world habits of various kinds of writers: poets, memoirists, fiction writers, essayists, etc.
- A study of specific writers' notebooks
- A study of our own writers' notebooks

### A Sense of Thoughtful, Deliberate Purpose about Their Work as Writers, and a Willingness to Linger with Those Purposes

- A study of how writers follow an idea through to publication
- A study of how writers "live with" a topic over time
- A study of how to conduct research for writing (firsthand and second-hand research)

### As Members of a Responsive, Literate Community

- A study of peer conferring and collaborative relationships
- A study of how writers work with other writers, editors, and publishers

**Ways of Reading Texts Like Writers, Developing
a Sense of Craft and Genre in Writing**

- A study of how to read texts like writers, both for structure and ways with words

- A study of a specific genre: poetry, memoir, literary nonfiction, fiction, drama, journalism, critique, editorials, picture books, descriptive, etc.

- A study of how writers "write" without words: looking at punctuation, spacing, layout, fonts, etc., in written texts

- A study of one writer's body of work

- A study of text-structure possibilities

- A study of ways-with-words possibilities

**A Sense of Audience and an Understanding of How
to Prepare Writing to Go into the World**

- A study of publishing opportunities for young writers

- A study of how writers edit their work for publication

- A study of what happens in the publishing process

As you look at these possibilities, remember that they are for units of study *over time*. During the year there will be curriculum outside these units of study that students will need in focus lessons or conferences to help them grow in different areas. For example, some students may need help with subject-verb agreement issues so that they can "prepare writing to go into the world," but subject-verb agreement would not be a whole unit of study. You want your units of study to be "big enough" to encompass understandings of some breadth in writers' lives.

# THINKING ABOUT UNITS OF STUDY ACROSS A YEAR

Even if you have not been organizing your writing workshop by units of study, you can probably imagine how you might lead your students in studies of this kind. In just the possibilities listed above, there is way more than a year's worth of curriculum. There is no "big brother" who has some magic answer to what you should study with your students in your writing workshop. You will need to select units of study that make the most sense for your teaching situation. There are several questions you can think about that will help you select your units of study.

### What Are My Strengths as a Teacher of Writing?

Whatever you absolutely love in writing, whatever you're best at, should become a unit of study in your classroom for the rest of your career. You may be the only teacher students ever have who is passionate about whatever it is, so go for it. Your love and knowledge in this area will help you teach well year after year. Every student I have ever had has studied Cynthia Rylant's writing for just this reason—because *I love her writing.*

### What Have My Students Studied Before in Writing?

From first grade onward, it is helpful to know as much as you can about what kind of writing instruction your students have had before they arrive in your classroom. What you know can impact your decisions about what you will teach, and you will need to plan with your students' expertise in mind, going "deep" when you know they have a lot of experience in an area. You will want to plan for studies that both *extend* what your students have been learning and studies that *introduce* them to important new ideas. Extending means that students might engage in similar units of study year after year—this is especially true of genre study. Students could study memoir or poetry every year of their lives and continue to extend their expertise each time. So aim for some studies that return students to familiar concepts and others that take them into new territory.

Sometimes knowing what is new territory for students can help you decide what studies you will need early in the year. If, for example, you have students in your fourth-grade classroom who have never been in a writing workshop, you will want to start with studies that build the most essential concepts necessary for their learning throughout the year—how writers gather ideas from the world and how to read like writers.

## What Are My Students Interested in? What Do They *Want* to Know as Writers?

This is a question that you probably cannot ask before the school year begins. You will have to get to know your students for a few weeks, or even months, to really answer this question. For this reason you will not want to plan out the entire year of study until after you have gotten to know your students. What you teach in April might depend on what your students seem very interested in. If there is a clear area of interest among many of your students, get behind the energy of this and go for it. I once had a class that got very interested in drama—they were quite the little actors and actresses. And so even though I would have not planned it on my own, a genre study of scriptwriting seemed appropriate with that group of students. The energy was there. You might have groups who are very interested in some author or genre or in getting published "in the real world"—whatever it is that catches your students' attention, follow along behind that and focus some of the study during the year around those interests.

## What Are My Colleagues Studying in Their Writing Workshops?

You may want to think about planning a unit of study along with other teachers in your school. If you have enough resources available, at some point during the year a "study-in-common" across several classrooms can provide many benefits. It gives you and your colleagues a chance to study this teaching together and share resources, and it gives students a chance to share their learning and ideas with students from other classrooms. These studies-in-common need not happen only at particular grade levels. Fifth graders and first graders, for example, might study literary nonfiction together in a co-genre study.

## What Resources Do I Have?

Sometimes decisions about units of study are made on the basis of resources you have available. I once planned a study of Patricia MacLachlan's writing because I knew she would be visiting in our area. If you have access to two writers who work together a lot, you might plan a unit of study on collaborative relationships, or if your best friend works at the newspaper you might plan a study around journalism. And then of course you will need to look at your library resources to see whether you have the texts you will need to support a particular study. This too can influence the planning decisions you make.

### For What Kind of Writing Will My Students Be Held Accountable?

If there is a particular kind of writing for which your students will be held accountable, you will want to plan a genre study of that kind of writing. This is often the case in states where writing is tested at various grade levels. Slow these studies down and really immerse students in *real examples* of the genre, having them read the examples like writers (describing how they are written) and studying how writers go about supporting their work in this genre. Also, if you have curriculum guides that you are accountable for, see if you can plan units of study that get at the objectives of the guide while still turning students' attention to writers for the learning they need in a given area.

The answers you find to these questions should help you plan some units of study to get your year started in the writing workshop. Remember, there are no "right answers" to what students should study at any given time during their school years as writers. What you want is to have good reasons for why you have decided to launch a unit of study in your classroom. Teachers can make the best informed decisions about what is right for their classrooms.

# UNITS OF STUDY OVER A SCHOOL YEAR

To help you picture units of study over a year, let's look now at two sample year-long layouts in writing workshops. The first is the layout of a year in an upper-elementary classroom, and the second is a year in a K–1 classroom. Notice that with each layout, we look at what kinds of writing students are doing alongside the study. You want to aim for a good mix of totally self-selected writing and required writing in specific genres under study. Topics, of course, are always self-selected, even when a genre is required. The exception to this on these layouts is a two-week genre study of testing in the upper grades, in which students learn to write for tests and in response to prompts.

**Table 11.1.**   Sample Year-Long Plan for Upper-Grades Writing Workshop

|  | Unit of Study | Students' Writing |
| --- | --- | --- |
| One week | Study of who we are as writers. Making plans for the year. | Self-selected |
| Three weeks | Study of what writers need to gather from the world to sustain a published writing life (notebooks). | Self-selected |
| Three weeks | Study of how to read texts like writers, both for structure and ways with words. | Self-selected |
| Four weeks | Poetry genre study. | Poetry |
| Two weeks | Study of peer conferring and collaborative relationships. | Self-selected |
| Three weeks | Author study of one writer's body of work. | Self-selected |
| Five weeks | Literary nonfiction genre study. | Literary nonfiction |
| Three weeks | Study of writing in professional lives (other than professional writers). | Self-selected |
| Three weeks | Author study of one writer's body of work. | Self-selected |
| Two weeks | Testing genre study. | Prompt writing |
| Four weeks | Historical fiction genre study. | Historical fiction |
| Three weeks | Memoir genre study. | Memoir |

**Table 11.2.**  Sample Year-Long Plan for K–1 Writing Workshop

|  | Unit of Study | Students' Writing |
|---|---|---|
| Two weeks | Study of different kinds of writing. Imagining what's possible. | Self-selected |
| Three weeks | Study of where writers get ideas and why writers write. | Self-selected |
| Three weeks | Study of how to read texts like writers. | Self-selected |
| Three weeks | Label books genre study. | Label books |
| Three weeks | Study of collaborative relationships (helping each other). | Self-selected |
| Three weeks | Study of writing for audiences. | Self-selected for a specific audience |
| Three weeks | Alphabet book genre study. | Alphabet books |
| Three weeks | Author study of one writer's body of work. | Self-selected |
| Three weeks | Poetry genre study. | Poetry |
| Three weeks | Study of how writers write without words: punctuation, spacing, layouts, fonts, etc. | Self-selected |
| Three weeks | Author study of one writer's body of work. | Self-selected |
| Three weeks | Study of simple text structures. | Self-selected choosing structures with intention |

So these are examples of what a year *could* look like. The time frames in these sample layouts are based on the assumption that the writing workshop happens every day, and even then they are very approximate. Sometimes there will be real energy for a unit of study, and it will make sense to stretch it out longer than you might have planned. Don't be afraid to study one thing for a very long time if the energy is there. These are the studies that students will remember for the rest of their lives.

Notice that several of the units of study are the same both at the upper grades and in the K–1 writing workshops. You will want to plan for these in developmentally appropriate ways. For example, I want to teach both first graders and fifth graders how to read texts like writers, but I will select different texts to introduce them to this idea. For the first graders I will need texts in which a lot of the crafting is in the print and the pictures and in very obvious text structures. Similarly, the concepts of genre study and author study are important across all grade levels, but I will choose the genres and the authors we'll study with the experience of the writers in mind.

Genre studies and author studies are planned in predictable ways. These studies always begin with some time devoted to *immersion* in the genre or the author's work. During this period of the study the students spend a good bit of their time in the writing workshop reading and sharing around the genre or author, getting a feel for the kind of writing under study. After immersion, students begin a period of *close study* of the genre or the author. During this time they will look closely at the craft of the office work and the craft of the texts they find in writers of this genre or by the author under study. These units of study always end with students *writing,* either in the genre or under the influence of the author they have studied. Once this way of working through a study is established in the workshop, students come to expect and own the process and the inquiry becomes a habit of mind for them.

One question that is often asked about planning for the writing workshop in this way is, "When in a scheme like this do I teach things like capitalization or comma splices?" And the answer is, "Whenever students need help with these things." Issues of convention aren't big enough by themselves to be units of study because what there is to know about them is fairly finite. If the whole class has to study all the capitalization rules, and half the students are using them just fine to begin with, then there is nothing in this study for those students to learn. Units of study need to be big enough that no matter what different students bring to the study, there will be new insights for all of them to gain.

Without a doubt, however, you will have students who will need help with various conventional issues. What help they need should be *your* unit of study.

Spend the first few weeks of school "looking over their shoulders" to see what kinds of help different ones need, and stay on the lookout for this throughout the year. In conferences and small groups, help students with explanations they need for various conventional issues. And if you see something that, truly, almost all your students seem to struggle with, then teach focus lessons on it until you see them beginning to understand. Just try not to fall into the easy trap of assumption—assuming that all your students will need help with something before you've really determined so from studying their writing.

# GATHERING RESOURCES FOR A UNIT OF STUDY

In units of study in a writing workshop, you will want to concentrate not so much on "*what* students will learn" as you will on "what can I get going in the room that my students can *learn from*." This is such an important distinction. Remember that you are teaching writers, not writing, so your focus is on creating an environment for your writers to inhabit where they can't help but learn. During a unit of study, you fill that environment with anything and everything you can think of related to the study that students can look at, ponder over, and talk about. When planning for any unit of study, there are several predictable resources I think about gathering.

## Writers' Voices

I want writers' voices to be a part of any unit of study, and for this reason I am a passionate collector of quotes. Whenever I hear a writer speak or read something that a writer has written or see an interview with a writer, I am on the lookout for quotes that I can file away to use in units of study. I like to "throw" relevant quotes into the room and let students discuss them. I paste quotes up around the room that relate to a unit of study. When assessing their own work, I'll ask students to mention quotes that have mattered to them in their learning as writers.

Articles about writers, interviews with writers, excerpts from books on writing (by writers), video interviews with writers, Internet conversations with writers—all of these get writers' voices into your room too, and all of them can be great resources for a unit of study. As you search out and come across these resources, learn to "listen" to writers with "curriculum ears"— reading them with an ear open for the big understandings they can help your students make about writing.

## Texts

Texts, texts, and more texts. Students need to be reading alongside their writing in any unit of study, and so gathering the best texts for a study is critical. Texts are selected for a unit of study on the basis of how they can help students develop the big understandings behind the study. So, depending on the focus of the study, I look for texts in different ways.

It is easy to think about text selection for a genre study—you need examples of texts written in the genre. Lots and lots of them. Never ask students to do any kind of writing without first *immersing* them in reading examples of the genre. A good portion of these examples should be *like* what the students might write. For example, if you are studying fiction with young writers, you will need many more examples of short fiction than you will of novel-length fiction. Your students won't be writing novels.

Outside of genre studies, there are a variety of kinds of texts I will select for other units of study. If I am teaching students to read like writers for the first time, I will select texts that are full of crafted ways with words and text structures. If I am teaching students about gathering ideas from the world, I will select texts that are written *about* everyday kinds of things and texts that are good meaning metaphors for the writing life. If we are studying how writers write without words (punctuation, spacing, fonts, etc.) then I will need to find texts that are full of examples of this. If we are studying collaborative relationships then I will look for texts that are co-authored. In other words, I look for writing that supports our study either through what it means or through how it is written.

## Real People

For many units of study there might be people I could invite into the classroom who can help us think about our area of focus. Writers themselves, of course, are nice, but we aren't all lucky enough to have professional writers at our immediate disposal. We do, however, probably have people near us who just love poetry, people who write as part of their professions, people who work in collaborative groups, people who learn to sew when they go to the mall in the same way we are learning to write from writers. With a little imagination you can probably think of all sorts of people who might visit your classroom and lend some insight to most any unit of study you would have. Real people help our students connect their learning to lives outside the classroom, and these connections build bridges to this world in powerful ways.

## Writing I Have Done

Another question I ask myself when planning is, "What writing have I done and what writing experiences have I had that I could share as part of this unit of study?" As my students learn to write from writers, I am an important writer in that learning. I can copy entries from my own writing notebooks, show stories and poems and letters I've written for my family members, tell stories of writing experiences I have had, share writing of my own that's in progress. Sometimes I will create experiences for myself as a writer so that I can know what they feel like and then later share them with students. For example, if I know I will be doing a genre study of fiction during the year, I may spend time in the summer deliberately trying to generate a notebook full of character, setting, and plot ideas so that I can learn about this process and have examples to share with students during our unit of study.

## Writing Students Have Done

I have kept drawers full of my students' writing throughout the years. With their permission I have copied notebook entries, drafts, and all kinds of finished writing projects in many different genres. I have saved their "writing about their writing" from portfolios and other assessments. In my notebooks I have saved powerful quotes from students about writing. I use student writing whenever I can in units of study, and, more than any other resource, student examples help young writers to see themselves mirrored in the work of other writers. You can think of the work your students are doing right now as having curriculum potential for future students. Ask yourself, "What are they doing that other students might learn from?"

# TEACHING DURING THE UNIT OF STUDY

When we think of setting up an environment that teaches during a unit of study in the writing workshop, we will need to broaden our understanding of our role in the teaching that happens there. While we will teach some things about the topic quite directly, at other times we will simply be guiding students to engage with materials and conversations and inquiries that we trust they will learn from.

The focus lesson each day will anchor the study by turning students' attention toward the topic. There are two main kinds of focus lessons I employ in a unit of study: focus lessons that share ideas or explain concepts, and focus lessons that set up inquiries.

## Focus Lessons That Share Ideas or Explain Concepts

Many, many focus lessons during the year will be simple, short lessons that share an idea or explain some concept about writing. During a unit of study, these lessons all relate to the topic under study. These focus lessons don't ask students to do anything in particular, though they might contain suggestions for things students might try. After these lessons students simply go to their independent writing time to continue to work on whatever projects they have going at the time.

Within a given unit of study I will want to have a number of lessons like this. In these lessons I might

- Share a quote of advice from a writer that helps me explain some idea about the process or products of writing.

- Explain how a crafting technique works, showing examples from texts.

- Show a piece of student writing that helps me explain some idea about the process or products of writing.

- Show a piece of my own writing that helps me explain some idea about the process or products of writing.

These lessons do not call for lots of student interaction. They are simply lessons which show and explain things about the unit of study in which we are engaged. As you plan your unit of study you will want to think about what focus lessons of this kind you can offer to students. You will want to go for quality. Ask yourself, "Of all that I might teach, what is likely to have the most impact on my students as writers?"

## Focus Lessons That Set Up Inquiry

The other type of focus lesson I plan for is the type in which I set students up for some inquiry. In these lessons I present some material that I ask students to look at or listen to with some focus related to our topic. They may be looking at texts like writers, reading articles about writers, listening to a quote from a writer they will discuss, or poring over samples of other student writing. Sometimes they provide the materials for inquiry: their writers' notebooks or their in-process drafts or their writing from several years ago. I simply plan a focus lesson that sets up a way for them to look at these things in relation to our topic. Here are a few examples of the types of inquiry I might set up during various units of study:

• In a study of our own lives and histories as writers, I might have students look through pieces of writing that they have done in the past, using Post-It notes to mark and comment on things they notice, and then discuss what they see with a small group, asking questions like, "What have we learned along the way?" and "How are we different now as writers than we used to be?"

• In a study of what writers need to gather from the world to sustain a published writing life, I might have students look through stacks of texts together and imagine (make theories about) where the writers got their ideas for those texts.

• In a study of writing processes, I might have students pore over articles by writers and dig out every mention they can find of writers describing their processes.

• In a study of how writers follow an idea through to publication, some students could look at magazines and study submission guidelines, while other students could study copies of *Writer's Market* to learn about book-submission guidelines.

- In a study of peer conferring, students might look at transcripts of conferences I have had (I always keep some of these) and study the kinds of teaching they see there, constructing theories about what does and doesn't work in conferences, and developing some guidelines they might want to follow in their own conferring.

- In an author study, students might spend a day just looking at leads across many different texts by the author, developing theories about how the author crafts leads.

- In a study of how writers edit their work for publication, I might have students look through pieces of my writing I have edited and develop questions and insights about my process, eventually interviewing me about my process.

- In a fiction genre study, students might interview people out in the world, using a question like, "Which means the most to you in fiction: plot, characters, or setting?" They could talk and develop theories about what they find in these interviews.

The teaching in these inquiry lessons spills over into students' independent work time because it asks students to engage with materials in some way. Basically, as I plan for these lessons I am thinking of this essential question: "What can I have students look at or listen to that will get them thinking and talking in meaningful ways about this topic?" Talk is so important to communities of writers who are engaged in a study together. Talk helps us to construct meanings that we wouldn't come to on our own. You will want to get your students very accustomed to talking things through in inquiry, having conversations about things that lead them to new understandings. You may even want to plan a unit of study on just that— exploratory conversation. In Chapters 5 and 6 I described a number of kinds of inquiry about both the craft of office work and the craft of texts which I use over and over again with writers.

After a focus lesson that sets up an inquiry, and after the inquiry itself, I usually plan on reconvening the workshop as a whole group to process the "big ideas" students have generated in their independent conversations and study. This may happen on the same day that the students engaged in the inquiry or it may happen on the next day. These processing conversations help us to develop some understandings in common, and often I return to some of these ideas in other focus lessons, building upon them and making new connections to them whenever I can.

To summarize, then, once I have gathered and gotten into the room everything I can think of for a unit of study in the writing workshop, I think about what I can teach and what I can get students engaged in that will teach them. In the spirit of true inquiry, I won't plan out an entire unit of study before it happens. I want to plan some engagements to get us started, and then I want to see what students are interested in within that. To put it simply, what I teach on Thursday during a unit of study has a lot to do with what happens on Monday.

## But Where Do I Start?

This is the question I am asked more than any other: *Where is the best place to start with all of this?* And the advice I always give is to start with the most essential understanding first. Teach your students to learn to write from writers. Explain the ideas of mentoring from writers right from the beginning. Get writers' personalities and voices into the room from the first day of school. Personally, I would start my units of study by focusing on the craft of writers' office work, looking closely at why writers write and how they go about living their lives in ways that lead them to writing. Next, I would study the craft of texts, training students' eyes to read like writers through a close study of a number of well-crafted texts. These two habits of mind, learning from the craft of office work and learning from the craft of texts, will permeate all your other studies throughout the year.

If your students come to you with these big ideas already in place, you might reconsider starting with these studies. You could start with them, searching for writers who can extend your students' understandings of office work and texts, but you might want to start somewhere else, with a powerful genre study or author study, or maybe a study of your students' own writing lives. Think of starting the writing workshop with something powerful enough that it will reverberate throughout all your teaching during the year. A good lead, in teaching as in writing, is hard to beat. A good lead will keep your students with you for a long, long time.

And no matter where you start the writing workshop, don't forget to let read-aloud time wrap its arms around your students' reading and writing lives at some point during the day. Read aloud is the single most important thing you can plan for the entire year.

# FOCUS LESSONS

## Filling the Writing Workshop with Craft Possibilities

Once students know how to read like writers and see craft for themselves, then the big time investment of lots of text study (as described in Chapter 6) will not be necessary. Instead, crafting possibilities will become a part of the curriculum offered through focus lessons in different units of study and in individual conferences.

In writing workshops at all grade levels, teachers have rituals for gathering students each day and offering them focused, whole-class instruction that covers a wide range of topics that writers need in order to grow and develop. As we gather our students to the couches and carpets in our classrooms, there will be many times during the year when we will want to direct their attention to various crafting techniques. The purpose of focus lessons on crafting techniques is to get possibilities in the room for things writers might try that will help them write well.

Filling a writing workshop with possibilities makes it a very exciting place to be. I like to think of it as being rather like filling a sewing room with all kinds of patterns and material and every sort of sewing notion imaginable, and then saying to those who enter, "Here, make something. Make something wonderful." I like the tone of these short, focused whole-class lessons on craft to sound something like, "Let me show you the coolest thing you can do when you write. It's a little something Gary Paulsen did and it's just so *cool.*"

Some of the crafting techniques I offer in these lessons may be ones that students have seen before in inquiry, or they may be techniques that are new to them. Basically, anything I have ever seen a writer do with writing can become curriculum for my writing workshop. Once my students know what it means to read like writers and learn from writers, focus lessons give my students and me a way to share this "curriculum of possibilities" in a very efficient, very predictable manner. I do much of the teaching in these lessons, but students are invited to teach others in this format too. Writing workshops become very "happening" places when they are filled with writers sharing interesting crafting possibilities.

No matter what the unit of study we have going in the writing workshop, focus lessons on crafting techniques make sense any time students have drafts underway, which is most of the time. These are the lessons that help them with the actual writing. I like to support them with focus lessons about text structures as they are planning for drafts, and then with lots of lessons on ways with words as they are into drafts and revisions.

## ORGANIZING FOCUS LESSONS

In the last chapter we talked about two kinds of focus lessons, those that share an idea or explain some concept and those that launch students into inquiry. Unless I am teaching students how to read like writers, most all of my focus lessons dealing with craft will be of this first kind—I will use the lesson to explain some crafting technique.

Focus lessons that explain are meant to be direct and to the point. Writers need to get back to their own writing, and so we can't take forty minutes of an hour-long workshop to explain something about how to write. As we plan, we always need to plan with a healthy balance of time in mind. But we do want our students "to get back to their own writing" with some new insight, and so it's important that our explanations in focus lessons are given with clarity and maximum efficiency. Planning well for these short lessons is very important.

As I plan for how I will explain a crafting technique in a focus lesson, I plan along the same familiar line of thinking we have used before in inquiry, reinforcing once again this habit of mind of learning from writers:

| Inquiry | Focus Lesson |
| --- | --- |
| *Notice* something about the craft of a text. | Show an example of a crafting technique. |
| *Talk* about it and *make a theory* about why a writer might use this craft. | Explain why the writer might have chosen to craft in this way. |
| Give the craft a *name*. | Give the craft a name. |
| Think of *other texts* you know. Have you seen this craft before? | Show other examples of the crafting technique in other texts. |
| Try and *envision* using this crafting in your own writing. | Envision this crafting technique in use in student writing. |

Now, though I want to cover all these bases because I want to maintain this line of thinking, I have to remember a focus lesson itself *is not* an inquiry. Because students are familiar with thinking about writer's craft along these lines, I use this familiar way of thinking to offer an explanation, but not to solicit student thinking. I am *showing how* in a focus lesson of this kind, and I do this very directly without a lot of student input.

While I make my focus-lesson plan to cover the entire line of thinking, there is no need to slavishly follow this order. For example, I might first show several examples of a technique in use (connections and noticing), go ahead and name it, and then describe how the writers are using the technique. Sometimes I might add a short piece to the focus lesson in which I have students try writing their own examples of the technique, either in the air or in their notebooks. But this isn't necessary. Focus lessons in workshops don't have to end with "guided and independent practice." The real work of writers serves as the "after-engagement" to focus lessons.

I do make sure I end each focus lesson on crafting techniques with this request: "If anyone tries this, be sure to let me know." When writers do try techniques I've shown in focus lessons or techniques they've found on their own in inquiry, I make a very big deal of it. I want students to know that I value their taking risks to try things in their writing. I usually have these students show the rest of the class their own examples of the technique alongside another writer's example. During the workshop I will also refer other students to those who've tried something to get advice on how to use a technique. I want students to feel that trying out crafting techniques gives them new expertise as writers, and so I treat them as if they have expertise when they have successfully crafted in specific ways.

The challenge for us in this directed, whole-class teaching of focus lessons on craft will be to keep it complex enough so that it matches the complexity writers really face when deciding how to craft their texts. You see, the focus lesson itself—explaining a certain way to use words or to structure a text, looking at examples of the technique, envisioning the technique in use—is the simple part. I mean, you could start at the beginning of the structures and ways with words from my library outlined in Chapters 7 and 8 and just teach them one at a time if you wished. The teaching part is fairly simple. The complex part is letting this curriculum go, letting writers take it over and make their own decisions about how to use it. You see, the point of this teaching about craft is never any one of the techniques itself. Students need to know a wide variety of crafting possibilities for texts, but the possibilities aren't the point. They are necessary, but they aren't the point. That students can use them to *make good decisions* about how to craft their texts is the point, and this is difficult for us as teachers.

We are accustomed to thinking of curriculum as being a set of ends in itself. We teach, we test. We teach, we test. Our familiarity with this makes us want to teach students a specific way to structure a text, say, and then require everyone to draft a piece using that structure—with topics of their own choosing, of course. How else will we know if they've "got it," we wonder. But the structure is not what we want to know if they've got. The structures and the ways with words are there to be *chosen amongst;* this is what real writers have to do. They have to make decisions. Forcing everyone into one structure takes this decision away, and so writers get no experience in the decision-making process. The crafting techniques we teach in focus lessons are means to another end—giving students a range of options to consider as they make decisions about their texts.

However, you might think that "if, during the course of the year, I have my students try out different crafting techniques that I've taught, then they will know these techniques better because I've guided them through them, so they therefore will make better use of them later when they make decisions on their own." There are problems with this kind of thinking. One is that *later* hardly ever comes in these situations. We know how readiness models of instruction often cut students off from any real engagements for years of their lives in school. We can always think of one more thing to teach before students get to do "the real thing." No, we have to use our focus lessons to get the curriculum of crafting possibilities into the classroom, but then we have to let it go. Let it go and then follow that curriculum we've offered out into our conferences as we help students "define and refine" their decisions about how they will craft their texts.

## FOCUS LESSONS THAT DEAL WITH TEXT STRUCTURES

Good writing is well structured, no doubt about it. In schools this fact has unfortunately manifested itself in artificial fill-in-the-blank formulas for writing that students are forced to plug into their (or someone else's) topics. It's a readiness model for learning to structure writing—let them try these simple structures now, and they can move on to something more sophisticated later. But sometimes *later* never comes, except to move from a five-sentence paragraph to a three-paragraph essay and then on to a five-paragraph essay. I may be exaggerating some here, but with the recent push in testing, I fear I am not. Formula writing has gotten a new head of steam because of testing, as many students are forced to write again and again in an artificial formula designed to help them do well on "The Test."

Though formula writing is a grossly oversimplified attempt to teach structure in writing, we cannot argue that students need to be guided to think structurally about their writing. They do. And we will need many focus lessons during the year that introduce or reintroduce (from inquiry) writers to structural possibilities for their drafts. In order to "think structurally about their writing," students will need exposure to a range of curriculum about structure. In any given year in a writing workshop, as parts of genre and author and crafting units of study, students should look at numerous possibilities for ways to structure whole texts or parts of texts in many different genres.

## Explaining a Way to Structure a Text

If I want to teach students about a certain way to structure a text, then I need to gather several examples of texts that use this structure. It helps if I can choose texts that students are already familiar with as readers, but if not, I will show them enough of how an unfamiliar text works in order for them to see the structure. I leave these texts in the room then for several days so that students may return to them on their own. If I were going to teach students about using repeating lines to hold pieces of text together, then I might bring in Cynthia Rylant's *When I Was Young in the Mountains* (1982), two of Bert Kitchen's books, *Somewhere Today* (1992) and *When Hunger Calls* (1994), and an overhead copy of John Grisham's opening pages of *The Partner* (1997), where he uses the repeating phrase, "They found him." I have lots of other texts I could show students, but in the interest of time I will need to be selective. I could follow up later with another focus lesson or two in which I show even more examples.

Next, I will need to think about how I will explain what these texts I have gathered have in common. What will I say about this structure across these texts? I need to phrase this so that it makes what these writers are doing available to writers in the room. I will say something like this:

> Basically, what these writers did was that they took one key thing that they wanted to say a lot about, one really big idea, and they used it again and again, to start each new part they would say about it. The repeating lines and phrases bring the reader back to that key thing as each new bit of information or detail is added.

Notice that I have now "untied" this explanation from the topic of any one of the texts. Just as this was important to do in inquiry (see Chapter 6), it is also important to do in focus lessons.

A few years ago I would have ended this lesson after showing the examples, naming and describing the technique, and saying something like:

> So, if any of you are writing something that has one central idea like this, holding everything together, you might want to try using a repeating line to show that, just as these writers did.

And I would usually (eventually) have a student who was able to make this big connection to his or her own writing and would try the technique out. Now, however, by adding the step of envisioning the technique in use with students at the end of these lessons, I am helping many more of them to think about what this would *really sound like* in another piece of writing.

As I envision the technique in use, I write some of it "in the air" so that students can actually hear it. I try to work the technique "around the room" a bit by using it with several different topics and genres of writing. I try to envision the technique with real topics and ideas that I know my students have, either in their notebooks, in their ideas, in in-progress drafts, or even in pieces of writing they have completed. My goal is simply to envision *us* using this technique in *our* writing. So, envisioning for the repeating-line structure might go something like this:

> Let's see, John, you know how you were wanting to write about your trip to camp last summer? You could easily use this structure for that. You might start each section with something like, "In the slow summertime days at Camp Boone, we . . ." and then use that to introduce descriptions of things you did there. You could tell a lot of different things that way. Or, let's see, Cara is writing her piece about tips for babysitting. Maybe she could use a repeating line to introduce each tip. I don't know, something like, "What you absolutely, positively must know about babysitting is . . ."—something like that for each one. Maribel is writing about the house she grew up in back in Texas; she might use a repeating line that is just something like, "In my first house, in my Texas house, we grew strawberries in the backyard." You know, introduce each thing she wants to tell with some kind of repeating line like that.

Notice that I actually suggest repeating lines as I envision these. Doing so helps the envisioning be very, very clear, and it helps me to know whether I can really envision this in use. I am demonstrating a way of thinking when I do this, showing students how a writer takes something she sees and imagines it as a *possibility*.

You may wonder why I don't use my own topics instead of theirs when I envision possibilities. I do sometimes, but I don't hesitate to use theirs either. I like to set a climate in the room of "batting around ideas" and let students get very comfortable with what this means. I want them to do this envisioning with each other too, and so often, after a focus lesson like this, I will suggest that they talk with each other as they work that day about ways they could see themselves using this text structure in their future writing. Again, I am trying to get them comfortable with the kind of batting around of ideas that all creative people engage in. What's neat is that once students are familiar with what I do as I envision in these lessons, I often don't even have to do this part anymore—they volunteer to do it for me.

You may wonder if I ever see any of these lines I've written "in the air" in actual drafts. Of course I do, and I don't mind one bit if students try something another student or I have imagined with their topics. We don't actually write things for each other—we simply have a workshop in which ideas are flying around everywhere, and we all help to generate them. I love the image of a writing workshop being this kind of place.

You may also wonder if I just make these up off the top of my head. The answer is yes, I do. I try not to think of them ahead of time because, remember, I am demonstrating to students a kind of thinking. I want it to really be the brainstorming, off-the-top-of-the-head, unfinished kind of thinking that I show them. I think that we don't let students see us do this often enough, and yet this kind of thinking is the hallmark of very creative people. So sometimes I struggle, and sometimes the things I envision for them come out sounding weird, but that's OK. I want them to see this.

## Exploring a Range of Structural Possibilities

When I want to teach students to think through a variety of possibilities for how they might write about a single topic, I will do a different sort of focus lesson. Instead of looking at one structural possibility across many different topic ideas, I will lead students in looking at one topic idea and envisioning writing it in several different structural ways. In a way, these lessons are more about envisioning than they are about any one text structure. Before I can do a lesson like this, students will need exposure to a number of different text structures. I want lessons like this to teach students that what they are learning should be giving them a range of options to consider as they draft and plan for drafts.

To teach this kind of lesson, I need a single-topic idea. I might ask for a volunteer, or I might just choose one. I like to work with an idea that has a quality in common with other ideas my students are choosing for writing. For example, if lots of students are writing personal narrative, then I would want a topic like that. If lots of them were writing descriptive pieces about things that interest them, then I'd want a topic like that.

Let's say that I choose a topic where a student wants to write about what it's like to visit at his grandmother's apartment in the city. I need texts nearby that use a variety of different text structures. Again, it helps if these are texts that students already know, but they don't have to be. I can just explain how one works, if need be. I like to be able to get my hands on example texts as I demonstrate envisioning to students. Doing so really helps reinforce the important idea of mentoring ourselves to other writers.

I explain to students that when they have a single idea for writing, the text structures they know offer them many different possibilities for how they might write about that topic. Then, I proceed to envision a single topic written several different ways. If the student has in mind to write about his grandmother's apartment in the city, he might write it in any one of these ways, for example:

- As a seesaw text like *No One Told the Aardvark* (1997) by Deborah Eaton and Susan Halter. He could move back and forth between contrasting things from his home and life in the country and his grandmother's home and life in the city.

- As a collection of photographs and poetry like Walter Dean Myers did in *Brown Angels* (1993). He could take pictures from her apartment and its surroundings and write poems to go with them.

- As a framing-question text like *I Want to Be* (1993) by Thylias Moss. He could start with a question such as, "What is it like to visit your grandmother in the city?" and then write a series of descriptive images that answer that question.

- As a guidebook like *The Pirate's Handbook* (1995) by Margaret Lincoln. He could have sections like "What to Pack to Go to Grandma's" and "Things to Be Sure NOT to Say at the Dinner Table at Grandma's House" and "Survival Tips for Spending a Week at Grandma's."

- As a narrative sequenced by a series of objects like *Aunt Flossie's Hats* (1991) by Elizabeth Howard. He could perhaps frame a story in which he unpacks his suitcase from a visit at grandma's and uses the objects he unpacks to tell about what it was like to be there.

- As a two-part text like *For the Love of the Game: Michael Jordan and Me* (1997) by Eloise Greenfield. He could have the first part be all about, say, mornings at his house in the country, and then switch and say, "But mornings at grandma's in the city are very different." The second half would describe those mornings in contrast.

- As an inanimate-voice text like *Cry Me a River* (1991) by Rodney McRae. He could let the apartment building where his grandmother lives or some object from her house like a clock on the wall or a kitchen table be the speaker and tell the story of what life is like there.

- As a series of short memoirs like *Walking the Log: Memories of a Southern Childhood* (1994) by Bessie Nickens. He could write a number of short, contained narratives about things he has experienced at his grandma's apartment, each one standing alone but combined in a volume about this one topic.

- As a text written like a diary as in *Catherine, Called Birdy* (1994) by Karen Cushman. He could make the text look and sound like actual diary entries. Each entry would capture some aspect of life at grandma's apartment.

- As a text with a series of vignettes connected by a repeating line like *When I Was Young in the Mountains* (1982) by Cynthia Rylant. Each vignette would capture some quality of life in the apartment in the city and tell a very short story about something that happened there.

- As a participatory text like Joanne Ryder's *Shark in the Sea* (1997). He would write the text in second person, asking his reader to become a part of life at his grandmother's apartment: "Walk up the stairs now and don't get tired. You have four flights to go. . . ."

- As a text with commentary embedded in it like Carolivia Herron's *Nappy Hair* (1997). As he tells about grandmother's apartment, other family members might add their "two cents" in comments around his text.

We could go on and on with ideas like these, but that's enough for you to get a feel for what I mean. I usually go through these rather quickly, occasionally writing some actual lines in the air for different ones if they seem appropriate. The purpose of a focus lesson like this is to help students see the *range of possibilities* for any one idea or topic for writing. After a lesson like this, I often suggest that students talk through with one another as many possibilities as they can think of for their ideas. I also suggest that they keep lists in their writer's notebooks of possibilities they envision for various texts they might write.

## FOCUS LESSONS THAT DEAL WITH WAYS WITH WORDS

Focus lessons on ways-with-words crafting are very similar to lessons about structure. Most every focus lesson I teach on ways with words simply follows the line of thinking used in inquiry—notice, describe, name, connect, and envision. This line works very efficiently to help me explain how a certain way with words is used by writers to make certain meanings or rhythms or sounds in texts.

To start these lessons I will need to gather some texts that have examples of the crafting technique in them. For example, if I am showing students the technique of placing an adjective in an unusual place, I might pull out *My Mama Had a Dancing Heart* (1995) by Libba Moore Gray, and show them examples like "we drank lemonade cold" and "hot tea spiced." Since I know it helps to show another writer using the same technique, I might also pull out Jane Yolen's *Miz Berlin Walks* (1997) and show them "But one rained into my hand and it was all over gold." I will either put these examples on an overhead or just read them and show them straight from the text.

Next I need to name and describe how these writers are using this technique and carefully untie it from their meanings. I might explain it this way:

> Basically, what these writers are doing is that they are playing with our ears. They know that we expect adjectives like these to come before the words they describe, that we expect to hear "cold lemonade" and "hot spiced tea" and "gold all over." They know that we expect this, and so they shake us up by moving the adjectives to another place. It makes the writing interesting, gives it an interesting sound. So if you wanted to try for this sound in your writing, you could try this—moving adjectives to unusual places.

Quickly, I move to envisioning some possibilities by writing a few quick examples in the air. Again, when I do this I try to work with familiar material, material that is very much in the room:

> Using this technique would be something like, "It was a night *dark* when I went camping by myself for the first time." Or maybe something like, "I saw a truck, *two-ton*, coming straight at me." Or Mary, in your piece about the pool, you might call it "water blue" instead of "blue water." You know, say, "I dove into the water blue for the first time."

One thing that I often do in ways-with-words lessons which I don't usually do in structure lessons is that I use actual texts to show how a crafting technique would look if we tried it. With structures, because so many parts of the text have to work together, it is hard to do rewrites as part of a focus lesson. But ways-with-words crafting is small and contained and easy to show in an example. I save texts of my own and texts from former students to use as examples for this teaching. As students look on, I rewrite a part of a text using the crafting technique I am explaining. These "demonstration texts" give me a way to show the larger meaning context for which a certain crafting technique would make sense.

With the technique above, for example, I might show students this part of a piece I wrote about my garden:

> I love my garden. It is a dream. Visions of lilacs. Smells of daisies. Soft petals from red roses and fat, purple hydrangea.

I could then show them how I might rewrite this part by using the crafting technique of putting adjectives in unexpected places. If I did, I could write it this way:

> I love my garden. It is a dream. Visions of lilacs. Smells of daisies. Petals soft from roses red and purple fat hydrangea.

When I actually rewrite some real text by using a certain crafting technique, I move the teaching beyond just envisioning. I move the teaching into *revision*. This gives students concrete examples of how writers can return to a draft and try out other possibilities. I think our students sit and stare blankly at drafts during revision because they don't know what kinds of things they might do with them. If we nudge these connections between crafting and revision a little more by using examples like the one above, students will come to see that what they are learning as part of their craft study does have potential for them when they revise. Revision can then become an almost playful revisiting of our drafts where we say to ourselves, "What cool stuff could I do to this to make this writing interesting?"

I will sometimes end a ways-with-words focus lesson by having students try to write an example of the technique in their writer's notebooks just to try it on for size. There is not a method to when I do this; usually it just has to do with whether I feel we have time to try it. I don't want to take too much of their work time in the focus lesson. I end by asking the students to do two things: first, to let me know if and when they use the crafting technique in an actual draft, and second, to be on the lookout as they help each other for places in their classmates' drafts where the crafting technique might work. "Don't be afraid to suggest it if another writer hasn't thought about using it," I tell them.

## Envisioning—So Important to This Teaching

You may have noticed that envisioning is such an important part of the teaching that happens around crafting techniques. And, you may be thinking that you'll never be very good at this "writing in the air" thing, that it's really very hard. I think that with time and experience you'll be surprised at how easy it will become for you and your students to envision crafting techniques in use with all kinds of topics. And you'll need to become experienced at it because it's one of the most important kinds of thinking you can demonstrate in your classroom. You'll want your students to have drafts and dreams of drafts floating around in their consciousness all the time, and their ability to envision craft in texts is what will make writing these drafts more and more automatic for them as they write throughout their lives.

## Reference

Grisham, John. 1997. *The Partner.* New York: Doubleday.

# BRAVE, BOLD TEACHING
## The Power of Suggestive Writing Conferences

**M**ichael had just gotten started drafting a story when I sat down to have a conference with him during the writing workshop in his third-grade classroom. It was a fantasy story, and he wasn't very far along:

The flying tiger.
One day There war
a tiger Named prince.
he helped The Birds
fix There house. The Birds
paid him By giving him
feathers.

*"The Flying Tiger": Michael's beginning*

Before I could do more than greet him, Michael launched into telling me his story idea. He explained that the birds were going to give the tiger so many feathers that he wouldn't know what to do with them all. As he talked on about all the feathers, a thought entered my mind. "He gives them fields. Fields and fields and fields," I thought. It's a line from Cynthia Rylant's *Dog Heaven* (1995), and I knew Michael and his classmates had been studying the craft in this and other Rylant texts. According to the description of his idea, Michael was at a perfect place in his text to use this technique of stretching out an idea by adding on repetitive items in a series. His *meaning* matched Rylant's *meaning*, though their topics were very different. I could see a copy of *Dog Heaven* nearby, so I went and got it. I found the "fields" page and I said:

> Michael, it sounds to me like you are in a perfect place to use this technique that Cynthia Rylant uses here. You know how she wants to show that there are just so many fields, so she adds on that part "fields and fields and fields"? Well, you are saying there are so many feathers, so maybe you could try that. You know, like, "The birds paid him by giving him feathers. Feathers and feathers and feathers." Then it would show that same thing that you were describing to me, that there are just so many of them. What do you think?

As you can see from his addition below, he thought it was worth a try, so he added on, "Feathers, feathers and more feathers":

*"The Flying Tiger," with Michael's addition*

That was our conference for the day. Five small words added to a draft, but a whole new strategy added to a growing repertoire of strategies that Michael knows which will help him craft writing for maximum effect.

You may think that calling this conference with Michael "brave, bold teaching" is a bit of a stretch, and maybe it is, but for me as a teacher it *feels* brave and it *feels* bold. You see, several years ago I would not have helped Michael in this way. I would not have suggested that he try writing a certain way in his draft. Studying the craft of writing alongside students in inquiry has changed my teaching dramatically. In my writing conferences I am suggesting more, nudging more, helping students with their actual drafts more than I ever have in the past.

## EXPANDING MY KNOWLEDGE BASE

You see, the main reason I wouldn't have helped Michael with his draft in this way several years ago is simply that I wouldn't have thought of this suggestion. Before I started studying the craft of writing, I didn't know any texts as a writer, I didn't know with any explicitness any techniques that writers use to make their writing come alive, so I wasn't in a position to suggest very much. It wasn't that I was holding back; I just didn't have anything much to hold back. My own history of writing instruction had left me with a few lame suggestions to "add more detail" or to "try making it flow better," but nothing much beyond that little blob of writing tips that, in their nebulousness, never helped anyone write well.

Studying the craft of writing has expanded my knowledge base exponentially in what I know about how good writing happens. I now know a whole repertoire of techniques for good writing that I didn't have in my first years of teaching. I now have a stack of texts that I know like the back of my hand. I know what kind of writing they have in them, and I have thought a lot about why the writers crafted the texts in those particular ways. As I move about the workshop and see what my students are trying to do as writers, these well-written texts and the things I know about them are never far from my thinking. I am taking Cynthia Rylant and others along with me as I teach now.

You see, in teaching terms, what I have to offer now is a lot more writing curriculum. Before I started studying craft, I couldn't have even considered helping students more with their writing because I didn't know how to help them. I just didn't know much about good writing. And what's really funny is, I didn't know I didn't know. I didn't know I wasn't helping my students as much as I might have. Because I didn't realize there were some very distinct understandings available about how to craft writing, I didn't know we were missing out on anything. The study of craft has helped me know how to help my students write well. By looking at craft across many, many kinds of different texts, professional writers have helped me to see what kinds of things I need to be teaching students how to do. The bottom line is that I couldn't teach what I didn't know, and now that I know so much more, my teaching has changed.

When I encountered Michael and his many feathers that morning, I thought immediately of a good writing technique I could teach him because I had that technique in my repertoire. I could tell that his meaning matched the meanings I had seen when other writers used this technique, so I saw an opportunity to teach him this move in a context I thought would make sense to him. The more you know of curriculum, the more opportunities you find to teach in very contextual ways in a writing workshop. You see what students are trying to do, you pull from what you know that will help them do it well, and then you show them how within the contexts of their individual texts, as I did with Michael.

Inquiry structures like those described in Chapter 6 generate all kinds of curriculum in crafting techniques for the writing workshop. The teaching challenge we face is to help students bring this curriculum out of the inquiry and into their real work as writers in our classrooms.

Writing conferences are the backbone of the writing workshop. Good conferences move the teaching of writing from the whole-class carpet gathering to the individual writer's desk. And what a big move it is. Conferencing is probably the hardest part of workshop teaching. We all have spent years learning to do it better and in more and more theoretical ways, and adding this new knowledge base about the craft of writing into this teaching has only made it more challenging. What are the best ways to help students come to know and use crafting techniques as they write? Before we answer this question, I believe it will be useful to think theoretically about the highly suggestive teaching like that in Michael's conference. For me, it took time and lots of deep thinking before I became comfortable working with students in this way, so I'd like to share some of this thinking with you.

## FINDING A NEW TEACHING ROLE

Over time, as I came to know more about good writing from my studies of craft, I was able to think of more ways I could help my students with their writing. I was excited about this, but I was still wary of suggestive teaching, especially in conferences with individual writers. You see, helping with the actual writing, the actual wording or structuring of a writer's piece, was something I had never really experienced as a writer or as a teacher. It felt very odd to me to suggest that a student should try a writing technique, even if that technique matched the student's meaning and would probably help him or her write well. Helping in specific ways with writing just seemed to me like something that took ownership of the writing away from the student. Because I had never known this kind of writing help, I had trouble envisioning how it might manifest itself in a writer's work.

Luckily, the vision I needed for this kind of teaching came to me in a very timely fashion while I was agonizing over how to best bring my new knowledge base to my teaching. As Lester Laminack and I were finishing our book *Spelling in Use* (1996) for NCTE, we were assigned an editor, and I had my first opportunity to work with someone in this capacity. The experience was, to put it mildly, revolutionary for me as a teacher of writing. I can define what our editor did for us quite simply: She looked at our drafts to see what we were trying to do, and then she made suggestions along the way for how to do it even *better*. It was obvious from the start that she knew a lot about writing, and this gave us the confidence to entrust our writing to her. And most everything she suggested we tried, and almost every time we realized, "Hey, that does work better." It was so helpful for us to have someone who was so knowledgeable about writing look at our drafts and make suggestions for things we could try. Not once did I feel like she had somehow taken the piece away from us. We had birthed the ideas with words; she helped us give compelling shape and form to those words. As a matter of fact, because we cared so much about our topic, we were honored to have help writing it as well as we possibly could.

This experience helped me to rethink my teaching role in the writing workshop. I knew that studying craft had taught me a lot about good writing, and knowing more, I wanted to help my students more. Our editor gave me a vision for how helping in constructive ways might be possible. She also helped me to realize what the challenge of this teaching would be. The challenge would be always to put my students' writing first—to always let my assessment of what they are trying to do lead me to the curriculum I offer them. You see, this is why the editor's help never felt like she was stealing the writing away from us, because she always, always based her suggestions on what she thought we were trying to do with the writing. She wasn't trying to get us to do something different—she was only showing us how to do what we were already doing *better*.

For this teaching to be successful, then, I would need to really listen to my students tell me about their drafts for writing. I would need to listen and get a handle on what they were trying to do, and then match that with writing techniques I know which help writers do that well. I could use my curriculum knowledge to help them write better, but I had to be sure that the curriculum never drove the helping. The student's intentions had to drive the helping.

What I needed, more than ever, was to remember to let assessment drive my one-on-one workshop teaching. Traditional teaching has been driven by a model that has curriculum as its first concern (What will I teach?), followed by instruction (How will I teach it?) and ending with assessment (Did they get it?). But the whole idea of the writing workshop—a place where writers write and where we teach into and around that writing—forces us to rearrange the order of these essential components when we think about our conferencing. When we confer, we need assessment first that looks at what students are doing as writers, what they know about what they are doing, and what they need to know to do it even better. We make curriculum decisions on the basis of what will help students most at that time or what would make the most sense in the context of their work as writers. And then, after we've matched curriculum to our assessments, we deliver instruction. Keeping this "order" in mind as we go about our conferring will help us engage in thoughtful instruction and not steal away students' intentions and purposes in writing.

To help make this "assessment-first" teaching order clear, we can think again about the conference with Michael. It had three essential components:

1. I listened to what he was trying to do (assessment).
2. I thought of what I knew that could help him do it well (curriculum).
3. I suggested something for him to try (instruction).

*Assessment.* First I listened as Michael described what he was drafting. I was listening in a particular way, not for the topic so much as for the meanings he was trying to make. I could tell that Michael had an intention to write about something that was amassing, something going on and on and growing bigger and bigger. I needed to separate this meaning from "feathers" in order to help Michael craft, and you can see that the way I stated it did not mention feathers. Why the separation? If you'll remember from our discussions of craft in earlier chapters, writers craft texts in certain ways because they are making certain meanings or trying for certain effects. For example, when writers craft a very long, runaway sentence, they are trying to show a sense of some extreme feeling—desperation, excitement, fear. You will see that this meaning is matched in example after example of this technique, though the topics will vary greatly. So my assessment needs to help me see what meanings Michael is trying to make with his topic.

*Curriculum.* I need to think of effective ways that I know to help Michael get his meanings across well in his writing. I am thinking of other texts I know where writers are making similar meanings, and in this case I think of Rylant's *Dog Heaven* (1995). Luckily, it's a book Michael has seen, and he has discussed the craft of it with his classmates. If he didn't know the text, I would still go quickly to the section where its meanings match his own and read him enough of it to show him the technique.

This is where an expanded knowledge base helps so much. Knowing crafting techniques and knowing where to find them helps you match them to your students' writing. Having a history of conversations in inquiry about why writers craft in certain ways across texts helps you to match meanings with your students' writing and to know which techniques make sense in context. When I work with students in these ways, someone almost always remarks, "You have to really know a lot of writing well to teach this way, don't you?" And the answer is "yes." You do have to know some texts and some techniques well enough so that you have them in your back pocket to help students when they need them. To help you confer well, there is no substitute for having a sound knowledge base in writing techniques and texts.

*Instruction.* The last part of this interaction was for me to suggest to Michael that he try this technique. You will notice that I explained why I thought the technique made sense, pointing out that it matched his meaning. This explanation is critical if I want Michael to own this technique in his future writing. He needs to know the kind of situation that might call for the crafting technique—to show something amassing, something going on and on and growing bigger and bigger—so that he will recognize it when he finds it again in his writing. I also showed him another writer using this same technique, giving him an example of it in use in another context, and then I wrote in the air some of his piece using the technique so he could hear how it sounded. It is important not to stop short of writing a little in the air because hearing some text crafted in the suggested way is what will really make it available to the writer.

You might have noticed that the essential components of the line of thinking for inquiry are all "covered" in subtle ways in a conference like this—notice, talk about and make a theory, name, other texts, envision. I return to these components again and again as I teach, and not just in inquiry. When we follow this predictable line in our teaching, we are doing more than helping students with a certain piece of writing at a certain time. Our ways of working with them also serve as consistent demonstrations of how to learn to write from writers. Our hope is that over time the process of matching meanings to the crafting techniques they know will become internalized for them, and they will be thinking in these ways on their own as they draft and revise.

## TEACHING IN THE "ZONE"

This kind of teaching, this helping students to write well, is highly theoretical. The great socio-psycholinguist Lev Vygotsky theorized that all children have a "zone of proximal development." This zone represents the range of tasks a child can perform in *collaboration with others*, a range that extends, of course, beyond what the child can do on his or her own. I have become comfortable with the idea that my students be allowed to work at their writing in their own zones of proximal development, not entirely left alone, but with guidance from me and from other writers in the room. I try to make my students comfortable with this idea too, erasing the stigma that can attach itself to a piece of writing if you know that "someone helped you with it." It's *fine* if someone helps you with it! You can do way better writing—do things you couldn't even imagine doing by yourself—if someone helps you with it.

This is a funny thing with teaching. Sometimes when I show writing samples from my students, teachers will say to me, "My students just never write anything like that." And my reply almost always is, "Maybe you aren't helping them enough." And then I get kind of a shocked look. For some reason, with writing we have gotten this idea that helping someone with anything more than a few editing checks is "cheating." But it's not. As long as you always work from the student's intentions and purposes, there is nothing wrong with helping a student know how to write something well. Writing is something we do, and it helps to have someone showing us how to do it along the way. Writers show us how it's done every time we read, and teachers who know things about writing can show us when they teach as well. As Lucy Calkins would say, "don't be afraid to teach."

Know that the help you give a child on an individual piece of writing will outlive that piece of writing. Remember that Vygotsky went on to say that what is in a child's zone of proximal development today will become something the child can do independently tomorrow. In other words, what Anna can do with your help today, she will be able to do by herself tomorrow. There may not be a more important understanding behind what we do in conferring than this one. If our teaching is to help students outgrow themselves, then we must teach within the "zone" and help them to accomplish today what they could not accomplish without our help, knowing that tomorrow this brave, bold teaching will lead them on their own to wondrous words.

## CRAFTING CONFERENCES

In the writing workshop, our students will need conferences when they are engaged in many different ways in the writing process. Sometimes they will need conferences that help them to develop a topic more or to know how to gather ideas for some good reason they have for writing. Sometimes they will need conferences that help them to establish better ways of working at their writing or conferences that help them to set goals for themselves as writers. Our students may need conferences that help them to decide on a genre or to know how to pursue a publishing opportunity. They may need conferences that help them to understand how subjects and verbs agree or how to check for end punctuation. All of these kinds of conferences work together during a year in a writing workshop to help students learn to write well.

Crafting conferences are those conferences that help students very specifically with actual text drafts, and their purpose is to help students write well, not just write adequately or correctly, but write *well*. These are the conferences in which we help students use, in their own drafts, the techniques of craft that they have seen in writers they admire. These are the conferences in which we bring down off the charts on the walls the things we have found in craft inquiry and help students to try them in their own drafts in ways that make sense.

The line of thinking we use for crafting conferences bears repeating again. In these conferences we

1. Listen to and look at what the child is trying to do (assessment).
2. Think of what we know that can help the child do this well (curriculum).
3. Suggest something for the child to try or help to refine what the student is trying (instruction).

Crafting conferences are really about helping writers think of good possibilities for their drafts or helping them refine the possibilities they are already trying. Some crafting conferences will deal more with text structures while other conferences (like Michael's) will deal more with specific ways with words. Conferences about structure may come at any point before or during the drafting process, but undoubtedly they are very effective when we have them just as writers are beginning to plan how they will write something. Conferences about specific ways with words will almost always happen when we catch writers in the middle of drafting or during revision after drafting.

## STRUCTURE CONFERENCES

Conferences about structure help students to decide how they will go about writing a piece or how they will refine a way of writing a piece that they are already trying. Will I write this piece with a beginning and ending that match? Will I write it as a series of diary entries, or will I have it move as vignettes connected to objects? Will I hold time still in the piece and move from place to place, or will I write the piece so that it jumps back in time? These are the kinds of questions writers will ask as we help them in these conferences. And because we know that good writing is structurally sound, these conferences are some of the most important crafting conferences we will have. These conferences are also the ones that help students to envision more than one kind of text possibility for their various reasons to write.

So that we can open up some thinking about crafting conferences, let's look now at two conferences about structure that I had in a fourth-grade classroom. The first conference is with Jovan.

**Katie:** Jovan, tell me about the seed idea you're working with.

**Jovan:** I'm doing this thing about my future. About what I want to be when I grow up—a pilot. *[He gets this big grin on his face when he says "pilot."]*

**Katie:** Ooo, that sounds exciting. What are you thinking about how you might write this piece? Do you know yet?

**Jovan:** I want to do it sort of like in the future, like start with that, when I am already a pilot. Then I want to go back in time and tell how I became a pilot, like all the stuff I had to do to get to be one.

*In structure conferences, some version of "How might you write this piece?" is a predictable question that students come to expect from me over time. The question is very much "in the room," as we have discussed it in both focus lessons and many conferences. Students know that it is a question of structure.*

**Katie:** Oh, so you're sort of dealing with a flashback kind of thing aren't you? Like you'll go backwards in time?

**Jovan:** Yeah, like that. Back to when, well like now, when I'm a kid and I'm first wanting to be a pilot.

**Katie:** Have you started drafting at all yet?

**Jovan:** Nope, not yet. I've just got this stuff about what you have to do to be a pilot. I'm going to start tomorrow, I think. *[Aren't we all going to start our drafts tomorrow!]*

**Katie:** OK, well let me just tell you the one main thing I know about flashback writing. Usually it has some kind of scene to it, like you landing a plane or you packing your bags for your next trip or something like that, and then in the scene there is a trigger. The trigger is what makes you think back in time. Like maybe you see an add for flight school or you find an old toy airplane you used to have. Something that takes you back in time. You know *Knots on a Counting Rope [Martin and Archambault 1987]* don't you? *[He nods yes.]* Well, in that book I think the trigger is when the little boy asks his grandfather about how he got his name. Remember that? *[He nods.]* Well, that's, like, the trigger. That's

*Jovan has a plan for what he wants to do. I name for him the structural technique he has described as a "flashback." Naming techniques for students is important in conferences. The names give the students language that makes it easier for them to talk about writing.*

*As soon I establish what Jovan is doing, I think of something I can tell him that might help him to do this. I draw from what I know about flashback writing. Notice that I define "scene" and "trigger" with actual examples. I just make these up and write them in the air so that Jovan can hear what I mean. I also try to think of another text I know that uses a flashback, and luckily I think of one that Jovan knows as well. In conferences I am always trying to connect students' writing to mentor writers.*

what I mean by that. So you'll need something like that in a scene to take you back.

**Jovan:** Yeah, I've been thinking about that. I'm going to start in the future and my alarm clock is going to go off and I wake up and realize I've forgotten my flight. That's like how I'm going to start it.

**Katie:** That sounds great. So all you'll need is a trigger in there to take you back. You could spend today thinking of some possibilities for how you might do that. I'd make a list of them in my notebook if I were you. This is a really neat idea, Jovan.

*So Jovan already had his opening scene in mind. My teaching just nudged him to think more specifically about how he was going to get out of this scene and move back in time. Notice that I leave Jovan with my enthusiasm for his plan and with an idea of what he might do next. I try not to leave a conference without the writer having some energy for what he will do next.*

The conference with Jovan is fairly typical of a conference with a writer who has a structure in mind for a draft. Jovan described to me what he was doing, a flashback structure, and I used the knowledge I had of this crafting technique to offer him advice and support on how to go about doing that. I had to pay attention to where he was in the process of writing (not yet drafted) and tailor my advice to fit his work at that time.

You might notice that once I knew what he was doing, I moved fairly quickly to the teaching. This is something I have learned to do. I used to struggle with the idea that if I talked to a writer for a longer period of time, I might find something better to teach. And I probably would have. But Jovan was one of *thirty-six* writers in this classroom, and even if he was only one of twenty (wouldn't that be grand), I would still have to manage my teaching time in ways that make sense. Finding "the best thing to teach" is not the goal of my conferring. Teaching in direct response to what this writer is saying to me is my goal. Direct response, that's my goal.

I have to take a leap of faith and just trust Jovan and my teaching. I asked a question, he answered it, I listened, and I helped. In crowded classrooms, quality in conferring comes not from the quantity of time we spend with each child, but from the fact that we really listen to them in the moments we are with them. Our interest in what they are saying and doing as writers, and our teaching, which is a very direct response to that—these things make all the difference. When we get frustrated that we can't give each child more of our time, we have to remember that the impact of teaching interactions *based on listening* is immense in students' lives.

Not all conferences about structure are as easy as the one with Jovan. Sometimes writers have no idea how they are going to write something. This second conference is with Ian, and it is very different from the preceding one. Ian had not started to draft yet either, but I knew that he did have a topic he wanted to pursue and that he had gathered a number of entries around this topic in his writer's notebook.

**Katie:** So Ian, remind me of what your seed idea is. I know you have one, but I can't remember.

**Ian:** My dog.

**Katie:** Oh yeah, Jazz. I forgot. *[Ian had written before about his dog Jazz; a published piece about Jazz's death.]* You've written about him before. You know, lots of writers work with the same seed idea over time. They do different kinds of pieces on the same topic. Patricia MacLachlan does that. She writes about the prairie a lot. Anyway, do you have an idea about how you are going to write about Jazz this time?

*I am capitalizing on an opportunity to match Ian's work as a writer to a mentor writer's work. The question, "How are you going to write it?" is a predictable one in structure conferences. I tailor it to the child's idea for writing.*

**Ian:** No. *[His body language says he's kind of de-energized by this. I wait a while, but he doesn't say anything else.]*

*Reading body language is very important in conferences. So is wait time. Often, if you just wait, writers will say more. Ian was just a young man of very few words this day. I think he really just didn't know what to say.*

**Katie:** Well, do you think you just need more time to think? Or do you want me to see if I can help you?

**Ian:** I don't know.

**Katie:** OK, why don't we see if I can help some. If you'll let me see some of what you've got, I'll see if I can help you think of some possibilities. *[Ian agrees, so we look at his notebook. He shows me the entry that tells the story of Jazz's death. Just below that entry he has written, "Jazz and me do a lot of special things together."]* Ian, this statement you wrote here, this statement says to me that you have a vignette or a snapshot thing in mind. It sounds like there must be a lot of little scenes in your head about those special times with Jazz. Am I right?

**Ian:** Yes.

**Katie:** I think you could probably play with that structure some and see what happens. You know, a piece about you and Jazz, sort of like Cynthia Rylant's that we looked at, *When I Was Young in the Mountains* [1982]. Remember how we talked about how it was written with all those little snapshot stories? You could do that with you and

*I'm thinking, "OK, now what do I do? He's not sending me away, but he hasn't exactly asked me to stay either." I decide to pursue helping him some. Again, reading his body language tells me that he has lost energy for what he's doing, and I don't think leaving him alone right now will help much.*

*It would not have helped for me to have left Ian with "more time to think," telling him I would return later to help him when he had some ideas. He needed help getting ideas for how he would write. As we looked at his notebook, I was looking for clues as to the kind of meanings he was making there about this topic. The kind of meanings would help me know the kind of text to suggest.*

*I connect the idea for the kind of text to one that Ian knows, and I explain how and why I see the one I envision for him as being like Rylant's. I go an extra step to define, with examples, what I mean by "little scenes," making some up that are typical dog scenes. I don't really have any idea as to what scenes he has in mind about Jazz. I'm just giving him examples of*

Jazz—little stuff like, I don't know, like him waiting for you at the door to come home or you and him at the park or playing with fake bones or something. You could probably think of a lot of little scenes like that couldn't you, scenes of those special times? *[Ian nods "yes."]*

**Katie:** OK, great! You'll need some way of tying them all together eventually, maybe a repeating line like Rylant uses. You could even use the line you have here—"Me and Jazz do a lot of special things together"—and write little scenes in between that. Or you could try some different lines, something like, "If dogs are man's best friend, Jazz was a real buddy." Something like that. *[Ian laughs at this line I've written in the air.]* You're laughing! *[I join him laughing for a moment.]* OK—it was kind of corny. Anyway, does this sound workable?

**Ian:** Yes. *[His body language has perked up considerably.]*

**Katie:** I'd do two things, then, first. I'd reread *When I Was Young in the Mountains* to see again how Rylant did this kind of text. Then I'd start a list in your notebook of ideas for little scenes you might write of you and Jazz. OK?

**Ian:** OK.

**Katie:** This sounds like a great idea. I can't wait.

*the kind of things I mean by "little scenes." Examples of what we mean are very important in conferences.*

*I remind him of a feature of many vignette texts, the repeating line. There are other ways I could suggest for how to tie vignettes together, but for the moment I feel that only one suggestion is enough to get him started "seeing" this text. Notice that I write in the air two repeating line possibilities so that he can hear what I mean by this. The laughter is good in the conference. It shows that Ian feels better. I don't want him agonizing over this, like he did at the start. "I'm here to help" is the message I like my conferences to have.*

*I leave this conference with Ian having a plan for exactly what to do next. Notice that I send him to the mentor text to review it as a writer.*

*It did sound like a great idea. I like to leave writers with my own enthusiasm for their plans.*

Now, I know what you may be thinking, because I thought the same thing when I looked at the transcript of this conference. You're wondering about that last note, that "leave writers with my own enthusiasm for *their* plans" part. You're thinking that this was really *my* plan rather than Ian's. You're noticing that I did most of the talking in this conference and just took Ian by the nose and dragged him to a vision for a vignette piece about his dog Jazz. My using this conference as an example makes you a little nervous, I know. It makes me really nervous.

I decided to go public with this conference because I want it in the public domain. I want people to talk about it. I want to generate conversations about how we work with writers like Ian, because we all have them in our writing workshops. It would be nice if we all had only writers like Jovan, if we all had only writers with big plans who just need a little of our input. But we don't. We also have writers like Ian. And because I write as well as teach, I know that any writer can have an "Ian" day, a stuck day. Ian was stuck at a time when all his classmates were preparing drafts for a publication day that was coming up in just a few short weeks. Ian needed help, and I have struggled for years trying to decide on the best ways to help writers like him. Lately, more and more of my conferences with writers like Ian are going a lot like this one.

A few years ago I wouldn't have had a conference like this. I would have told Ian that I would come back to him later when he had more time to think about what he would like to do. But my new repertoire of understandings about the craft of texts has given me confidence to help writers like Ian more when they are stuck. If they can show me even the tiniest glimpse of the meanings they are trying to make, I can usually help them match those meanings to a kind of writing that might work for them. Ian directed me to the page in his notebook that had the vignette statement on it: "Me and Jazz had a lot of special times together." This statement was my information about what meanings he was trying to make. I tried to help him see the amazing potential in that one line, and the plan for writing—the plan I helped Ian *a lot* with—was based on *his* meanings. I believe that sometimes my teaching in conferences has to help students see what's not there yet. I used Ian's meanings to help him see this and to find direction that he didn't have before the conference.

One issue I have struggled with is whether the tone I like in conferring—the "I'm here to help" tone—might make some students (like Ian) too dependent on me. I'm still unsure about this and really think that the answer probably varies with different writers. I need to consider each conference I have with a child in the context of *all* the conferences I have had with him. And with each student that I teach, I need to ask myself the questions, "What is my teaching relationship with this child? Does our relationship as teacher and student have a healthy mix of support and independence?" If it does, then there may very well be times when I help a lot, and other times when I just blow some wind into sails that are already unfurled and moving forward.

In addition to watching out for dependency in individuals, I also have some "rules of thumb" I follow when working with writers like Ian. One is that I will not help writers decide on what meanings they will make. I will give them all kinds of advice and curriculum about how other writers go about finding reasons to write, but in the end, writers must say to me, "I want to write about this" or "I want to say this" or "This is the idea I want to work with." Before I will help, students have to make their own moves toward ideas that matter to them. I am adamant about this. Writing is about having something to say, and that something must come from the writer. Once the writer knows what that is, then yes, I will help him or her think about what to do with this thing that needs saying.

The other rule I follow is that when I help, I have to make sure my help is "bigger" than the piece of writing. The help has to explain something that will stay with the writer for the future. Jovan's help had to be about *flashbacks*, and Ian's help had to be about *vignette pieces*, knowledge they can take to other pieces someday. Lucy Calkins says, "Teach the writer, not the writing," and this is so true if our helping is to be transformed into teaching. If I can be confident that I have really taught a writer something and not just pulled him out of a bind, then my helping becomes about the thing he has learned, not about "Since you can't do this, I'll do it for you."

When having conferences about text structures, your knowledge base will be very important. Carry what you know of different ways to structure texts to your conferences as students are drafting or planning for drafting. Use your knowledge to help direct them to mentor texts, plan their next moves, rethink a structural technique, or decide on a structure for their ideas if they don't have one. Whatever kind of help they need, be ready to pull from what you know of how writers structure texts.

In my conferences about structure,

- I ask questions designed to get writers talking about their visions for the structure of a piece. The question I use most frequently is simply, "How are you thinking you are going to write this?"

- I listen closely for the kinds of meanings the writer is wanting to make.

- I find out if a writer has a structure in mind for a draft. If so then my only job is to help the writer make the structure work well. I listen to find out if the writer needs any further explanation of how a structure works. I try to think of mentor texts that are structured in similar ways and suggest the child look at these.

- I sometimes come to a writer who can think of several ways to structure a piece of writing, but cannot decide which one would be best. I listen to each one and tell the writer the advantages and disadvantages I see with each idea. I'm not afraid to say which one I think would work best. I explain why I think this. In this case I sometimes suggest the writer draft the beginning of each one in a different structure and then we'll look at them and see which one is working best.

- I often encounter writers who have a topic idea but really don't know how to go about writing it. In these cases I first listen to what the child is wanting to do with the topic. Does it sound like the writer wants to write a descriptive piece ("My Grandmother's Garden"), or an informative piece ("Tips for Jet Skiing"), a vignette piece ("Good Times with My Dog"), a single-story piece ("My Trip to Mesa Verde"), a contrast piece ("Being an Only Child/Having a New Sister"), and so on? On the basis of the type of piece it sounds like the writer is wanting to draft, I suggest a few structures that I think might work. With any structure I suggest, I write a little in the air to help the writer really envision what the piece might sound like cast in this structure.

- Sometimes a writer will describe to me a structure he or she is planning to use, and I think as I hear it, "This probably isn't going to work." I usually tell the writer this and explain my misgivings. Sometimes the writer tells me more that I didn't know, which makes the structure make sense, but often I find that the writer agrees and is relieved to have a problematic draft steered in another direction before too much work is done on it. I try and help the writer to think of another possibility that might match the meaning better and work more effectively.

- Once the structure of how the draft will work is established, I try and get mentor texts into the writer's hands that have similar structures.

- I like to keep the tone of possibility very strong in these conferences. I often find myself saying things like, "You know, what would be really cool is if you tried . . ." I want students to know that these conferences are about helping them to make the coolest, grooviest, most radical pieces of writing they can.

## WAYS-WITH-WORDS CONFERENCES

Unlike conferences about structure, ways-with-words conferences almost always happen once students have drafts in hands. These are the conferences that teach students how to match the meanings inside their texts with specific crafting techniques that will bring the writing to life. The conference with Michael at the beginning of this chapter was a ways-with-words conference. In these conferences we look at what writers are doing inside their drafts and we make suggestions for crafting techniques on the basis of what we see.

Let's look at one ways-with-words conference, also from a fourth-grade classroom, which I had with Carlos as he was drafting a piece about his friends called, "My Yearbook":

**Katie:** Carlos, tell me a little about this draft. What are you doing with it?

**Carlos:** I'm doing this story where I find this old yearbook and start looking at it. And I see these pictures of my friends in it, and when I see one, I tell about that friend. I'm

*I don't start these conferences by looking at the draft. I always start by having the writer "tell me about it." I want to hear the writer describe it so that when I do look at the draft, I can make some judgments about whether the writing is in fact matching the writer's meanings. I am care-*

just going to do four friends, or maybe five, I'm not sure. I've got three so far.

**Katie:** Oh that's *so* cool. So it's like you made up the yearbook story so you could tell about your friends, and not just boring tell about them blah, blah, blah, but you know, do it with a story.

**Carlos:** Yeah.

**Katie:** Groovy. May I look at a little bit of it? *[He lets me look at the draft. I quickly read through some of the text he's got so far.]* This kind of thing you're doing reminds me of Gary Soto's book *Snapshots from the Wedding [1997]*. Do you know this book? *[He shakes he head "no."]* OK, well, I'll try and get it for you here in the next day or two. But I can explain to you what I'm thinking. In that book he writes it like he is showing you the photos from the wedding. And he writes stuff along the way that sounds like that, like he's showing you. He tells you stuff just like someone showing you real pictures would tell you. I'm thinking that in your draft you might try putting in some stuff that is like someone who was really looking at a yearbook would say. Like on this page, instead of just going straight to John's picture next, you could write something like, "Oh look,

*ful to look at the writer when I ask this question, not at the draft.*

*I show enthusiasm for what Carlos is doing, and I also sort of define what he's doing for him. When we confirm the way that a student is going about something, it helps to say back to him how he's doing it. This helps to make the technique he is using even more explicit for him and more available for his future use.*

*I connect what Carlos is doing to another writer I know who has written a text with a matching meaning—writing alongside photographs—and I use this connection to show Carlos a crafting technique that can help him with his piece. Notice that I actually write a line in the air for his text that is an example of what I am explaining, so that he can hear what I mean.*

there's a picture of John." So it sounds to the reader like you just saw it and are surprised by it. Does that make sense? To add in comments like that?

**Carlos:** I think so.

**Katie:** OK. Well, I'll get that book for you so you can see how Gary Soto does this, and if you want to try it, I think it might really work nicely in this piece. So if you want to just keep drafting now, I'll see if I can find that. It won't be hard to add this stuff in if you decide you want it.

**Carlos:** OK.

*I leave Carlos with a promise to find him this mentor text, and with the option to try this technique if he likes it after seeing it in another text. I also leave him with advice on what to do next as he's drafting.*

Ways-with-words conferences are about helping students to imagine new possibilities for their texts. Just as in conferences about structure, I have to bring all that I know of different ways-with-words techniques to these conferences, sit this curriculum down alongside my students' writing, and then see what makes sense to teach in the context of the pieces at hand. In these conferences it is also very important that I listen to the kinds of meanings writers are trying to make in their drafts. I want to suggest techniques that match these meanings. This points up the need again for me to know more than just ways-with-words techniques; I need to know the *reasons* writers use them. Students can come to own many crafting techniques fairly easily if I am ready to help them see reasons and opportunities to use them in their actual drafts. This is smart, good-sense teaching, but it requires me both to have a strong knowledge base about craft and to know how to work with students in conferences.

In my conferences about ways with words,

- I have these conferences while students are engaged in drafting or while they are revising.
- I look at the draft and help the writer imagine crafting possibilities on the basis of what he or she is trying to do.

- I'm not afraid to make very specific suggestions. When I do suggest something, I explain why I think the technique would be effective in that part of the text. These explanations are what will help writers come to know when to use certain crafting techniques in future texts. I write a little in the air of what I've suggested so that the writer can hear what it would sound like.

- Whenever possible, I pull a mentor text example so that the writer can see how the crafting technique I am suggesting is used in another text.

- I never suggest more than one or two things in a ways-with-words conference. I don't have time for more, and I don't want to overwhelm the student.

- Again, I like to keep the tone of possibility very strong in these conferences. I often find myself saying things like, "You know, what would be really cool is if you tried . . ." I want students to know that these conferences are about helping them to make the coolest, grooviest, most radical pieces of writing they can.

## CONFERENCES AS DEMONSTRATIONS

As we move about the room conferring with students, we need to remember that we are in fact offering two "chunks" of curriculum for students as we do this. One chunk is the obvious content of the conference, delivered in direct response to the writer's needs. But every time we confer we also offer students a "how-to" course in how writers can work together to help each other. This is "teaching between the lines," but very powerful and real nonetheless. Students will learn a lot about how to help writers from watching us help them and others.

This learning will take place vicariously whether we encourage it or not. All teachers of especially young children have had the experience of hearing their words coming out of students' mouths as they work together. But I want more than vicarious learning to happen. I want students to be intentional in learning from me how to work better with one another as they confer together in the writing workshop. So I tell them this. I encourage them to help each other in the ways I help them, really listening to their classmates and suggesting possibilities for others when they see them. Sometimes I will "fishbowl" conferences for students, gathering them around to watch a conference and take notes on what they see happening. Then we study these notes and think about guidelines we want to follow as we help. Often, I share with students my own theories about the best ways to help—the same information I have shared throughout this chapter.

My vision for the writing workshop is that it be a place where we all pool all that we know to help each other write well. While everyone will have his or her ongoing projects to pursue, no one will be left to "face the writing" alone. We have writers on the bookshelves and writers at the desks next to us, and we are all learning how to learn from each other. The growing, learning, helpful place that is the writing workshop is a great place to be.

## References

Laminack, Lester L., and Katie Wood. 1996. *Spelling in Use: Looking Closely at Spelling Instruction in Whole Language Classrooms.* Urbana, IL: National Council of Teachers of English.

Vygotsky, L. S. 1962. *Thought and Language.* Edited and translated by Eugenia Hanfmann and Gertrude Vakar. Cambridge, MA: MIT Press.

# 14

# Assessment That Focuses Our Eyes on Craft

Imagine this. Imagine you are walking down the halls of an elementary school in the midst of a week-long celebration of children's publishing. The walls are lined from top to bottom with stories and poems and memoirs, essays and letters and alphabet books. The children have written about ponies and super heroes, grandparents and sisters and brothers, dreams for a different world. They have published on posters and in cardboard books, some with glitter and markers and fabulous illustrations, others on simple paper from a word processor. Imagine now that you stop to read a piece that a fourth-grade boy has written entitled "The Wolf."

### The Wolf

It is night. The bright stars shine like diamonds, and all is quiet. Deep in the woods, a wolf tilts its head and howls at the moon. To let the others know that he is king.

He is also inviting the other wolves and saying it is time to look for food. The sun has awakened by the time they are all together. The forest has completed its rest. Now it is time for the wolf to take over the forest.

As they lurk around the forest alert, and ready, ready to strike at movement of any kind. The fierce but shy creature lurks in the forest. Scouting the grounds for tracks of any kind.

The mother must get food for her cubs because without it they could not survive the winter frost. The mother knows she must hurry and find food. It is so cold but she must find food. It is like her body is one big ice cube. But she keeps on going and going until her mission in complete.

Finally night falls and the mother lays to rest with her cubs. She listens to the crickets chirp. She is thinking of tomorrow because she knows that tomorrow is another day. And another fight for survival.

Zachary Harkins

What do you think when you finish reading Zachary's piece? If you are a zoologist you might read "The Wolf" and find yourself critiquing the accuracy of the "facts" about wolves that inform the piece. If you are a lover of wolves, as my husband is, you might find yourself very moved by the motherly survival instincts Zachary conveys so well in the piece. If you are not one to embrace the developmental nature of children's writing and you look at it as he wrote it (facing page), you will likely focus on the spelling approximations and you'll think, "This shouldn't have been put up like this." But if you are a writer, a real writer with a love for words, you are definitely thinking, "This boy is like me. This boy is *a writer*." I mean, just look at what he is doing in this piece.

The very first time I read "The Wolf," what blew me away was the subtle weaving of repetition throughout the piece, the careful close echoes of words which give the piece such rhythm and match the meaning of the daily, repetitive fight for survival in the wild. As I reread, I noticed other, equally stunning features like the simple, three-word beginning, "It is night." I noticed the willingness to personify the sun and the forest, an even more sophisticated writer's move than personifying the wolves, which he also does. I noticed the piece was written in third person with present-tense verbs, a challenging voice for young writers to master. I noticed a writer who really understands that punctuation can help him make meaning, inserting commas and full-period stops between ideas that match the way I imagine Zachary *heard* the piece as he read it to himself. I noticed that the piece was structurally very sound, moving in a full circle from night to night. And I

2-27-97 The Wolf Zachary

It is night. The bright stars shine like
dimonds, and all is quiet. Deep in the
woods, a wolfe tilts its head and howls
at the moon. To let the others know he
is king.

He is also inviting the other wolfs
and saying it is time to look for food.
The sun has awaken by the time they are
all together. The forest has completed it rest.
Now it is time for the wolf to take
over the forest.

As they lerk around the forest
alert, and ready, ready to strike at
movement of any kind. The fierce but
shy creature lerks in the forest. Scouting
the grounds for tracks of any kind.

The mother must get food for her
cubs because without it they could not
survive the winter frost. The mother knows
she must hurry and find food. It is so
cold but she must find food. It is like
her body is one big iceicube. But she
keeps on going and going until her
mission is complete.

Finaly night falls and the mother
lay to rest with her cubs. She listens
to the crickets chirp. She is thinking
of tommorow because she knows. that tomorow
is another day. And another fight for
survival

*"The Wolf," by Zachary*

noticed that Zachary, like so many other accomplished writers, has learned
the power of the conjunctive ending, "And another fight for survival."

As a teacher, my ability to read like a writer has necessarily changed the
way I look at students' writing. The study of craft has given me new eyes to
see things I couldn't see before in my students' ways with words. I am sure

that the Zacharys in my classrooms have been writing amazing things like this for years—I have just missed so much of it because I didn't know how to see it. Once you understand the crafts that cross genres and topics and help writers write well, once these crafts become a part of the language you speak about writing, you will have so much more to look for and so many new things to value in students' writing. Once you have studied craft, you can never walk down that hall (or stay in your classroom) and look at children's writing in the same way.

## ASSESSMENT MATCHES OUR VALUES

Our assessment of student writing, what we can see in what our students do, teaches them so much about what we value in writing. And in many ways, these values we communicate through our assessments come to shape so much of what students believe about writing themselves. Think of the many adults who came to believe writing was a horrible process of exposing all you didn't know to outside readers. This belief was shaped by years of assessment that only looked at what they—as writers—didn't know. Hardly anyone looked to see what they did know. To put it simply, we can ask ourselves this question: "What is the message of what I see in student writing?" Our responsive assessments send very strong messages, and so it is critical that we think carefully and specifically about what we are looking for as we assess student writing.

Assessment should match what we value, and I value many things in a student's development as a writer. I value that a writer has a strong sense of self, and that he or she writes thoughtfully and with purpose using a process that is workable. I value that a writer knows how to be a part of a literate community in which writers take and give response with ease and learn from other writers. I value that a writer knows how to read the world for ideas and use those ideas to write in different genres. I value that a writer knows how to prepare a piece of writing for an audience. I value that a writer uses the knowledge of crafting techniques to strive not just to write adequately, but to write well. These values guide all of my curriculum, instruction, and assessment decisions in the writing workshop. Knowledge of crafting techniques hasn't replaced any of the other values—it is an addition to them—so in this chapter it is this specific value that I would like to consider as an aspect of assessment. What are the signs in our students' work as writers that show us they are using their knowledge of crafting techniques?

## Signs of Intentionality

One sign that I look for in student writing is very evident in Zachary's piece. It is a sign of *intentionality*. What is so obvious in "The Wolf" is Zachary's intention to write this piece well, to write this piece as *literature*. The layers of ways with words that he uses in the piece make it clear that he wasn't just trying to "write something about wolves"; he was trying to capture attention for his piece about wolves, to write well about wolves. I can see very clearly in "The Wolf" an unwritten but very strong message, a message between the lines, if you will, that says to me, "I care about this. I care about what I am writing about, and I want you [the reader] to know that."

The "message between the lines" is evident in the many decisions Zachary made for how he would write the piece. "The Wolf" doesn't sound like talk or thinking or notes on wolves just written down, the kind of writing you get in a notebook. The piece has a deliberately literate tone which separates it from that kind of writing. Zachary used a variety of crafting techniques that he knows, probably explicitly and implicitly, to write the piece as literature. For teachers who encourage students to mentor themselves to experienced writers, signs of this kind of intentionality in a writer's work are very important, and they can be seen at all grade levels. Consider this piece by five-year-old Nicholas Lowe, entitled "Watch How the Wind Blows":

**Watch How the Wind Blows**

Hey bomber man watch how the wind blows!
Hey fireball man watch how the wind blows!
Hey bird watch how the wind blows!

Look at the craft in this piece! Nicholas has taken a passion in his life, a passion many of us roll our eyes at (but probably need to understand as part of the culture of childhood), a passion known as video games, and he's

*"Watch How the Wind Blows," by Nicholas*

*"Hey bomber man watch how the wind blows!"*

turned it into a piece of literature. Nicholas is doing something very different than the five-year-old (or seven-, eight-, or nine-year-old) who writes, "I like to play video games. They are fun." He has sentences that match structurally, a repetitive phrase, and a carefully chosen mark of punctuation which he repeats as well. He shows us that he knows as a writer that he can do more with an idea than just write *about* it; he can use that idea to fashion text into literature, a very sophisticated understanding. Our "eyes for craft" need to help us see what an amazing piece this is. Our long-searching eyes as teachers need to help us see what this moment in time means to Nicholas's development as a writer. What kind of writer will he be in ten or twenty years if he is writing with this kind of intention when he is *five*?

As you look at the products of student writing in your classroom, look for signs that students are crafting in ways that transform their writing into literature, that show they anticipate audience, that are clearly something more than "just writing." Look for signs that they see their writing as belonging on the shelves of your classroom library or on the pages of your magazines and newspapers. Look for students who are trying to write well, on purpose and with intention, using techniques they have learned from reading like writers.

Notice that the emphasis here is not on looking for any specific crafting techniques; the techniques themselves only serve as markers of students' intentions, and it is these intentions that we are most interested in. The curriculum of crafting techniques is only a means to another end, and the "end" is the student who is using this curriculum to fulfill his or her own purposes as a writer. As Lucy Calkins has reminded us so often, we teach the writer, not the writing, and our assessment needs to ultimately look past the writing to the writer. Think of the pieces of writing students produce as providing you with information *about them as writers.*

This kind of focus on information about writers is very different from the check-sheet mentality of so much traditional assessment. In the check-sheet, traditional kind of assessment, we check to be sure students *know certain things* rather than seeing *what things students know.* Now, those two kinds of checking may sound very similar, but moving that word "know" to come after "students" actually shifts our whole paradigm from assessment that is curriculum centered to assessment that is student centered. This shift doesn't mean that curriculum isn't important. It is. This whole book is about filling writing workshops with curriculum that will help students write well. We simply must remember that the curriculum itself is never the point. It's important, but it's not the point. We have to put curriculum into the room and then let it go, let it go into the hands of writers at work.

You see, letting curriculum go lets us know that when we see this curriculum show up in student writing, we have really, truly achieved our goal—to help students write well about what matters to them. What does it matter if we teach everyone to use a repeating line (as Nicholas did), have them all write a piece with a repeating line in it, and check them all off on knowing how to do this? This doesn't show us what we really need to know about what our students can do as writers. What we need to know is whether Nicholas can take a reason of his own to write, choose crafting techniques he knows for writing well, and fulfill his purpose. Our assessment needs to answer *that* question for us. We will want to look very closely at the crafting techniques which individual students are choosing to use as they write—so that we will know what *they know* about what is helping them to write well. Crafting techniques in use in student writing are our best signs that what we value is manifesting itself in our students' intentions as writers.

# CRAFTING TECHNIQUES—SIGNS OF STUDENT INTENTIONS

When you value crafting techniques as signs that students are trying to write well, so many small things they do will become so *big*. You might find that you get really excited about things in student writing that other people read right past. To illustrate, let's look at some writing from Lisa Cleaveland's kindergarten classroom in Brevard, North Carolina. Lisa is a brilliant teacher who, from day one in her writing workshop, leads her very young writers in the study of craft and in learning to write from writers.

Take, for example, this piece by five-year-old Sam Irvin, entitled "The Biggest House":

### The Biggest House

Once upon a time there was a little man that wanted a big house and he kept on building and building and then he finally stopped and rested and then went back to work and building and he thought a minute and he just said "hmm" and just went back to work and building and building and building and building until finally he stopped and rested and went back to work building until . . . he had the biggest house of all. But he wasn't done so he went back to work. The end.

Those ellipsis points, carefully placed after the word "until" and forcing you to turn the page to find out "until what?" are such a *big* deal. In a way, these marks let Lisa inside Sam's head as a writer. They show her that Sam is really

*"and rested and went back to work building*
*until . . .", from "The Biggest House," by Sam*

anticipating readers, anticipating his marks coaxing readers to turn the page and find out what will happen next. What Sam knows about these marks is no different than what Debra Frasier knows. She uses them in *On the Day You Were Born* (1991) again and again, just as Sam does, to connect pages like this:

> you slipped out of the dark quiet
> where suddenly you could hear . . .
> . . . a circle of people singing (n.p.)

Nearby in Lisa's classroom, other young writers are using crafting techniques of their own, and Lisa is ever-watchful for these signs of writers' intentions. Nikolas Shepard uses a repeating line to write about life during the frequent snows they've been having in his small mountain town:

**When it Snows**

When it snows I go sledding.
When it snows I build snowmen.
When it snows I have school.
When it snows it feels cold.
The end.

This piece gives Lisa very important information about Nikolas's knowledge of craft and how he is using it. Nicholas knows that if he has a vignette piece in mind—in this case, all the different things he does when it snows—he can use a repeating line to hold those vignettes together. It's the same knowledge that Cynthia Rylant used in writing *When I Was Young in the Mountains* (1982) and Bert Kitchen used in writing *When Hunger Calls* (1994). Nearby, Nikeyta MacCall uses ellipses, a repeating phrase, a thread-back ending and musical notes to write her "singable book" entitled "I Love My Mom."

**I Love My Mom**

I love . . . my mom.
I love . . . dad.
I love . . . Shelbi.
I love mom, I love dad, I love Shelbi.
The end.

*"When it snows," by Nikolas*

*"When it snows I go sledding"*

*"When it snows I build snowmen"*

*"When it snows I have school"*

*"When it snows it feels cold"*

*"The end"*

*"I love my mom," by Nikeyta*     *"I love . . . my mom"*     *"I love mom, I love dad,
I love Shelbi"*

Lisa will make notes on the sophisticated techniques she sees Nikeyta using in this single piece, adding to her growing storehouse of information about what Nikeyta knows as a writer.

Lisa is blown away when she sees the book that Amanda Whitlock is assembling for publication. It's entitled "I Like the Sun," and it is full of signs that Amanda is intentionally crafting the writing for an audience:

**I Like the Sun**

Written and illustrated by Amanda Whitlock

Dedicated to Ali

When I was five years old I was not in this book stuff.

The sun comes out in the day.
The moon comes out in the night.
The stars come out in the night too.

In addition to the well-crafted structural soundness of the text, Amanda has included other signs in the byline and dedication that let Lisa inside her head and show her teacher that she is making intentional decisions as a

"I like the sun," written and illustrated by
Amanda Whitlock

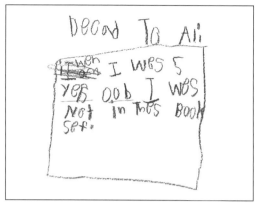

"Dedicated to Ali"
"When I was five years old I was not in
this book stuff."

"The sun comes out in the day"

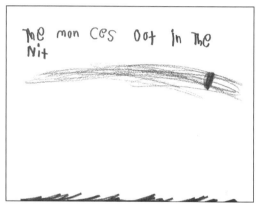

"The moon comes out in the night"

"The stars come out in the night too"

writer. Her "About the Author" statement provides incredibly important assessment information, showing Lisa that Amanda sees her own growth as a writer on a time line of changes.

The ability to see crafting decisions in the work of these young writers is what makes Lisa such an amazing teacher. She understands their work as five-year-olds in a much broader context, envisioning what their work today means to their tomorrows as writers. Her knowledge of craft across many different types of texts allows her to see how incredibly smart her students really are and to trust them with very sophisticated curriculum. Lisa understands that her young writers are doing the same exact things as very experienced, adult writers—they are simply doing them as five-year-olds. But the things themselves are not different—five-year-olds and fifty-five-year-olds understand many of the same things about writing.

Take Nikolas's text "When It Snows." Nikolas knows exactly the same thing that Gary Smith knew when he started six sentences in a row with the same words, "It begins with . . ." in his article in *Sports Illustrated* (see Chapter 2). Both writers understand that you can use a repeating phrase in a text to connect a series of items that go together, together. Nikolas may or may not be able to articulate what he knows, but his writing clearly indicates he understands this crafting technique which Gary Smith uses for a part of his text, and which Nikolas uses for his entire text. Because Lisa knows what this technique looks like in writing by adults, she knows how significant it is when she sees it in the writing of children. Her developmental understanding of craft across texts has given her new eyes for looking at her students' writing.

Lisa's new eyes for craft cause her to see evidence of students mentoring themselves to writers all the time in her classroom. Look at one page from conference notes that she took over two days in her classroom in February (shown on page 282).

Notice the many references to genres (flip-up books and singable books and baggy books); authors (Rod Campbell, Eric Carle); texts (*Amazing Anthony Ant* and *On Top of Spaghetti* and *Oh Dear*); crafting techniques (repeating lines, speech bubbles, musical notes); and aspects of writers' processes (prewriting, co-authoring, taping, continued writing). Notice that she obviously asks her students about their intentions, their

# Writing Workshop: Feb. 27th, 28th
## (also some center time)

| | | | | |
|---|---|---|---|---|
| **Ali** | **Amanda** 2-27 while writing her own flip up book (like Rod Campbell's <u>Dear</u> and <u>Dear Zoo</u>) was singing <u>On Top of Spaghetti</u>—singable book we just read. | **Bryce** 2/28 Making a book at writing center. | **Devin** | **Hanna** 2-27 Brought book from home for me. Making a book like Rod Campbell—A flip up book. After reading to the class she said "I'm going to make a book like that"—I praised her for prewriting/making her own. She mention re-occurring line. |
| **Jacob** | **Jesse** 2-27—made a speech bubble w/words—said he learned how through comic books 2-28—Making a book—a flip up book. Using <u>lots</u> of tape. | **Jessica** | **Jonathan** | **Kari** |
| **Kenny** | **Kyle** | **Larke** 2/28 Wrote about a surprise b-day party for her mom— Kept using a repeating line— "Just because I want it to look nice" still writing at rest time | **Maggie** 2/28 Making a book w/ Maria. She is doing the writing and Maria is illustrating. Reads book—about friends. | **Maria** 2/28 illustrating a book w/ Maggie—during center time |
| **Matthew** | **Melissa** | **Nicholas** 2-28 Writing at center time—making a book "Watch how the wind blows." Said—"I have a repeating line in my book—it is watch how the wind blows" | **Nikeyta** 2/27 wrote about her mom & dad—made sure she put by on front. Made a bookmark for it too. Very proud. Wants to read it to class. Put a yellow dot on it. 2/28—Made a singable book w/ Shelbi—put notes in. Wrote it 1st thing in morning when came to school | **Nikolas** |
| **Sam I** 2/27 had pencil behind his ear—said "I look like a writer" I just think before I write. | **Sam J** 2/28 Sam J co-wrote a book w/ Sam I <u>Sonic goes to the beach.</u> S. J. has been writing about rainbows & the beach a lot. | **Sarah** 2/27 Wanted to make her book a baggy book—feels like an author | **Shelbi** 2-28 Started writing a singable book—sang it and I asked her about what other books look like w/music for singable books. Went and got <u>Amazing Anthony Ant</u> and made musical notes in book | **Taylor** 2-27—said Sam I's sunshine looked like Eric Carle's. |

*Lisa's conference notes*

audiences, their writing mentors, and their crafting decisions. Notice that she thinks about what she already knows about students as writers, commenting on Sam J's current topics and Sarah's feeling like an author. Notice that Sam I's comment about his pencil behind his ear making him "look like a writer" was important assessment information for Lisa, important enough to include in her notes, showing her that Sam is thinking of himself as a writer.

As I watch Lisa teach and talk with her about her teaching, I am impressed with the fact that she seems so often to find what she is looking for in her students' writing. I believe there are two reasons for this. One is that, again, she knows craft well and is able to recognize it in many different texts because she has seen and studied it in many forms. She has done the all-important work of not only coming to know craft herself, but also of coming to understand what that craft looks like developmentally in the writing of the students she teaches. With assessment, there is no substitute for having a strong knowledge base about the many facets of writing and the writing process. The more you know, the more you see in your students' writing.

I believe the other reason Lisa so often finds her very young students trying to craft their writing is that her students know she *expects* them to write in these ways. She asks them repeatedly in conferences about their crafting decisions, and so they begin to see themselves as the kinds of writers who would have answers to those questions. They go to their writing each day knowing they will be asked about how the piece of writing came to be, questions like, "Why did you decide to use a repeating line here?" and "What do other books with music in them look like?" You can see responses to these questions in the notes Lisa took as she worked alongside her young writers. The "hidden curriculum" in the assessment questions Lisa asks during conferences is that students will be decisive writers—and in many ways, assessment *becomes* curriculum in classrooms like Lisa's, the questions she asks again and again teaching students ways to think about their work as writers.

As students get older, the assessment questions we ask about how they are crafting their writing become even more critical. These questions continue to teach older students to think of themselves as writers who would have answers for them. Many upper-grade teachers now incorporate questions about crafting decisions into portfolios and other student self-assessments, asking students to explain crafting decisions they made or places in their texts where they are mentoring other writers. Some really good assessment questions (related to crafting) appear below:

### Before Projects

- How do you envision writing this project?
- How are you planning to use your notebook to support this project?
- What are you reading to help you get ready to write this project?
- Who do you think your audience will be?

On the facing page, you'll see an example of a middle school student planning a writing project by thinking through some of these questions, and you'll see my response to her plans.

I have found that a proposal like this one is a very good management and assessment tool. I have students address questions that teach them a way of envisioning and planning for their writing that is significant to their development as writers. The proposal also serves a contractual function, forcing the writer to say, "This is what I am working on." Often, I will have students give themselves working deadlines on these proposals, much as writers under contract to a publisher are asked to do. Notice that I respond in ways that confirm and extend the writer's plans, trying to maintain the tone of one writer helping out another. Later, when the project is completed, I will have the writer reflect on her plans and comment on how well they did or did not work for her. That's what Sharon, a fifth grader, has done around her plans, shown on pages 286 and 287. These reflections can help young writers gain more and more control over their own writing processes as they are able to reflect and revise after each major project.

Using Post-It notes, I ask students to make process notes all over their drafts and even their final copies of projects. I want them to use these notes to explain things about how the projects came to be—from ideas to final pieces. By asking students to address the same guiding questions again and again as they "Post-It" their drafts, I am teaching them a way of thinking

### My Poetry Project Proposal
#### by Rebecca Pargas

**How do I envision my project?**

My project would be a poetry booklet, with a variety of poems. Most of them would probably be self-reflective or about nature. They might include memories I have from childhood. I'm not sure if there will be a specific theme yet. I will probably submit it for publication to different magazines, just to see how far it can take me. My audience will probably be teenagers like myself, because I will probably include things in this booklet that they could relate to. I am also going to include poems that I could share with my family, because they would be about memories that they would remember and could relate to. If my sister agrees and likes this project, I am hoping that she will illustrate it!

**How am I going to use my notebook?**

I have many different entries about my memories and different problems and topics that I think about at my age. I will take those ideas and some of those exact phrases to make this booklet.

**What stuff will I read to prepare for this?**

I am reading *The House on Mango Street* right now. I am also planning on reading some of Cynthia Rylant's books, which deal with her life and memories from childhood. I will definitely read more poetry and memoirs.

Rebecca,
This sounds like a great project. Let me share something I have done on several occasions. I have made memoir projects as gifts for members of my family and they are the most special gifts in the world. You may want to think about this, especially if your sister is willing to illustrate it. The reading you are doing is right on target for a project like this — also I'll bring some more books week after next. Good luck! ☺ Katie

*Rebecca's project proposal*

> ( This didn't *really* work . ! )
>
> ## Times to work on my project (hopefully)
>
> **MONDAY** WORK ON THIS AND TOPICS OF MY BOOK FOR A WHILE (1/2 TO 2 HOURS
>
> *This worked*
>
> **TUESDAY** TOPIC AND (MAYBE) 1ST DRAFT
>
> **WEDNESDAY** BY NOW I SHOULD AT LEAST HAVE THE TOPIC DECIDED ON, SO I SHOULD DEFINENTLY BE WORKING ON MY 1ST DRAFT AND MAYBE START THINKING ABOUT THE PICTURES
>
> **THURSDAY** TRY TO WORK ON 1ST DRAFT AND MAYBE FINAL COPY, AFTER READING IT TO SOMEONE AND MAKING CHANGES
>
> **FRIDAY** FINAL COPY AND WORK ON PICTURES
>
> *This didn't*
>
> **SATURDAY** FINISH HALF OF BOOK (THIS MIGHT TAKE A WHILE)
>
> **SUNDAY** FINISH OTHER HALF, WORK ON COVER
>
> **MONDAY** FINISH COVER
>
> *** THURSDAY AND DOWN- WORK ON PUTTING NOTES BY EVERYTHING ***

*Sharon's project schedule*

that I hope will permeate the actual process of writing. Here are some of the kinds of questions I ask students to address with these notes:

### During and After Drafting

- Why were you writing this? Where did you get your reason to write?
- What things are you trying in your writing?
- Who are the writers you are learning from? How and what are you learning from them?

# WRITING PROJECT
### A PICTURE BOOK

JUNE
15 and 16
1995

### ***HOW DO I ENVISION MY PROJECT?***

**1.) HOW WILL I USE MY NOTEBOOK TO DO MY PROJECT?**
I will try to use different entries for ideas and try to think of different ideas to write down.

**2.) WHAT WILL I READ THAT WILL GET ME TO WRITE?**
Different kinds of picture books.

**3.) WHAT KIND OF AUDIENCE WILL I HAVE?**
Probably younger children, anywhere from 4 to 8 years old.

**4.) HOW WILL IT BE PUBLISHED?**
As a single book, not in a series or a magazine or anything.

**5.) WHAT HAVE I READ THAT IS LIKE THIS?**

*I liked the pictures*

1.) <u>WHEN I WAS LITTLE</u>  by Jamie Lee Curtis
2.) <u>A CHAIR FOR MY MOTHER</u> by Vera B. Williams
3.) <u>THE RELATIVES CAME</u>  by Cynthia Rylant
4.) <u>THE SALAMANDER ROOM</u> by Anne Mazer

**WHAT I LIKED ABOUT THESE STORIES**
**1.)** it was funny; good pictures
**2.)** pictures were descriptive
**3.)** all of the above
**4.)** pictures were descriptive

\* Normally I like past tense but for my project I did present tense. \*

### °°°THE FIRST THREE STORIES WERE IN 1ST PERSON°°°
and I liked that.

*Sharon's project proposal*

- Where are the places in this piece where you really tried to craft the writing?

- What decisions did you make as you were writing?

- What can you tell me about your beginning (ending, structure, audience, etc.)?

On pages 288–290, you can see some process notes on two of Rebecca's poems in her poetry anthology.

**Just a Game**

She steps behind the line,
like so many times before.
Takes a deep breath,
sweat glistening on her forehead.
Shaking with excitement,
nervousness,
anxiety,
fear.
The crowd is quiet,
she looks up at them.
Where is everyone?
All her supporters,
her loved ones?
She squints,
but finds no one.
No one.
She is all alone.
So important
so intense,
Her breath comes in raspy, short
gulps.
This is it.
They are all depending on her, and
It is time, now.
She tosses up the ball,
Striking it with all her might.
It glides through the air,
a bullet toward
The Enemy.
Perfect, aimed.
But, as it
travels over the net,
it touches it
so slightly.
Tickles it
so slightly.

June 25, '95
Draft #1

I really don't know
how or where I got the
idea for this, especially
because I love volleyball!
The idea just came,
and the words just
flowed into my head
and then onto the
paper one quiet,
Sunday morning.

I used a lot of
repitition in this
poem for emphasis.

This got long really
fast! I couldn't
figure out how to
shorten it

*Rebecca's poem "Just a Game"*

Devastation beyond belief.
"It's okay."
they console her.
"There's more to play. Besides,
it's just a game."
Just a Game.
Yes, she tells herself,
But, if only, she thinks.
If only.
And it troubles her in her sleep
when she relives it
again and again.
Just a Game, she tells herself.
But she can never love it
again.
Cowers from any sport, competition, challenge
until she
forgets how it all started.
All that's left is the fear,
Lives with a gnawing fear,
yet she knows not why.
But her memory will whisper to her again,
Late at night
When the action of life
Cannot protect her.
Just a game, it taunts,
Just a Game.
Or is it?

*Rebecca's poem "Just a Game" (continued)*

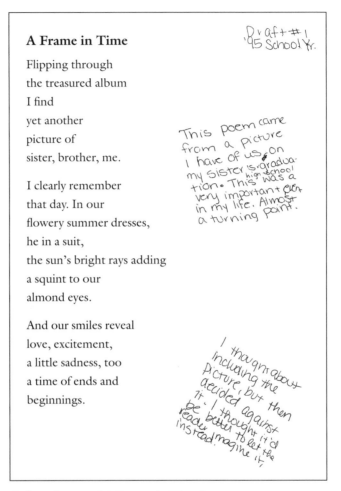

**A Frame in Time**

Flipping through
the treasured album
I find
yet another
picture of
sister, brother, me.

I clearly remember
that day. In our
flowery summer dresses,
he in a suit,
the sun's bright rays adding
a squint to our
almond eyes.

And our smiles reveal
love, excitement,
a little sadness, too
a time of ends and
beginnings.

Draft #1
'95 School Yr.

This poem came from a picture I have of us on my sister's graduation. This was a very important event in my life. Almost a turning point.

I thought about including the picture, but then decided against it. I thought it'd be better to let the reader imagine it instead.

*Rebecca's poem "A Frame in Time"*

When students think about their writing in these ways, they are really required to think of each piece as *something that came to be* in their writing lives, not just as a writing sample, not just another piece of school paper. As they talk about how the pieces came to be, the story of each piece becomes an important chapter in the unfolding story of their writing lives. And so while this serves an important assessment function, the process is also curriculum, teaching students a way of thinking about their writing that they can carry with them to other pieces, other purposes.

# KNOWING WHAT STUDENTS KNOW

Questions about crafting decisions also help teachers know what writers understand about the crafting techniques they are using. I am frequently asked about students using more risky crafting techniques: "How do I know if the sentence fragment this student used was intentional or not?" You ask the student. Students should be using this kind of crafting technique with intention, not by accident because they don't understand conventional sentence structure. So ask them. I am careful to ask them in just this way. I say, "Tell me about this part of your draft," and I point to the part where the sentence fragment is located in the text. I listen for intention in the student's response and can usually tell rather easily whether something was intentional. There are usually four scenarios that will follow:

1. The fragment (or any other more risky technique) wasn't intentional but works well in the text. In this case I explain to the student the crafting technique he or she has used, why it works in the text, and how it is often used.

2. The fragment was not intentional, and it doesn't work well in the text. In this case I show the student how to make it a conventional sentence and explain why it doesn't work in the text.

3. The fragment was intentional, but it doesn't really work in the text. In this case I explain why I think it doesn't work well so that the student can consider a rewrite.

4. The fragment was intentional and works well in the text. In this case, we celebrate!

This kind of assessment about, especially, the more risky techniques gives me the peace of mind that I need as a teacher to know that students really own the techniques they are using. If a student can use a sentence fragment for effect *on purpose* and can articulate this to me, then he or she can also be purposeful in *not* writing sentence fragments if the situation and audience warrant it. Remember, again, to look past the writing to the writer. Use your assessment to invite students to help you understand what they know about the writing you see.

## ASSESSMENT THAT EMPOWERS YOUNG WRITERS

When we think of assessment, we can't help but think historically, and in writing so many of us remember assessment as something aimed at putting us squarely in our place, something that would show us all we didn't do and didn't know. Now, as teachers, we still use assessment to help us see what students need to know, but our response to that doesn't have to make students feel stupid or small. Our response can be one of helpfulness. The more we know about writing, the easier it is to respond as a helper. I think that in the past, many responses were not helpful because we responded out of frustration; we didn't really know *how* to help students, even if we had wanted to help. Learning to write from writers has given us a greater repertoire for helpfulness, and we can use that to our students' advantage.

In addition to showing what students need to know, assessment can and should help us see what students *already know*, and it should help them to see this too. The more we as teachers know about writing, the more we can see of what our students know, and we can use what we see to respond to them in ways that are empowering. When assessment is an invitation to our students to think decisively about their own writing, they will show us again and again how they are thinking and growing and living as writers.

## AND AFTER "THE END" WE RESPOND

Response. I have come to believe it is the single most important factor in my relationship with the student writers I teach. How I respond to them in inquiry, in conferences, in small and large groups, is absolutely critical. If I really value their developing identities as writers, as I say I do, then my responses have to show them I value this. My responses have to show them, every day, that I really think of them as writers. And perhaps there is no time when this is more important than after they have written, "The End."

If we spend our school years teaching students to learn to write from writers, then it is essential that we respond to their work in just the same way that we respond to any other writer. Once their writing is finished, there is nothing left for us to be but *readers*. Our last response to student projects has to be a literary response. We need to let students know that they have moved us with words, caused us to laugh or sigh or remember. We need to respond in ways that show students we have looked at their writing as *literature*.

Two summers ago I taught a writing workshop for middle school students in South Carolina. During the month-long workshop we kept notebooks, studied the craft of writers' office work and the craft of all kinds of beautiful texts. We took part in response groups, and we wrote and wrote and wrote alongside the great writers on our library shelves. Each student in that workshop developed one major writing project for the summer. Some wrote historical fiction, some science fiction, some realistic fiction, some picture books, and several made poetry anthologies. All along the way these students received all kinds of assessment response to their work-in-progress, from me and from the other students. But when it was all said and done, when my time to stop teaching had come to its end, I took each of their project portfolios and I sat at my computer and I wrote every one of them a response, straight from my reading, living heart.

Aaron was in between fifth and sixth grade, and he had done a poetry anthology for his project. In his portfolio he included over twenty-five final poems, drafts of the poems, and copies of notebook entries that led to the poems. Here is the response I wrote to Aaron:

June 29

Dear Aaron,

I first looked through the copies from your notebook and I was so moved by the two pages that led to the roller coaster poem. The first one—the entry when you work through finding your own richness—and then the poem draft that captures so well the heart of what you were trying to say about your life. This is a writer's notebook at its best—thoughts leading you to drafts.

Next, I looked quickly for the nature poem because I was anxious to see how it had evolved. I like the way the speaker in the poem is sitting right in the middle of all the nature things that are happening—like the speaker is wrapped up in it—in the wind and the weeds and the sun—like we really are by nature. And this helps to get across the idea of how man's feelings can also be so pushed and pulled by what's happening in nature. Very nice.

I loved the mouthwash poem when you read it to us yesterday, and I loved seeing it on the page. It reminds me of a mystery sort of poem and could very well be one if you chose not to tell the reader that it's mouthwash you are talking about. The taking something ordinary and making it significant is so much what poetry is about—finding the significance in ordinary things—and you've certainly done that here.

In the poem "Beauty and Love" there are certain phrases that made me stop and read them again because they were striking: "deep look" and "breathe in the beauty" and "noisy silence" and "spreading meadow" were a few that really struck me. These phrases remind me of what I've learned about Cynthia Rylant and how she doesn't use a lot of describing words but the ones she does use she chooses with great care. You choose with great care here too.

I felt very connected when I read the poem about your brother Nate. I guess this is because I got to meet him yesterday and was very impressed with him—he seems just the way you describe him in this poem and I can see why you look up to him. One of the powers I hope you never forget is how writing can help us sustain relationships by helping us say what really needs saying sometimes.

The poem "Freedom" with the illustration of the eagle was really interesting because, of course, the eagle made me wonder if this was an eagle speaking in the poem. Which if it is gives it many layers of meaning which make me think. I wonder what the flame is that needs quenching—a willful spirit maybe?

Finally I'm going to comment on "Rain" because it will help me to explain what I've noticed about you as a writer and a poet. The thing that really defines you (for me) as a writer, and especially as a poet, is that you don't just see things and write about them—you see yourself *into* and *onto* things. Everything you observe seems to make you think about what's of value in your life. Like the rain making "the wanting creep" over you and "the lightening" crashing at your back. In this poem these elements feel so lonely as you translate yourself onto them. It is a very powerful poem, Aaron.

Keep writing!

Fondly,
Katie


Try and imagine that you are an eleven-year-old boy reading this response to your writing. How would you feel? How do you think you would feel the next time you embarked on a writing project? Can you imagine how you would return to your writing each time if you received responses like this to what you had done?

There is nothing that makes us feel like writers more than to have someone respond to what we have written as *readers*. If we want our students to understand this function of published writing—this function to entertain, delight, appall, inform, anger, or sadden readers—then we must respond to the writing they do in our classrooms in ways that show them this. Maybe I think more of my teaching than I should, but I really believe that the fifteen minutes or so it took me to write this response to Aaron is a fifteen-minute investment that will change his life. I believe that teaching is that big. I believe that it matters that much.

## Learning to Respond

When I look closely at what I write in response to students' projects, I see that there are a few predictable kinds of responses I make, and you can see almost all of them in the letter to Aaron because it is a long response to a major project. When I write a response I might

- Connect the student's writing to the writing of another author.
- Comment specifically on craft, quoting phrases and words that are striking.
- Name for the student something I see him or her doing with the writing.
- Make a comment about how the piece fits into the body of the student's work over time.
- Mention the parts that really sound good to me, quoting actual parts of the writing.
- Tell the student what the writing makes me think about, remember.
- Share what I may have learned from the content of the piece.
- Share questions that the writing raised for me.

You might look back through the letter to Aaron and see if you can identify these various kinds of responses.

Notice that not once do I say any direct form of "Good work" or "Marvelous job" or "Fabulous." These expressions of praise are empty. They don't really say anything about the writing at all. These aren't responses. They are *labels for responses*—the teaching equivalent of "telling instead of showing."

Several years ago I heard Donald Graves speak and he said, "Praise never helps a writer." And I remember being taken aback by that. I remember thinking, "Well I think praise really helps me as a writer!" But as I've grown as a writer and a teacher, I have come to understand what this much wiser teacher meant. And I believe he was right. Students don't need me to sing them my empty praises. They need me to tell them what moves me when I read what they have written, tell them what words won't stop thundering in my ears, tell them what images have curled up inside my mind's eye. My students need me to be a reader for them. A reader who loves their work, yes. But a reader, not a cheerleader shouting meaningless sideline praises.

## Our Responses Teach

Your responses to writing can serve as demonstrations for students of how to respond to each other's writing. You can share lists like the one above and actually teach students about how to respond. I like for writers to get as many readerly responses to their writing as possible, but students sometimes need help knowing how to do this for one another. Over time, though, your responses to each one of them will show them how this is done.

I believe that *writing* responses for students is really important. A written response gives writers something tangible to hold in their hands, something to take away, to share with others, and to read again and again. Of course, with my youngest writers, I might have to read them the response I have written, but I still think it is important that they can hold my response in their little writers' hands.

Many responses to completed projects are much shorter than the one to Aaron. They don't have to be long to be powerful. What matters is the quality of what you say, the reading-response quality that shows students you think of their writing as literature. Let's look now at some shorter responses to single pieces completed by a group of fourth-grade writers.

Justin had completed a writing project about eagles, his favorite animal. The genre was memoir, and in the piece Justin told about once having an eagle for a pet. Here is the response I gave him:

Dear Justin,

I've never known anyone who had an eagle for a pet! He must be an amazing creature to watch and play with. I couldn't get over how much you said he eats. Was he just really hungry that time, or do eagles eat that much usually? I love the line, "I then took him out for a fly." Very clever, playful language—a play on "taking him out for a walk." Also, when you used the question to the readers asking them if they've ever taken care of an eagle, that's a really neat writing technique, sort of talking right to the reader.

Good luck and keep writing.

Notice the direct response to the content of Justin's piece, opening with an exclamation that shows him he's amazed me. I honor his expertise by sharing with him that he taught me something I didn't know about eagles. I quote from his text, defining for him what he has done with his play on words and his direct contact with the reader.

Christie writes a descriptive piece about spring bunnies in a field, and in this response to her writing I let her know which parts are especially visual and descriptive for me as a reader. I like to quote very directly from students' writing in my responses. Notice that I begin this note that way. There is no other honor quite like being quoted as a writer. I comment specifically on a technique she has used, and compare her use of the circling effect with Cynthia Rylant's writing. Notice again that I'm naming things I see her doing, extending response into teaching by confirming these techniques:

Dear Christie,

"Yellow daisies that grow in patches in the fields." I love this line. It is very visual. You made these rabbits come to life—just doing as they please. I love the way you have "scampering" at the beginning and the end. This is a neat writing technique. It reminds me of Cynthia Rylant's *The Relatives Came*. She does that same thing—begins and ends the same way. The opening "Let's hop down" is neat too. Sort of like talking right to your reader.

    Good luck and keep writing.

My response to Sara's nature poetry shows that she has really captured my emotional attention, and I don't shy away from letting students know that they've tugged at my heart:

Dear Sara,

You write like an artist, each line, each phrase a carefully painted picture. I am wondering, do you visualize these things before you write them? It seems like you must really see them and then use the words as a paintbrush to capture what you see. The line "it is like you can't describe the feeling of your heart" really spoke to me. I know just what you mean. Sometimes life is so beautiful it's like the words just aren't big enough. You have a poet's heart, Sara.

    Good luck and keep writing.

In this response I ask Sara a question about her process "do you visualize things before you write them?"—which shows I am truly impressed with whatever process she has used to help her to these words. These questions have the tone of one writer speaking to another writer, a tone of "I'd really like to know how you do what you do." I show Sara that she has captured a big meaning for me, stating for her my connection that sometimes the words just aren't big enough. And finally, I tell Sara something very directly that I believe about her, that she has a poet's heart.

    I stand in awe at the power our words as teachers can have in students' lives. I am fearful of the strength of one negative word and how it can live with someone forever. But I rejoice at the idea that just a few simple, honest words of support and belief can also stay with someone for a very long time. "You have a poet's heart, Sara." Words to build a life upon.

# 15

# NEVER TO TEACH ALONE AGAIN

Jolene loved animals; anyone could tell. She wore wolves on her T-shirts, birds on her homework folder, a ring made of tiny dolphins. She talked about animals and dreamed about animals and drew pictures of animals she longed to see someday. In ten short years of her life, she had found a passion for living things.

As I visited in her fifth-grade classroom over time, I came to know her as "the girl who loves animals," and she came to know me as "that lady who loves writing." And when we met one morning, two passionate people in a writing workshop, I couldn't have known then what I know now—that the encounter with Jolene would become a benchmark in my teaching life.

Jolene came over to where I was sitting and she handed me a piece of paper. Then she said just exactly this:

Look at this poem I wrote. It doesn't make any sense, but it rhymes.

And just at that moment, just as she finished saying it, my eyes looked down and I saw the title of the poem, "Dolphins." And what I have to tell you is that before I even read the poem, my heart sank. My heart sank because "the girl who loves animals" had written a poem about dolphins that *didn't make any sense*. I mean, animals made more sense to Jolene than to anyone I knew. She understood their beauty, their freedom to roam and swim and fly high above her. Jolene *loved* animals. Why would she write about dolphins and not make any sense? I was *teachless*. No words came out as a response to what she had said about the piece in front of me, so I went ahead and quietly read her poem.

### Dolphins

I know a dolphin
He was so sweet
He is a mammal
Just like a camel
He might eat meat
He swims in the ocean
with a lot of motion
They swim together
They don't have any feathers.

After I read "Dolphins," Jolene's comment about it seemed even more perplexing to me. Actually, it did make some sense. The poem showed that Jolene knew things about dolphins—they are mammals, they swim in the ocean, and they don't have feathers. It certainly wasn't what I would call a nonsense poem. So why would she say it doesn't make any sense? Not know-

*Jolene's poem "Dolphins"*

ing exactly where to go with the situation, I decided to see if I could use Jolene's own words to nudge her in a different direction. I said,

> Jolene, this is very interesting, especially what you said about it—that it rhymes but doesn't make any sense. You must have concentrated very hard on making it rhyme. [She nods "yes" in response to this.] You know what I'm wondering? I'm wondering if you could do just the opposite. If you could write a poem that makes sense but doesn't rhyme, because I know you really love dolphins and know a lot about them, so you would know lots of things to say.

At first, a look crossed over Jolene's face like she wanted to say, "Why on earth would anyone want to do that? Write a poem that doesn't rhyme?" But then she kind of shrugged her shoulders and said, "OK. I could try that." We agreed to meet again a little later to see what she came up with.

Before long, Jolene motioned to me from across the room that she had something, and as quickly as I could I went to check in with her. She had done it. She showed me proudly a new dolphins poem that did, in fact, make sense and not rhyme.

### Dolphins

Dolphins live in the ocean
They swim in schools
They are very intelligent creatures
Also mammals.

As I read through the new poem draft, my heart sank back down again. Jolene had done exactly as I suggested and had ended up with a poem as dry

*Jolene's second dolphin poem*

as toast. I mean, it just didn't *sound* like poetry anymore. At least the first one had been fun to read. As I read it aloud to her, I could tell she would think I was crazy if I suggested that somehow this was an improvement. I had gotten us into this mess, and it was up to me to get us out. Would she let me nudge her one more time? I had to try, at least. I really wanted Jolene to learn (today, by George) that poetry was a way to express real things, true things. So I said:

> Well, you did it, Jolene. *This one* makes sense. [There's a long dramatic pause here as I let this sink in and think what I will say next. I decide to take the honest approach.] I'm really thinking that now we just need one more thing. We need some pretty words for what you want to say, some words that show you don't just know things about dolphins, but that you also really like them. Do you know what I mean? [Her look says, "Maybe, but I'm not sure." I decide to show her what I mean.] Like instead of saying "They swim," you might say "they dance through the waves." Stuff like that to give it a poetry sound and show how you feel about them. Do you think you could try it that way, one more time?

And with unbelievable patience for that lady who loves writing, the girl who loves animals went away to write her poem about dolphins for the *third* time that morning. When she returned a few minutes later she showed me this:

**Dolphins**

Deep below the sea where there are
many wonders lives the dolphin
The graceful dancers play together
The creatures are intelligent as well as beautiful
They are like us. Mammals.

I picked my heart up off the floor, gave Jolene a big hug, and said, "I knew you had it in you. Just *look* at what you've done here. Just listen to what you've written." And I read it aloud to her in my best read-aloud voice, and she smiled.

*Jolene's final dolphin poem*

Driving back to the university that morning, I thought about what Jolene had said about her first dolphins poem: "It doesn't make any sense." I think that what Jolene was trying to say was this: "This poem in no way represents anything I would ever really want to say about dolphins." She wasn't *trying* to make sense as she wrote it—she was trying to rhyme. She thought this was what poets do. And so even though I helped her rewrite until she had something a little better, the teaching was sort of misdirected because Jolene hadn't started out trying to say anything meaningful about dolphins. I had made the writing better, but had I really taught the writer anything?

Jolene was a young woman just full of passion who wanted to write poetry. She needed more than just help using "pretty language." She needed mentors who could show her how passionate people write poetry. I could help her here and there with single poems, maybe, but to really grow and develop as a writer of poems she would need more than I could give her. I found myself, once again, loading all my poetry books into boxes, hauling them in the back of my truck to yet another school.

I left the books in Jolene's classroom with not much more than a "Here, read these" bit of advice. It would be almost two weeks before I would be able to return to be a part of their writing workshop, but I wanted Jolene and her friends to have a chance to read as much poetry as they could in the meantime. Just a few days after leaving the books, I was working in my office at the university, when one of my college students stopped by. Sara was an intern in Jolene's fifth-grade classroom. She handed me a folded-up piece of paper. "Jolene sent this to you," she said. I opened it. A new poem.

## Save Our Animals and the Earth

Save the animals. They need us,
And we need them.
Venus has no life nor any other planet but Earth.
Earth is our home. We need to save it.

The world will be nothing if we don't save it.
Has our mind gone? Do we have no sense?
Earth is our home. We need to save it.

A Do-Do Bird is an animal, and there are no more of them. Why?
Need I say?
It is we who are killers, all of us.
Mankind could come to an end soon
And this is because of cars, hunting, litter, and more.
Lucky we are! The earth has not come to an end already.
So, if you were listening, earth is our home. We need to save it.

Anything can live now, but we are on the edge of destruction.
Need I not remind you
Do not sit back. Earth is our home. We have little time to save it.

The machines we have now are for relaxation, but we need to—
Have to—pick up our act ourselves. We made it and we are too lazy to pick it up.
Everything is not ours, but the earth is our home, and we have little time to save it.

Everything on earth is not ours
And we destroy everything like it can be replaced.
Right. Am I right. Is that how you feel. Well let me tell you something, buddy,
That is the wrong thing to think on this planet.
Have you any sense? The earth is our home, and we have little time to save it.

Now are you still listening to me? Get
Out there and start picking up.
Wow! You listen to me. I've been saying to you that earth is our home and we
need to start saving it.

Now get to work and stop listening to me.

—Jolene Mae Jurss

There she is. The girl who loves animals. Making sense, lots and lots of sense.

This time my heart didn't sink. This time my heart took a huge leap, turned a cartwheel inside my chest. Writing under the influence of poets like Eloise Greenfield, Nikki Grimes, Georgia Heard, Marilyn Singer, Joyce Carol Thomas, Jane Yolen, Lee Bennett Hopkins, and scores of others, Jolene had discovered that poetry offered her a powerful way to let her passionate voice be heard. In this poem she was making, quite possibly, more sense than she had ever made before in her writing life. Jolene had become a living, breathing poet with big, important things to say.

And as for that lady who loves writing, well, let's just say you won't catch her out in a classroom anymore without her beloved books. She's bought a cart to haul them in. She's shopping for a bigger truck. . . .

# Bibliography

Aardema, Verna. 1981. *Bringing the Rain to Kipiti Plain: A Nandi Tale*. Illustrated by Beatriz Vidal. New York: Dial.

Arnold, Katja, with Sam Swope. 1997. *Katja's Book of Mushrooms*. New York: Holt.

Asch, Frank, and Ted Levine. 1998. *Cactus Poems*. San Diego: Harcourt Brace.

Baylor, Byrd, and Peter Parnell. 1978. *The Other Way to Listen*. New York: Scribner.

Bedard, Michael. 1997. *The Divide*. Illustrated by Emily Arnold McCully. New York: Doubleday.

Berry, James. 1996. *Rough Sketch Beginning*. Illustrated by Robert Florczak. San Diego: Harcourt Brace.

Bouchard, David. 1995. *If You're Not from the Prairie*. Illustrated by Henry Ripplinger. New York: Atheneum.

Brown, Margaret Wise. 1949. *The Important Book*. Illustrated by Leonard Weisgard. New York: Harper and Row.

Bruchac, Joseph. 1997. *Many Nations: An Alphabet of Native America*. Illustrated by Robert Goetzl. Philadelphia: Bridgewater.

Bunting, Eve. 1994. *Night of the Gargoyles*. Illustrated by David Wiesner. New York: Clarion.

———. 1996. *The Blue and the Gray*. Illustrated by Ned Bittinger. New York: Scholastic.

———. 1996. *Secret Place*. Illustrated by Ted Rand. New York: Clarion.

———. 1997. *Moonstick: The Seasons of the Sioux*. Illustrated by John Sandford. New York: HarperCollins.

Burleigh, Robert. 1998. *Home Run*. Illustrated by Mike Wimmer. San Diego: Harcourt Brace.

Cabrera, Jane. 1997. *Cat's Colors*. New York: Dial.

Cadnum, Michael. 1997. *The Lost and Found House*. Illustrated by Steve Johnson and Lou Fancher. New York: Viking.

Carle, Eric. 1987. *The Very Hungry Caterpillar*. New York: Philomel.

Carlson, Nancy L. 1997. *ABC I Like Me!* New York: Viking.

———. 1998. *It's Going to Be Perfect*. New York: Viking.

Carlstrom, Nancy White. 1997. *Raven and River*. Illustrated by Jon Van Zyle. New York: Little, Brown.

Cisneros, Sandra. 1991. *House on Mango Street*. New York: Vintage.

Collard, Sneed B. 1992. *Do They Scare You?* Illustrated by Kristin Kest. Watertown, MA: Charlesbridge.

Conrad, Pam. 1995. *Our House: Stories of Levittown*. New York: Scholastic.

Cooke, Trish. 1994. *So Much*. Illustrated by Helen Oxenbury. Cambridge, MA: Candlewick.

Curtis, Jamie Lee. 1993. *When I Was Little*. Illustrated by Laura Cornell. New York: HarperCollins.

———. 1996. *Tell Me Again about the Night I Was Born*. Illustrated by Laura Cornell. New York: HarperCollins.

Cushman, Karen. 1994. *Catherine, Called Birdy*. New York: Harper.

Davies, Nicola. 1997. *Big Blue Whale*. Illustrated by Nick Maland. Cambridge: MA: Candlewick.

Davol, Marguerite W. 1996. *How the Snake Got His Hiss*. Illustrated by Mercedes McDonald. New York: Orchard.

Dewey, Jennifer Owings.1998. *Mud Matters: Stories from a Mud Lover*. New York: Cavendish.

Draper, Sharon. 1996. *Tears of a Tiger*. New York: Aladdin.

Dunbar, Joyce, and Gary Blythe. 1996. *This Is the Star*. New York: Harcourt Brace.

Dunphy, Madeleine. 1995. *Here is the Southwestern Desert*. Illustrated by Anne Coe. New York: Hyperion.

Eaton, Deborah, and Susan Halter. 1997. *No One Told the Aardvark*. Illustrated by Jim Spense. Watertown, MA: Charlesbridge.

Erickson, Paul. 1997. *Daily Life in a Covered Wagon*. New York: Puffin.

Fleming, Denise. 1996. *Where Once There Was a Wood*. New York: Holt.

Fletcher, Ralph. 1997. *Twilight Comes Twice*. Illustrated by Kate Kiesler. New York: Clarion.

Florian, Douglas. 1998. *Insectlopedia*. San Diego: Harcourt Brace.

Fox, Mem. 1985. *Wilfrid Gordon McDonald Partridge*. Illustrated by Julie Vivas. Brooklyn: Miller.

———. 1994. *Sophie*. Illustrated by Aminah Brenda Lynn Robinson. New York: Harcourt Brace.

———. 1994. *Tough Boris*. Illustrated by Kathryn Brown. San Diego: Harcourt Brace Jovanovich.

———. 1997. *Whoever You Are*. Illustrated by Leslie Staub. San Diego: Harcourt Brace.

Frasier, Debra. 1991. *On the Day You Were Born*. San Diego: Harcourt Brace Jovanovich.

———. 1998. *Out of the Ocean*. San Diego: Harcourt.

Garza, Carmen Lomas. 1996. *In My Family/En Mi Familia*. San Francisco: Children's Book.

George, Jean Craighead. 1993. *Dear Rebecca, Winter Is Here*. Illustrated by Loretta Krupinski. New York: HarperCollins.

———. 1995. *Everglades*. Illustrated by Wendell Minor. San Francisco: HarperCollins.

———. 1997. *Look to the North: A Wolf Pup's Diary*. Illustrated by Lucia Washburn. San Francisco: HarperCollins.

Gilchrist, Jan Spivey. 1997. *Madelia*. New York: Dial.

Gillette, J. Lynett. 1997. *Dinosaur Ghosts: The Mystery of Coelophysis*. Illustrated by Doug Henderson. New York: Dial.

Gravett, Christopher. 1997. *The Knight's Handbook*. New York: Cobblehill.

Gray, Libba Moore. 1995. *My Mama Had a Dancing Heart*. Illustrated by Raúl Colón. New York: Orchard.

Greenfield, Eloise. 1986. *Honey, I Love, and Other Love Poems*. Illustrated by Diane and Leo Dillon. New York: Harper.

———. 1988. *Nathaniel Talking*. Illustrated by Jan Spivey Gilchrist. New York: Black Butterfly.

———. 1993. *Childtimes*. New York: Harper.

———. 1997. *For the Love of the Game: Michael Jordan and Me*. Illustrated by Jan Spivey Gilchrist. New York: HarperCollins.

Grimes, Nikki. 1994. *Meet Danitra Brown*. Illustrated by Floyd Cooper. New York: Trumpet.

———. 1996. *Come Sunday*. Illustrated by Michael Bryant. Grand Rapids, MI: Eerdmans.

———. 1997. *It's Raining Laughter*. Photographs by Myles C. Pinkney. New York: Dial.

Hall, Donald. 1994. *I Am the Dog, I Am the Cat*. Illustrated by Barry Moser. New York: Dial.

Haynes, Max. 1997. *In the Driver's Seat*. New York: Bantam.

Heard, Georgia. 1992. *Creatures of Earth, Sea, and Sky: Poems*. Illustrated by Jennifer Owings Dewey. Honesdale, PA: Wordsong.

Herron, Carolivia. 1997. *Nappy Hair*. Illustrated by Joe Cepeda. New York: Knopf.

Hesse, Karen. 1997. *Out of the Dust*. New York: Scholastic.

Hopkins, Lee Bennett. 1995. *Been to Yesterdays: Poems of a Life*. Illustrated by Charlene Rendeiro. Honesdale, PA: Wordsong/Boyds Mills.

Houston, Gloria. 1992. *My Great Aunt Arizona*. Illustrated by Susan Condie Lamb. New York: HarperCollins.

Howard, Elizabeth F. 1991. *Aunt Flossie's Hats (and Crabcakes Later)*. Illustrated by James Ransom. New York: Clarion.

James, Simon. 1991. *Dear Mr. Blueberry*. New York: McElderry.

Janeczko, Paul B. 1998. *That Sweet Diamond*. Illustrated by Carole Katchen. New York: Atheneum.

Jessup, Harley. 1997. *What's Alice Up To?* New York: Viking.

Johnson, Angela. 1996. *The Aunt in Our House.* Illustrated by David Soman. New York: Orchard.

Johnson, Paul Brett, and Celeste Lewis. 1996. *Lost.* New York: Orchard.

Joosse, Barbara. 1998. *Lewis and Papa: Adventure on the Sante Fe Trail.* Illustrated by Jon Van Zyle. San Francisco: Chronicle.

King-Smith, Dick. 1993. *All Pigs Are Beautiful.* Illustrated by Anita Jeram. Cambridge, MA: Candlewick.

Kitchen, Bert. 1992. *Somewhere Today.* Cambridge, MA: Candlewick.

———. 1994. *When Hunger Calls.* Cambridge, MA: Candlewick.

Kroll, Virginia. 1994. *The Seasons and Someone.* Illustrated by Tatsuro Kiuchi. New York: Harcourt Brace.

Krupinski, Loretta. 1992. *Celia's Island Journal.* Boston: Little, Brown.

Kurijan, Judy. 1993. *In My Own Backyard.* Illustrated by David R. Wagner. Watertown, MA: Charlesbridge.

Laminack, Lester L. 1998. *The Sunsets of Miss Olivia Wiggins.* Illustrated by Constance Rummel Bergum. Atlanta: Peachtree.

———. 1998. *Trevor's Wiggly Wobbly Tooth.* Illustrated by Kathi Garry McCord. Atlanta: Peachtree.

Lasky, Kathryn. 1995. *Pond Year.* Illustrated by Mike Bostock. Cambridge, MA: Candlewick.

———, and Meribah Knight. 1993. *Searching for Laura Ingalls.* Photographs by Christopher Knight. New York: Macmillan.

Lincoln, Margaret. 1995. *The Pirate's Handbook.* New York: Cobblehill.

Lindbergh, Reeve. 1994. *What Is the Sun?* Illustrated by Stephen Lambert. Cambridge, MA: Candlewick.

———. 1997. *North Country Spring.* Illustrated by Liz Sivertson. Boston: Houghton Mifflin.

Little, Jean. 1987. *Little by Little: A Writer's Education.* New York: Viking.

Locker, Thomas. 1990. *Snow Toward Evening.* New York: Puffin/Pied Piper.

———. 1995. *Sky Tree.* New York: HarperCollins.

———. 1997. *Water Dance.* New York: Harcourt Brace.

———. 1998. *Home: A Journey through America.* San Diego: Harcourt Brace.

Loewer, Peter, and Jean Loewer. 1997. *Moonflower.* Atlanta: Peachtree.

London, Jonathan. 1998. *Dream Weaver*. Illustrated by Rocco Baviera. San Diego: Harcourt Brace.

Lyon, George Ella. 1993. *Dreamplace*. Illustrated by Peter Catalonotto. New York: Orchard.

MacLachlan, Patricia. 1993. *Baby*. New York: Delacorte.

———. 1994. *All the Places to Love*. Illustrated by Mike Wimmer. New York: HarperCollins.

———. 1995. *What You Know First*. Illustrated by Barry Moser. New York: HarperCollins.

Mallory, Kenneth. 1995. *Families of the Deep Blue Sea*. Illustrated by Marshall Peck III. Watertown, MA: Charlesbridge.

Manning, Mick, and Brita Granstorm. 1996. *The World Is Full of Babies*. New York: Doubleday.

Martin, Bill Jr., and John Archambault. 1987. *Knots on a Counting Rope*. Illus. by Ted Rand. New York: Trumpet.

Maynard, Bill. 1997. *Santa's Time Off: Poems by Santa as Told to Bill Maynard*. Illustrated by Tom Browning. New York: Putnam.

McDonnell, Flora.1994. *I Love Animals*. Cambridge, MA: Candlewick.

———. 1995. *I Love Boats*. Cambridge, MA: Candlewick.

McLerran, Alice. 1991. *Roxaboxen*. Illus. by Barbara Cooney. New York: Puffin.

McRae, Rodney. 1991. *Cry Me a River*. New York: Angus and Robertson.

Melmed, Laura Krauss. 1993. *The First Song Ever Sung*. Illustrated by Ed Young. New York: Lothrop, Lee and Shepard.

Minters, Frances.1994. *Cinderelli*. Illustrated by G. Brian Karas. New York: Viking.

Mora, Pat. 1998. *This Big Sky*. Illustrated by Steve Jenkins. New York: Scholastic.

Moses, Will. 1997. *Silent Night*. New York: Philomel.

Moss, Thylias. 1993. *I Want To Be*. Illustrated by Jerry Pinkney. New York: Dial.

Murphy, Mary. 1997. *I Like It When . . .* San Diego: Harcourt Brace.

Myers, Walter Dean. 1993. *Brown Angels*. New York: HarperCollins.

Nickens, Bessie. 1994. *Walking the Log: Memories of a Southern Childhood*. New York: Rizzoli.

Ogburn, Jacqueline K. 1997. *The Reptile Ball*. Illustrated by John O'Brien. New York: Dial.

Onyefulu, Ifeoma. 1993. *A Is for Africa*. New York: Cobblehill.

———. 1997. *Chidi Only Likes Blue*. New York: Cobblehill.

Pallotta, Jerry. 1994. *The Desert Alphabet Book*. Illustrated by Mark Astrella. Watertown, MA: Charlesbridge.

Paulsen, Gary. 1990. *Canyons*. New York: Delacorte.

———. 1990. *Woodsong*. Scarsdale, NY: Bradbury.

———. 1993. *Dogteam*. Illustrated by Ruth Wright Paulsen. New York: Delacorte.

———. 1995. *The Rifle*. New York: Harcourt Brace.

———. 1995. *The Tent*. New York: Harcourt Brace.

Priceman, Marjorie. 1994. *How to Make an American Pie and See the World*. New York: Knopf.

Quattlebaum, Mary. 1997. *Underground Train*. Illustrated by Cat Bowman Smith. New York: Doubleday.

Radin, Ruth Yaffe. 1982. *A Winter Place*. Illustrated by Mattie Lou O'Kelley. Boston: Little, Brown.

———.1989. *High in the Mountains*. Illustrated by Ed Young. New York: Macmillan.

Rand, Gloria. 1997. *Baby in a Basket*. Illustrated by Ted Rand. New York: Cobblehill.

Raschka, Christopher. 1993. *Yo! Yes?* New York: Orchard.

Ray, Mary Lyn. 1996. *Mud*. San Diego: Harcourt Brace.

Reiser, Lynn. 1993. *Tomorrow on Rocky Pond*. New York: Greenwillow.

Robinson, Aminah Brenda Lynn. 1997. *A Street Called Home*. San Diego: Harcourt Brace.

Ruurs, Margriet. 1996. *A Mountain Alphabet*. Illustrated by Andrew Kiss. Toronto: Tundra.

Ryder, Joanne. 1991. *Winter Whale*. Illustrated by Michael Rothman. New York: Morrow.

———. 1997. *Shark in the Sea*. Illustrated by Michael Rothman. New York: Morrow.

Ryder, Nora Leigh. 1997. *In the Wild*. New York: Holt.

Rylant, Cynthia. 1982. *When I Was Young in the Mountains*. Illustrated by Diane Goode. New York: Dutton.

———. 1984. *This Year's Garden*. Illustrated by Mary Szilagyi. Scarsdale, NY: Aladdin.

———. 1984. *Waiting to Waltz, A Childhood: Poems*. Illustrated by Stephen Gammell. Scarsdale, NY: Bradbury.

———. 1985. *The Relatives Came*. Illustrated by Stephen Gammell. Scarsdale, NY: Bradbury.

———. 1986. *Night in the Country*. Illustrated by Mary Szilagyi. Scarsdale, NY: Bradbury.

———. 1989. *But I'll Be Back Again*. New York: Orchard.

———. 1990. *Soda Jerk*. Illustrated by Peter Catalanotto. New York: Orchard.

———. 1992. *An Angel for Solomon Singer*. Illustrated by Peter Catalanotto. New York: Orchard.

———. 1992. *Missing May*. New York: Orchard.

———. 1993. *I Had Seen Castles*. New York: Harcourt Brace.

———. 1995. *Dog Heaven*. New York: Blue Sky.

———. 1996. *The Whales*. New York: Scholastic.

———. 1998. *Scarecrow*. Illustrated by Laura Stringer. New York: Harcourt Brace.

———. 1998. *Tulip Sees America*. Illustrated by Lisa Desimini. New York: Scholastic.

Rylant, Cynthia, and Walker Evans. 1994. *Something Permanent*. Poetry by Cynthia Rylant. Photography by Walker Evans. New York: Harcourt Brace.

San Souci, Robert D. 1997. *The Hired Hand: An African-American Folktale*. Illustrated by Jerry Pinkney. New York: Dial.

Schaefer, Carol Lexa. 1996. *The Squiggle*. Illustrated by Pierr Morgan. New York: Crown.

Schertle, Alice. 1995. *Down the Road*. Illustrated by E. B. Lewis. San Diego: Browndeer.

Schnur, Steven. 1997. *Autumn Acrostics*. Illustrated by Leslie Evans. New York: Clarion.

Seibert, Diane. 1988. *Mojave*. Illustrated by Wendell Minor. New York: HarperCollins.

Seymour, Tres. 1996. *The Gulls of the Edmund Fitzgerald*. New York: Orchard.

Shannon, George. 1997. *This Is the Bird*. New York: Houghton Mifflin.

Shelby, Ann. 1995. *Homeplace*. Illustrated by Wendy Anderson Halperin. New York: Orchard.

———. 1996. *The Someday House*. Illustrated by Rosanne Litzinger. New York: Orchard.

Shields, Carol Diggory. 1995. *Lunch Money and Other Poems about School*. Illustrated by Paul Meisei. New York: Puffin.

Shuett, Stacy. 1995. *Somewhere in the World Right Now*. New York: Knopf.

Singer, Marilyn. 1994. *Family Reunion*. New York: Macmillan.

———. 1994. *Sky Words*. Illustrated by Deborah Kogan Ray. New York: Macmillan.

Sis, Peter. 1996. *Starry Messenger*. New York: Farrar, Straus and Giroux.

Sorensen, Henry. 1996. *Your First Step*. New York: Lothrop, Lee and Shepard.

Soto, Gary. 1997. *Snapshots from the Wedding*. Illustrated by Stephanie Garcia. New York: Putnam.

Spinelli, Eileen. 1993. *If You Want to Find Golden*. Illustrated by Stacy Schuett. Morton Grove, IL: Whitman.

Spinelli, Jerry. 1990. *Maniac Magee: A Novel*. Boston: Little, Brown.

Stafford, Kim. 1994. *We Got Here Together*. Illustrated by Debra Frasier. New York: Harcourt Brace.

Stewart, Sarah. 1997. *The Gardener*. Illustrated by David Small. New York: Farrar, Straus and Giroux.

Stolz, Mary. 1993. *Say Something*. Illustrated by Alexander Koshkin. New York: HarperCollins.

Stutson, Caroline. 1993. *On the River ABC*. Illustrated by Anna-Maria Crum. Boulder, CO: Roberts Rinehart.

Suen, Anastasia. 1997. *Man on the Moon*. Illustrated by Benrei Huang. New York: Viking.

Sullivan, Silky. 1996. *Grandpa Was a Cowboy*. Illustrated by Bert Dodson. New York: Orchard.

Taylor, Mildred. 1978. *Roll of Thunder, Hear My Cry*. New York: Bantam.

Tucker, Kathy. 1997. *Do Cowboys Ride Bikes?* Illustrated by Nadine Bernard Westcott. Morton Grove, IL: Whitman.

Turner, Ann. 1987. *Nettie's Trip South*. Illustrated by Ronald Himler. New York: Macmillan.

———. 1992. *Rainflowers*. Illus. by Robert J. Blake. New York: Zolotow.

———. 1997. *Mississippi Mud: Three Prairie Journals*. Illustrated by Robert J. Blake. San Francisco: HarperCollins.

Walsh, Jill Payton, and Stephen Lambert. 1997. *When I Was Little Like You*. New York: Viking.

Woodson, Jacqueline. 1997. *We Had a Picnic This Sunday Past*. Illustrated by Diane Greenseid. New York: Hyperion.

Yolen, Jane. 1987. *Owl Moon*. Illustrated by John Schoenherr. New York: Philomel.

———. 1992. *Letting Swift River Go*. Illustrated by Barbara Cooney. Boston: Little, Brown.

———. 1993. *Welcome to the Green House*. Illustrated by Laura Regan. New York: Putnam.

———. 1994. *Grandad Bill's Song*. Illustrated by Melissa Bay Mathis. New York: Philomel.

———. 1995. *Here There Be Witches*. Illustrated by David Wilgus. New York: Harcourt Brace.

———. 1995. *Water Music*. Photography by Jason Stemple. Honesdale, PA: Boyds Mills.

———. 1996. *Sacred Places*. Illustrated by David Shannon. New York: Harcourt Brace.

———. 1997. *Miz Berlin Walks*. Illustrated by Floyd Cooper. New York: Philomel.

———. 1997. *Nocturne*. Illustrated by Anne Hunter. New York: Harcourt Brace.

———. 1998. *Welcome to the Ice House*. Illustrated by Laura Regan. New York: Putnam.

Zamorano, Ana. 1996. *Let's Eat*. Illustrated by Julie Vivas. New York: Scholastic.

Zolotow, Charlotte. 1992. *The Seashore Book*. Illustrated by Wendell Minor. New York: HarperCollins.

———. 1993. *The Moon Was the Best*. Photography by Tana Hoban. New York: Greenwillow.

# Author

*Photo by Mark Haskett*

Katie Wood Ray is assistant professor in the Department of Elementary and Middle Grades Education at Western Carolina University, where she teaches undergraduate and graduate courses in language arts and children's literature. She is co-author of another NCTE publication, *Spelling in Use: Looking Closely at Spelling in Whole Language Classrooms* and is currently serving as co-editor of *Primary Voices K–6*. She lives with her husband and their two wolves high on the side of a mountain, where the view makes it easy to find wondrous words.

WONDROUS WORDS

Composed by Precision Graphics in Galliard and Papyrus.
Typeface used on the cover was Papyrus.
Printed by Versa Press on 60-lb. Finch.